Journal of the Society of

Christian

Ethics

VOLUME 31, NO. 2 • FALL/WINTER 2011

Contents

Book Reviews

Contributors

Preface

The 2011 Annual Meeting of the Society of Christian Ethics (SCE) was held in New Orleans, Louisiana, a city known for its cultural diversity as much as for its jazz, food, climate, and both respectful and raucous hospitality. The Big Easy is also known for its exposure of the underside of corruption and neglect—sadly, neglect that includes the devastating aftermath of the 2005 hurricane season and Hurricane Katrina as well as the long summer of 2010 that witnessed the British Petroleum–Deepwater Horizons Gulf of Mexico oil spill. As these words are written, a spring thaw is wreaking havoc along the Mississippi River from East St. Louis, Illinois, and Memphis, Tennessee, to Greenville, Mississippi, and Baton Rouge, Louisiana. This time it appears that New Orleans will be spared by the opening of the Morganza Spillway while many smaller rural communities will be inundated, with peoples' homes and businesses washed south toward the Gulf of Mexico.

Neither the environmental nor the Katrina stories of New Orleans were lost on SCE members. Eighty-four SCE colleagues participated in the January 6 preconvention ecojustice tour of New Orleans organized by environmental ethics and theology interest group co-convener Dawn M. Nothwehr. Narration for the tour was supplied by experts from Catholic Charities of the Archdiocese of New Orleans and the staff of the sites visited: Providence Community Housing Center, Rebuild Center, Café Hope, and PACE Center for the Elderly. The four-hour tour culminated with the panel presentation "Disrupting Environmental Degradation," which concluded that an "ignorance-based worldview" for restoration of coastal Louisiana wetlands, a perspective that emphasizes what is not known, can serve the central norms of Christian environmental ethics that actively seeks new knowledge.[1] Another premeeting tour, focusing on post-Katrina New Orleans, will be highlighted in the preface of the *JSCE* 32, no. 1 (2012).

The president of the SCE invited members to consider certain themes as they developed proposals in response to the call for papers. The themes for the 2011 meeting included a question about how ethics might be considered theological in diverse traditions. That question was explored by three plenary speakers, each of whom is published here. Other themes for this meeting were engaged by both premeeting tours. Still other themes raised the human and environmental costs of natural disasters, taking as a point of reflection the devastating earthquake in Port-au-Prince, Haiti, January 12, 2010. Likewise, the call for papers raised the ongoing concerns of race, poverty, and political agency, each having incarnate value in New Orleans.

This issue begins with Douglas Ottati's interest in the question of the intersection of theology and ethics. In many ways, his essay anticipates the work of Charles Curran and the presentation, not included in this issue, of Susan Frank Parsons toward a conclusion worthy of both: that a theological ethics can be Christian if it is directed in service to the life of faith. Ottati assumes that Christianity (and other religious traditions) matter to ethics, and that such mattering deserves arguments foundational to what is important about faith as well as to the practical difference such faith might make to human life. Charles Curran considers a similar question through a significantly different lens than Ottati's argument. (Both he and Parsons were invited by President Ottati to consider the question of the relationship between theology and ethics.) Curran offers his thinking on and questions about what distinctive contributions the Christian tradition can bring to the discipline of ethics, recognizing insight from nontheological as well as other religious wisdom traditions. He considers the predominance of quandry ethics and then follows with a systematic overview of how the distinctive content of Christian ethics can most profitably and practically be used today. Ottati and Curran, along with Parsons, did more than wonder, simply, about how theological ethics is theological, Christian, and the inquiry itself to be done. Each offered their points of view in unique though familiar ways as we members of the guild were challenged and encouraged to persevere against a climate of irrelevance (if not irreverence) among our colleagues in other professional disciplines. The intersection remains critical and the future seemingly precarious (especially where colleges, universities, and seminaries consider their budgets in less than optimal economies), will a faith-based ethics survive?

The issue turns next to an icon of liberty in the United States—President Abraham Lincoln. The bicentennial of Lincoln's birth was celebrated throughout 2009, and that commemoration as well as other reasons prompted Lloyd Steffen to ask what religious ethicists might learn from examining Lincoln's legacy. Steffen finds an unorthodox religionist in Lincoln, who remained humble in his convictions that no one tradition—religious or philosophical—held the market on truth. Lincoln was, as Steffen argues, duty-bound to charity of an intellectual and religious kind as the need and ethical requirement incumbent on us all.

In a similar vein, two other essays in this issue explore the question of the place of one's religious convictions in the public sphere, but in quite divergent cultural contexts. John Burgess takes the agenda of H. Richard Niebuhr's *Christ and Culture* to contemporary Russian Orthodoxy and there finds a sixth type—Christ in culture—embodied among the Orthodox. This development recognizes the Orthodox mode of survival amidst the preceding communist church-destructive program and calls the Orthodox to an "in-churching" commemoration, education, and social outreach that would follow the model of the historic church community. Tommy Givens revisits John Howard Yoder's work on the Jewish/Christian schism to suggest that some of Yoder's thinking precludes Yoder's own program of peace. Rather, Givens argues that the ethical integrity of the Christian community, like that of the Jewish community, is predicated on their having been and being the people of God's own election.

The next two essays raise questions about the criminal justice system in the United States. Amy Levad asks how the sacramental tradition of Catholicism might provide an alternative to the models of punishment found in monastic and ecclesiastical prisons and thereby contribute to restorative conceptions of justice and rehabilitation programs. She argues, contra the conclusions of Andrew Skotnicki, that the sacramental core of Catholicism and the peace, forgiveness, love, and justice of God's reign provide robust support for penal reform that protects public safety, promotes the common good, and restores community inclusive of the criminal offender. Kathryn Getek Soltis challenges Christian complacency in the face of the staggering rates of incarceration in the United States and the impact such imprisonment bears on families, especially upon those who are most vulnerable. Insofar as our criminal justice system exacerbates class divisions, it likewise places additional burdens on individuals and the communities to which they belong who are already marginalized, burdens that not even the *lex talionis* would have exercised as blindly.

The final essays tackle the questions of distributive justice and children's labor. Michael Turner places in conversation the work of John Calvin and John Rawls, asking who deserves social and material goods and on what grounds. Turner examines a fundamental objection to desert in an effort to reconsider the principle's theological warrant from God's grace to one's moral worth and entitlement. Cristina Traina ventures into what many would consider the underside of the global economy, the underpaid work of children. While scholars in the United States and elsewhere rightly decry the often deplorable conditions of child labor, Traina does not shy away from the real needs in these real times to develop a robust ethical description of children as intentional social and economic agents—as workers—and to articulate both their right to work and their rights as workers in a way that protects their flourishing rather than exacerbates their exploitation.

The issue concludes with reviews of books authored or recommended by members of the Society of Christian Ethics. Some of the reviews combine two or three texts of similar subject matter and may signal an innovative approach to the way the work of different authors may be profitably compared. Members of the SCE are invited to submit their books to Lois Malcolm, the book review editor, for review assignment. For more information about the *JSCE*, please visit http://scethics.org/, click on the "Journal" tab, and follow the links for FAQs, publication criteria, IRB regulations, review procedures, and information on serving as a referee or editorial board member.

Finally, the table below shows that the *JSCE* remains competitive among its peers for the academic excellence and timely as well as time-tested subject matter of its essays. As what has become the custom of our editorial work, the results of the electronic demographic surveys requested of those who submit proposals to the call for papers are published in the second issue of a volume year, following the determinations of acceptance from the Society's January meeting presentations.[2] (The first issue of a volume year includes the second half of papers accepted from the previous year's meeting.) There were 120 proposals submitted in response to the call (for individual papers, panels, and interest/working group sessions); from those proposals, 70 questionnaires were completed. The table charts proposals submitted for papers accepted from the New Orleans meeting, including papers and submissions from the Society of Jewish Ethics and the Pacific section meeting of the SCE. The *JSCE* maintains an average acceptance rate of 16 percent; this rate is calculated from the start of the review process with the submission of proposals in response to the call (120 this year, plus 4 papers submitted from the Pacific section meeting and 1 from the Society of Jewish Ethics) through the meeting presentations and final papers submitted. Many other professional societies who have a journal attached to their meetings follow this same formula for calculating their acceptance rates. Among such organizations see, for example, the Association for Moral Education and its *Journal of Moral Education*.[3] For those societies and journals that offer two routes to publication—one through direct submission, the other through the proposal in response to a call then to a meeting and followed by final review—see the following among the "Allied Academies": *Academy of Educational Leadership Journal; Business Studies Journal; Journal of International Business Research; Journal of Legal, Ethical, and Regulatory Issues*; and *Journal of the International Academy for Case Studies*, among others.[4]

Notes

1. In environmentally sensitive work, scientists hold two among other views or perspectives as the foundation of their thinking on the likely environmental or ecological impact of this or that project. The current dominant view is the knowledge-based worldview; the other is the ignorance-based worldview. See R. Eugene Turner, "Doubt and the Values of an Ignorance-Based World View for Restoration: Coastal Louisiana Wetlands," *Estuaries and Coasts* 32, no. 6 (2009): 1054–68.

2. Please note a correction to the demographic distribution results reported in *JSCE* 30, no. 2 (2010): x. The byline indicating "Proposals Submitted for the 2009 Annual Meeting . . . (Demographic data 2008 . . .)" should read "Proposals Submitted for the 2010 Annual

Meeting . . . (Demographic Data 2009 . . .)". The actual data presented in the table, however, are correct.

3. See the Association for Moral Education, Call for Proposals to "Cultivating Morality," the International Conference on Moral Education, meeting in Nanjing, China, October 24–28, 2011. "Proposals will be considered by the NJ2011 Programme Committee which comprises members of the *Journal of Moral Education* editorial board and its peer-review referee list, Association for Moral Education Board, Asia Pacific Network for Moral Education Committee, together with colleagues from the Research Institute for Moral Education, Nanjing Normal University and the National Centre for Ethical Studies, Renmin University of China, Beijing," www.nanjing2011.org/proposal-submission/index.html.

4. For information regarding the Allied Academies and their conference and publication activities, go to http://alliedacademies.org/Public/Default.aspx, http://alliedacademies.org/Public/Conferences/2011VegasCall.aspx, and http://alliedacademies.org/Public/Journals/Journals.aspx.

Demographic Distribution Results
Proposals Submitted for the 2011 Annual Meeting of the Society of Christian Ethics through Papers Accepted by the *Journal of the Society of Christian Ethics* (Demographic data 2010–2011; 70 of 120 proposals*)

	Gender		Membership			Ethnic-Racial Group							Education		Tradition			Total
	F	M	S	F	L	AR	AS	AA/A	HL	NA/A	W	O	DC	P	C	J	O	
Proposals Submitted*	26	44	23	47			7	1			62		23	47	68	1		70*/120
Submission Occurrence*																		
First	12	17	16	13			5				23	1	16	13				29
Second	8	9	6	11			1				15		6	11				17
Third or more	6	18	1	23			1				23		1	23				24
Decisions**																		
Proposals Accepted	26	50	21	55			4	1			70	1						76**
Papers Submitted	19	34	17	36			4				49							53
Papers Accepted	7	13	5	15			1				19				19	1		20
Gender**																		
Female	26		9	17			3	1			22		9	17	26	1		26
Male		50	14	36			4				45	1	14	36	49	1		50

Membership: S=Student, F=Full, L=Life

Ethnic–Racial Group: Ar=Arabic, As=Asian, AA/A=African American/African, HL=Hispanic/Latino(a), NA/A=Native American/Alaskan, W=White, O=Other (per the survey, respondents could check all that apply)

Education: M=MA/MTS (included in DC or PhD), Dv=MDiv/STL (included in DC or PhD), DC=PhD Candidate, P=PhD (per the survey, respondents checked highest degree earned)

Tradition: C=Christianity, J=Judaism, O=Other

*70 persons completed the demographic survey out of 120 proposals received; occurrence history and gender reflect this return.

**61 paper and 15 panel proposals were accepted out of 120 submissions. These decisions and gender information were established with the raw data from the survey, correlation of authors with proposals, correlation of authors with papers presented at the New Orleans meeting, and papers subsequently accepted for publication (including authors from the SJE, and Pacific section meetings).

Selected Essays

How Can Theological Ethics Be Christian?

Douglas F. Ottati

THIS ESSAY PRESENTS THE ARGUMENT THAT A THEOLOGICAL ETHIC CAN be Christian if it is shaped by a Christian theology or a reflective attempt to articulate a Christian worldview in the service of the life of faith. But there is no generic Christian theology, only historical varieties, many of which shape our ethics differently and also include distinctive self-critical resources. Therefore, although theology is not all you need, you must also be your own theologian to be a critical, interesting, and ecclesially relevant Christian ethicist.

Some years ago, my teacher James M. Gustafson asked, "Can ethics be Christian?"[1] He argued that aspects of Christian believing can qualify important dimensions of ethics. For example, faith in a loving God may dispose one toward becoming a loving sort of person. Believing that God commands—or, more broadly, that we should respond faithfully to divine activity—may shape our motives or reasons for being moral. Convictions about divine activity, such as "God liberates" or "God judges," may influence interpretations of historical circumstances that call for moral involvement. Emphases on love and reconciliation anchored in narratives about God's dealings with God's people or in stories about Jesus may also qualify our understandings of certain moral principles or norms such as justice as well as our understanding of how to apply them. The unique norm of radical discipleship may authorize a strict Christian pacifism that differs substantially from behaviors authorized by approaches that leave more room for self-regard. On these grounds, Gustafson answered his question in the affirmative. Ethics can indeed be distinctively Christian, although important aspects of Christian ethics often overlap with other ethics.

The question I ask here, as well as the answer I give and explore, owes a good deal to Gustafson's earlier argument. I assume that *theological* ethics can be Christian. My initial question is simply how they can be? That is, I assume theology matters for ethics. I assume that a picture of human life and the world in relation to God can make a difference for our practical orientations and stances in life. And I assume that a Christian theology can qualify our ethics and practical stances in distinctive ways.

My starting point also owes much to an argument made by another Gustafson student, John P. Reeder Jr., in his article "What Is a Religious Ethic?" Drawing on the work of Clifford Geertz and William Christian Sr., Reeder argued that religions furnish visions of the good and the real, worldviews that locate us in relation to what is important and to the possibilities afforded by the nature of things. We may therefore compare and contrast the worldviews offered by different religious communities and their traditions. We may also compare them with the pictures of what is important and possible offered by Marxists, existentialists, and others. A difference between Reeder's concern and mine is that he focuses on religious ethics whereas I am concerned chiefly with theological ethics and, within that designation, theological ethics that are *Christian*. But I agree that what I call theological ethics as well as what I call Christian theological ethics are species of religious ethics (more or less) as Reeder describes them. Indeed, I subscribe to a signal implication of both Gustafson's and Reeder's arguments. If you want to articulate a Christian ethic in full, or "all the way down," as it were, you need to not only identify moral norms and interpret circumstances; you also need to articulate a comprehensive doctrine, worldview, or theological vision.[2]

My initial question, then, is, how can *theological* ethics be *Christian*? My answer, predictably enough, is that a theological ethic can be Christian if it works with a Christian theology. But the significance of this answer only becomes apparent when we probe it further, when we ask just what Christian theology is and does, when we note ethically significant historical varieties of Christian theology, and when we explore how these varieties may include resources for self-criticism. Once we do these things, in fact, we shall be in a position to make observations about the enterprise of Christian ethics and what it means to be a Christian ethicist.

What Christian Theology Is and Does

Theology is logos of *theos*, or discourse and reflection about god or the gods. It is the reflective attempt to understand god or the gods more truly. A discourse is theological if it has something to do with god or the gods.

Many statements may be about matters of genuine importance, such as personal fulfillment, politics, or life in the cosmos, and yet not be theological. Conversely, statements about very many matters, including personal life, politics, and planetary ecologies, may be theological if they refer to god or the gods, or if they are made in a context that refers to god or the gods. Gustafson says he once attended a party where a colleague in chemistry challenged him to say something theological. He responded by saying, "God," and he regards theology (rightly, I think) as an attempt to understand things in their appropriate relations to God.[3] Thomas Aquinas wrote likewise that theology (*sacra doctrina*) expresses judgments about God and about creatures in relation to God.[4] Relatedness to God is what defines theological reflections.

Even at this early stage in our inquiry, then, we may hazard a generalization. Theological ethics situate human life and the world in relation to something more that we do not entirely comprehend or control. They appreciate, as Gordon D. Kaufman might say, that we live "in face of Mystery," and they tend to orient life toward a point of reference that lies beyond church, nation, ethnic group, or species.[5] Indeed, when they do, theological ethics do not envision what is important and what is possible simply as functions of humanity on its own, which is why they sometimes seem troubling from the perspective of secular and humanistic ethics.

As a historical matter of fact, however, most theology is not freewheeling discourse about things in relation to god or the gods. It is also discourse and reflection in the service of the teachings and doctrines of particular religious communities.[6] This is why there is no generic theology, and why we may speak of doctrinal reflections among Jewish communities, Islamic communities, and others that engage the historic teachings and sense-making resources of their respective traditions. Likewise, Christian communities have engaged in doctrinal reflections with the aid of the historic resources of the Christian movement. Through the centuries they have stated their teachings and doctrine in creeds, catechisms, and confessions, and Christian theologians from Origen of Alexandria to the present often have regarded themselves as teachers in the church.

The persistent connection of Christian theology with church teaching illumines its practical nature. Broadly speaking, Christian teaching and instruction is training in a way of living, a New Testament theme also taken up in early postcanonical literature. It is training intended to help people interact with others, objects, situations, and realities in a manner that is faithfully responsive to the God disclosed in Jesus Christ. The church teaches as it helps its members interact with families, possessions, governments, forests, and more in a manner that is also faithfully responsive to God. The church teaches because its pastoral aim is the faithful formation of the people of God.

A critical point is that building up people in a faithful way of life requires reflective activity. We need a picture of things in relation to God if we are to know how to interact with them in a manner that is faithfully responsive to God. If we are to interact with families, possessions, governments, and natural environments in a manner that is faithfully responsive to God, then we need to have some picture of how they are related to God. This is where Christian theology comes in. Christian theology is the reflective attempt to picture or envision ourselves as well as the many objects and others with which we interact in relation to the God disclosed in Jesus Christ. It is the reflective attempt to articulate a Christian worldview in the service of the life of faith. In short, it is a comprehensive doctrine that helps us to envision God, the world, and ourselves.

Varieties of Christian Theology

The connection with church teaching also illumines the historical nature of Christian theology and the emergence of distinct subtraditions. Indeed, the rise of theological subtraditions is endemic to the dynamics of faithful formation. By means of preaching, teaching, and pastoral care, communities try to form people at particular places and times. They train people to interact with things in a manner that is faithfully responsive to the God disclosed in Jesus Christ at Antioch in 380, Paris in 1270, and Cape Town in 2011. But at these places and times, the specific circumstances and realities, the challenges and the intellectual resources with which Christians interact differ, change, and develop. Over time, then, subcommunities and subtraditions emerge that are characterized by distinctive lines of faithful formation, practice, and theological reflection. It cannot be otherwise if Christian communities undertake the practical and pastoral business of faithful formation in history.

In addition, partly because so many biblical texts were written in the service of practical and pastoral aims, there is also plurality in the Bible itself.[7] Subsequent communities therefore find themselves having to formulate normative and characteristic approaches to interpreting Jesus Christ and the scriptures (since there is, for example, no single unified Christology in the New Testament). Under the pastoral pressures of forming faithful persons at particular places and times, they select and develop different themes, images, and ideas from biblical portraits and texts. Consider, for example, Roman Catholic emphases on the Gospel of John, incarnation, nature, and grace; Lutheran emphases on Paul, crucifixion, law, and gospel; and Mennonite emphases on the synoptic gospels, Jesus's reign, and radical discipleship.

This helps to explain why there is no generic Christianity or Christian theology. It also indicates why claims that a particular position is or is not "orthodox," or that a given theology does or does not affirm "the God of Jesus Christ," rarely advance scholarly debates. We need to know whose orthodoxies and which Christologies are at issue, how they compare, and what counts for and against them.[8] When it comes to Christian theology, one size never fits all since the dynamics of Christian theology and church teaching make for a historical plurality of Christian theologies.[9]

Indeed, the subtraditions also continue to develop. This leads to significant emendations of received stances, such as Roger Williams's creative revision of

Calvinist ideas of civil society, religious liberty, and fairness in seventeenth-century Rhode Island, or Karl Barth's sharp christocentric turn in twentieth-century Europe.[10] Further subdivisions and strands therefore emerge within longer-standing theological subtraditions. In recent years, feminist varieties of Roman Catholic theology have emerged that support revised stances on marriage and family, justice, and priesthood that some other Catholics do not share. This, in fact, is how one might read Rosemary Radford Ruether's classic book *Sexism and God-Talk*.[11] Similar observations hold for appropriations of liberal, evangelical, and liberationist themes by Lutherans, Baptists, and others. Just as there is no generic Christian theology, there is also no generic Roman Catholic, Orthodox, Lutheran, Reformed, or Baptist theology.

We are ready now to make a further point. Historical varieties of Christian theology become significant for Christian ethics when they support appreciably different practical stances. They become ethically significant when they qualify dimensions of ethics in distinguishable ways: when they dispose us toward different reasons for being moral, when they suggest different estimates of human possibilities and limits, when they encourage us to interpret circumstances differently, and when they influence us to understand and apply moral norms differently.

An Extended Illustration

John Calvin published nine editions of *The Institutes of the Christian Religion* from 1536 until 1559, when it finally had become a 1,500-page tome intended for students at the Academy of Geneva. However, it always concluded with a chapter on civil government where, in the later editions, Calvin contrasted his reflections with those of Peter Rideman, a Hutterite who published his *Account of Our Religion, Doctrine and Faith* in 1545.

Rideman's take on Christian faithfulness stressed a holy community that obeys Christ's reign, holds possessions in common, and participates in civil society in a comparatively restricted way.[12] Civil government, he said, is from God's wrath; it is an enterprise by which God permits the godless to discipline, punish, and restrain the wicked by means of the sword. By contrast, Christ's disciples put off all worldly glory. "Thus no Christian is a ruler and no ruler is a Christian, for the child of blessing cannot be the servant of wrath." Moreover, "a Christian neither wages war nor wields the worldly sword to practice vengeance." Christian citizens pay general taxes, but refuse to pay special taxes levied for war. "Neither can they make weapons," sit as judges, or participate in civil courts. In sum, for the occasionally imprisoned Protestant radical, civil government "has its place outside Christ, but not in Christ."[13]

The contrast with Calvin was nearly total. The humanist student of law railed against "certain fanatics" who boast that once we are in Christ and "are transported to God's Kingdom . . . it is a thing unworthy of us . . . to be occupied with . . . vile and worldly cares."[14] He claimed that God has established civil government to provide for the public manifestation of religion and so "that humanity may be maintained among men." Moreover, he said, its function "is no less than that of bread, water, sun, and air." Discussing magistrates, Calvin claimed, "God has entrusted to them the business of serving him through their office," and "civil authority is a calling, not only lawful before God, but also . . . by far the most honorable of all callings, in the whole life of mortal men." It is the responsibility of magistrates to represent "some image of divine providence, protection, goodness, benevolence, and justice."[15]

Unlike Rideman, Calvin also thought it worthwhile to distinguish better and worse forms of civil government. Much depends on circumstances, he said, but because kings very rarely control themselves "so that their will never disagrees with what is just and right," and because some kings are not especially wise, "a system compounded of aristocracy and democracy, far excels all others." That is, human failings and shortcomings make it safer and more bearable where a number exercise government and therefore help, teach, admonish, and restrain one another.[16] Calvin commended "restraint and humanity in war"; he claimed that magistrates properly exercise violent means "to restrain the misdeeds of private individuals" and "also to defend the dominions entrusted to their safekeeping, if at any time they are under enemy attack."[17] Turning to civil laws, he noted that God is a lawgiver, that varied historical constitutions are founded on natural equity, and that Christians should not reject the judicial process.[18]

My reason for eavesdropping on this debate is that we have here two specific varieties of Christian theology whose differences are significant for Christian ethics. The varieties offer dramatically different construals in relation to God of civil government, a basic reality with which faithful Christians interact. These different portraits in turn reflect different primary images of Christian faithfulness and our reasons for being moral. Rideman saw civil government in terms of a fundamental conflict between Christ's rule and the reign of fallen principalities and powers. He therefore regarded government service and the rest as instruments of divine wrath to be exercised only by the ungodly to restrain the wicked. This correlates with Rideman's view of Christian faithfulness as the commitment to follow Jesus rather than other (and alien) lords. Calvin saw Christian faithfulness as a response to God's universal reign, a reign disclosed in Jesus Christ but one in which civil government may mediate God's providence, goodness, and justice. His understanding of civil society was representative of a spirit of faithful participation in God's world that yields a "worldly Christianity." Government service, soldiering, the legal profession, and more were therefore understood by Calvin and later Puritans as legitimate callings, ways of pursuing justice and combating injustice, lines of both faithful and public service before God.[19]

The difference persists. Somewhat like Rideman, John Howard Yoder, whose thinking has influenced Stanley Hauerwas and others, claimed that Jesus brings a way, pattern, or direction of living that founds the church and contrasts pointedly with fallen principalities and powers.[20] The emphasis, to quote Hauerwas, is on the church as "the only true polity we can know in this life."[21] Somewhat like Calvin, the Dutch theologian and prime minister Abraham Kuyper, whose thinking has influenced Max L. Stackhouse and others, claimed that God's single government of the world takes place by means of differentiated spheres that are structured by appropriate institutions, such as politics and civil government, religion and the church, scholarship and the university.[22] Kuyper's spheres accord with what Robin W. Lovin calls a "pluralist realism." They emphasize diverse institutions such as corporation, family, church, government, and culture that constitute distinguishable contexts for responsibility.[23]

These differences are also at work in recent debates over the participation of Christians in civil politics and public discourse in pluralistic democracies. Many agree that the different comprehensive views of human life, its possibilities and limits that cultural and religious communities support, make it difficult to elaborate political conceptions of justice. Many today also are more keenly aware than were their classical forebears that cultural and religious differences tempt civil governments to enforce settlements against the wishes and wisdom of particular groups.[24] Even so, working from my own appropriation of the Reformed subtradition, I am comfortable arguing that Christians should participate in conversations aimed at political agreements and cooperative ventures among different communities.

I find considerable merit in Lovin's recent analysis of social contexts of responsibility, public forums, and the possible contributions of comprehensive doctrines to public discourse in pluralist democracies. I also believe he is correct to note that, although they may not be required to do so, some churches and theological traditions may formulate important claims in ways that use points of contact with other groups and institutions.[25] In fact, I think that Christian subtraditions such as my own have forthrightly "unapologetic" reasons to do so. I find merit, too, in Jeffrey Stout's somewhat pragmatic call for a democratic exchange of reasons and mutual accountability and responsibility in democratic life.[26] Critically understood, I think there is also merit in John Rawls's revised, comparatively flexible, and inclusive account of "public reason" that admits shareable religious reasons as well as religious doctrines with analogues in other comprehensive outlooks.[27]

These proposals differ, and estimates of them will depend partly on judgments that do not reduce to theology. Is pluralism or antireligious ideology the driving force of modern secularity and liberal democracy?[28] How does the development in modern democracies of differentiated and internally complex contexts and institutions shape circumstances for conversations and public deliberations? Even so, proposals such as those made by Lovin, Stout, and the later Rawls at times allow, encourage, and even require religious persons and communities to think both in their own confessional theological idioms and also in broader political terms. As Nigel Biggar notes, they call for religious persons and communities who are open to negotiations in which we listen to and reformulate each other's points of view.[29] Ethicists indebted to a theological subtradition such as Rideman's may have deep confessional reasons to resist this call on the grounds that it threatens, corrodes, and perhaps even destroys the integrity of genuine Christian faith and community through an unholy compromise with principalities and powers. However, I am inclined to regard it as a call for religious persons and communities to pursue the social good of principled cooperation under certain contemporary conditions—a good that Reformed theology disposes me to value and accept. Indeed, Calvin's own theologically based argument in favor of "a system compounded of aristocracy and democracy" pursues this good. His argument expresses core doctrines of his comprehensive outlook; it is couched in broader political terms and is compatible with a willingness to exchange of shareable reasons. Moreover, to the extent that Calvin backs robust participation in the civil and public realm, his theology suggests unapologetic reasons for taking up the responsibility of framing a workable civil politics and discourse in later pluralistic settings. This trajectory in Reformed theology will only be strengthened if we attend, as James Calvin Davis has done, to Roger Williams's arguments in response to religious and moral pluralism in different and later circumstances.[30]

I am a theological ethicist who believes and is willing to argue for these things. Bully for me. But my main point here is simply that my posture on these matters has much to do with my appropriation of ethically significant strands within my particular Christian subtradition.[31]

Resources for Self-Criticism

Christian theology is a practical wisdom that develops differently in specific Christian communities and subtraditions as it serves the pastoral and ecclesial aims of faithful formation. Moreover, some historic varieties of Christian theology make for appreciably different stances in ethics. This is what I have argued thus far, and it tags me as a kind of a historicist. Have I also made a contemporary case for an isolated and noncritical traditionalism? Not at all, and so now I want to indicate that varieties of Christian theology often include resources for self-criticism. If I am correct, then there is little reason to assume that sustained attention to historic theological resources necessarily repristinates cherished creeds and authorities. My procedure will be to outline three critical resources in my own appropriation of the Reformed subtradition and note overlaps, analogies, and comparisons with other varieties of Christian theology.

Church Teachings Are Subject to Criticism

Because I am a Reformed theologian of a comparatively ecumenical and liberal sort, I hope you will not mind if I begin with a statement made by my Roman Catholic teacher, David Tracy. There is no innocent tradition (and, I should add, no innocent subtradition either).[32] This insight is one with which a good Reformed theology will concur.

"As we do not rashly condemn what good men, assembled together in general councils lawfully gathered, have set before us; so we do not receive uncritically whatever has been declared to men under the name of the general councils, for it is plain that, being human, some of them have manifestly erred, and that in matters of great weight and importance. So far then as the council confirms its decrees by the plain Word of God, so far do we reverence and embrace them."[33] These are the opening sentences of the chapter in the Scots Confession of 1560 on general councils, their power, and authority. These sentences express not only typical Scottish contrariness but also a classical Protestant idea that Reformed theologians share with Lutherans and others: church teaching and tradition are subordinate to scripture and subject to criticism in light of scripture. Moreover, as the deliberations and decisions of all persons, communities, and institutions not only draw upon limited insight but also are subject to the skewing effects of sin, all church statements, including those made by general councils, are fallible, a point that connects with the refusal of Calvin and the company of Genevan pastors to sign the Nicene Creed as a test of orthodoxy in a disputation at Lausanne in 1537.[34]

Part of the Protestant idea is that we may go back behind accumulated teachings and traditions to the original documents of the Christian movement as the standard of criticism. These classic originals also stand in need of interpretation,[35] so the Scots' easy confidence that they will be able to confirm or deny conciliar decrees "by the plain Word of God" may justifiably be regarded as a recurrent Protestant hubris. Still, the critical regard for church teaching not only draws on convictions about the priority of scripture and the universality of sin. It also reflects the humanism of Calvin and other Swiss Reformers, such as Ulrich Zwingli, who shared Erasmus's concern to work from the best editions of classical texts rather than only from later glosses and interpretations.[36] Moreover, as is typical of other Reformed Protestants, the Scots continue to affirm a role for theological teaching and tradition (otherwise, why write a confession at all?). The net result is that appeals to church teaching are understood to contribute to inquiries of a certain kind. The broader theological conversation is never simply about (authoritative) tradition per se; appeals to church teachings and traditions are significant to the extent that they help us to get at the truth of the gospel.

Respect for the Arts and Sciences

Reformed theology has high regard for the arts and sciences, and willingly engages them. This is part of faithfully engaging society and world. Calvin himself regarded the arts and sciences as God's good gifts, maintaining, "If we regard the Spirit of God as the sole fountain of truth, we shall neither reject the truth itself, nor despise it wherever it shall be found, unless we wish to dishonor the Spirit of God"—an affirmation he shared in substance with much Roman Catholic tradition.[37] On this basis, Calvin commended writings of ancient jurists, philosophers (especially the Stoics), mathematicians, and physicians. He also claimed that astronomy, medicine, and natural science behold evidences of God's "wonderful wisdom."[38] Again, Jonathan Edwards pondered, drew, and described the movements of spiders partly because he regarded natural philosophy as the study of the manner of God's acting in the world.[39]

The upshot is that Reformed communities have supported educational institutions and often refused to insulate theology from other inquiries. Where this impetus was combined with ideas about covenantal checks, balances, and the dispersal of powers, the preference was for schools that foster free and unfettered inquiry. Recall Kuyper's claim that God rules human life through differentiated spheres and their appropriate institutions, including religion and church, scientific inquiry and university. Add his further claim that each institution in its appropriate sphere should be free from domination by the others lest we usurp God's sovereignty. The result? Free investigation and inquiry in the university should be supported even though it "leads to collisions."[40]

Obviously, the Reformed Christian subtradition has had its share of disagreements and conflicts over freethinking and inquiry. Calvin prepared charges against Servetus, even if it is true that Roger Williams's likeness appears on the Reformation wall at the University of Geneva. This is also a Christian subtradition that later found itself torn by the fundamentalist controversy. Nevertheless, in my judgment the liberal wing that comes to expression in the work of Friedrich Schleiermacher and others has been largely correct to intensify its critical impulses by advancing commitments to free thinking and by engaging well-attested scientific findings in fields such as evolutionary biology and modern cosmology on the theological ground that God is the source of all truth. In fact, the fidelity of the liberal wing to historic Calvinist principles in this regard has been routinely underestimated. A decision for it also entails a willingness to deploy methods of modern historical scholarship in the study of the Bible and church history, a development that finally led Union Seminary in New

York to sever relations with Presbyterian synods in the case of Charles Briggs and that necessarily leads to the rejection of overly sharp Protestant distinctions between the Bible and tradition. The Bible now is seen to be early tradition, a collection of charter documents produced by particular writers and communities. This observation, when leavened by postmodern liberationist, feminist, and womanist perspectives, opens the way to interpret the Bible with a dose of suspicion. Indeed, it pushes us toward Tracy's further observation that there is no innocent classic (including the scriptures).

An Ecumenical Appreciation for Plurality

Reformed theology harbors an ecumenical recognition of plurality that is based in ideas that emerged during scholastic debates between Lutherans and Calvinists.[41] Reformed theologians such as Francis Turretin, maintained that God the Son was active also beyond the flesh of the man Jesus, before, during, and after the incarnation. The upshot, as far as they were concerned, is that the infinite truly manifests itself in the finite, but the finite cannot entirely contain or comprehend the infinite. This essential dialectic of theocentric Christology encourages ecumenical theologies that are open to continuing conversations. Why? Because, although it insists that we have no access to God apart from historical particulars, it also recognizes that there is more to God than any one particular contains. Therefore, no subtradition or theology encompasses and adequately represents all there is to know about God and the Word of God. All remain partial and incomplete.

The solution? Put the subtraditions and theological visions into conversation with one another and encourage them to reach out to the *oikoumene*, or the entire inhabited world. By means of these conversations, ecumenical Reformed theologians expect to encounter productive tensions and to become more aware of their own tradition's distinctiveness. They do not try to supersede Christian subtraditions; neither do they endorse dogmatic isolation. Instead, they engage their own particular subtradition, bring it into conversation with other equally particular and partial subtraditions, and remain open to the possibility that these conversations may lead to vital and faithful emendations of Reformed theology.

Ecumenical theologians also appreciate the importance of conversations among broader faith traditions. They suspect that efforts to construct a single world theology fail to estimate sufficiently the importance of particular media and historical traditions of interpretation. They suspect further that world theologies almost inevitably entail attempts to formulate common or generic concepts, and that these attempts may sacrifice depth, foreclosing conversations about the meaning and adequacy of the many symbols and interpretive heritages borne by the multitude of particular religious traditions and subtraditions.[42] At the same time, they also reject exclusionary stances that do not recognize the limitations of our own traditions and do not allow for valid knowledge of God beyond the bounds of Christianity.

The idea is to put traditions into conversations that help us to appreciate distinctive features and doctrines as well as commonalities. Perhaps these conversations will also keep us questioning the adequacy of our own doctrines in the light of insights offered by others. The aim is neither a common world theology nor a defense of Christianity but rather illuminating conversation with worthy partners in our quests to know God more truly.

These critical resources of Reformed theology—an insistence that church teaching is fallible, a high regard for the arts and sciences, and an ecumenical appreciation for plurality—have roots in convictions about God. All express a theocentric bias. No created reality is infallible because no created reality, including the church, is God. Human competence in the arts and sciences is the gift of God, the source and fountain of all truth. God manifests Godself in historical particulars, but no finite reality entirely comprehends the infinite God. Therefore, genuine knowledge of God should be respected wherever it is found, and we should not equate our own tradition (or any other) with all there is to know about God. Other Christian subtraditions operate differently. Thus, Yoder grounded self-critical impulses Christocentrically when he argued against church tradition that violates principles of discipleship based in the teaching of Jesus.[43]

Theistic Humanism?

I turn now to a question I have been encouraged to raise by conversations with William Schweiker. Is there a fourth critical resource in the theistic humanism sometimes put forward by Reformed theologians?[44] I believe there is and that it represents considerably more than a commitment to work from critical editions and to adopt certain methods of text analysis. At its best, the theistic humanism intimated by Reformed theology is a baseline for construing God and humans in their appropriate interrelations.

A key insight is that human life is eccentric.[45] It finds itself in the midst of interrelations with other things, but it is not itself at the center of things. Indeed, it is equipped to see that the value of other things is not merely a function of human needs, wants, and desires, and that the main point of human life lies beyond itself. This comes through in related affirmations of classical Reformed theology articulated by Edwards and by the Westminster Shorter Catechism.[46] God's chief end in creating the world is God's own glory, and, according to Edwards, the glory of the God who creates and redeems is not God in isolation but God in relation to all things. The chief end of the human being, says Westminster, is to glorify God and enjoy God forever, or to be oriented not simply toward oneself but, if we accept Edwards' point, toward the encompassing reality of God and all things in which we participate. The theocentric bias of Reformed Christianity thereby furnishes a basis on which to criticize reductive anthropocentrisms that celebrate humanity on its own and encourage a destructive attention to what is good for humans in isolation. Theistic humanism envisions people in the context of a Cosmic Passage or divine creativity whose wider activities and ends extend far beyond the frame of human realities. This is its "displacing" movement.

But the "displacing" movement also begins a "relocating" movement, a drive toward a theological estimate of the distinctive place and worth of humans. Reformed theistic humanism puts people in their place by insisting that, in the context of the divine creativity, the world beyond humans has value in relation to God. However, it also insists that the good gift of human life has a place and a time in God's cosmos and is endowed with impressive capacities of appreciation and intervention. It claims that humans have worth not as the primary point of God's cosmos but as distinctive and worthy participants. Theistic humanism affirms that human worth is not something that we, whether as individuals, communities, or institutions, simply devise, construct, or bestow. The value of humans as worthy participants in relation to God and to others is rather a reality we are called upon to recognize and acknowledge.

After teaching Calvin for many years, I observe that, on this score, his theology harbors considerable tensions. The *Institutes* begin with a balanced theistic humanism that emphasizes the relational character of the knowledge of God and of ourselves.[47] Calvin's point is roughly that the classical dictum "Know thyself" is helpful but insufficient. For "Christian philosophy," as he sometimes calls it, the saying should rather be "Know God. Know thyself." Without knowledge of self and our gifts, limitations, and corruptions, there is no true knowledge of God: without knowledge of God, there is no true knowledge of self. This twofold knowledge, Calvin maintains, is the essential dynamic of true wisdom.

Occasionally, however, Calvin articulates a full-blown theological anthropocentrism, affirming at one point that "God himself has shown by the order of Creation that he created all things for man's sake."[48] At the same time, he portrays the divine agent in a manner that threatens to render God the only reality, insisting that God determines all (including human actions), and he issues God a metaphysical blank check: God works in and through intermediaries, apart from all intermediaries, and even contrary to every intermediary.[49] Still, when it comes to the worth of humans, Calvin insists that God finds something to love even in sinners and that the atonement is not the cause of God's mercy but its demonstration.[50] Exposing the Christian life and the sixth commandment, he is adamant that we respect the image of God in all people, including ourselves.[51] Nevertheless, and as almost every theological student knows, Calvin upholds a doctrine of double predestination, which, no matter how he labors to integrate it with his theology of grace and justice, seems plainly misanthropic.[52]

Tensions persist in Reformed theology on these points. Edwards affirmed divine determinism and double predestination, but he offered a more detailed and profound account of human agency than did the Genevan Reformer.[53] Schleiermacher claimed divine determinism never operates apart from mundane causes; because he could not fathom a pious apprehension of God's goodness that supports a dual decree, he also allowed for the restoration of all.[54] Barth believed Calvin went astray by making God great at the expense of humanity and world.[55] Should Reformed theologians, even those of us who may find Schleiermacher's and Barth's resolutions flawed, and especially as we engage in ecumenical conversations with Catholic and Methodist friends, work to identify and construct theocentric bases for a robust theistic humanism that can counterbalance destructive impulses toward both hyperhumanism and hypertheism?[56] Yes, I believe we should.

Conclusions

Now for some conclusions about Christian ethics and what it means to be a Christian ethicist. A theological ethic, I maintain, can be Christian if it works with and is shaped by a Christian theology. Even so, I have no intention of arguing that, when it comes to Christian ethics, theology is all you need. It is not, largely because important elements of ethics are not determined by theology alone. Other disciplines, many of them empirical, go into interpreting circumstances calling for moral action—for example, the devastation wrought by Hurricane Katrina and our nation's flawed response. Again, in addition to theology, our estimates of human possibilities and limits are responsive to philosophical perspectives, interpretations of biological bases for agency, and so on, not to mention insights garnered from biographies and novels. Multiple lines of reflection contribute to our understandings of moral norms such as fairness, justice, and care for the weak and dependent.

Thus, rather than argue theology is all you need, I am arguing this. If you are a Christian ethicist, then you also need to be your own theologian. Why? For one thing, your ethic can be Christian if it works with a Christian theology, but there is no generic Christian theology available for you to adopt, and many of the available varieties support different stances in ethics. You cannot lift yourself out of history, and you probably began to be formed by a Christian tradition before you understood it. Nevertheless, without considerable theological study, you can only continue to consent to it (or not) uncritically.

Indeed, you are likely to work with a specific version of your subtradition without accounting for alternative voices within it. You are also unlikely to develop a deep appreciation for your own tradition's self-critical resources, and this will play into the hands of those who regard theology as nothing more than a form of special pleading.

But there is more. Without sustained attention to ethically significant varieties of Christian theology, you will fail to understand adequately not only historical differences in Christian ethics but also some important contemporary debates, say, over public conversations in pluralist democracies. You will miss a pronounced sense for the distinctiveness of your own theology and the ways it influences your ethics. You will miss opportunities to rethink and perhaps revise significant aspects of your own theological ethic in the light of productive tensions and conversations with other theologies, and you will miss the measure of humility that often accompanies the recognition that your own stance is one among many.

Let me also underscore two additional benefits that may accrue to Christian ethicists who are their own theologians, who engage the arts and sciences, and who are ecumenically inclined. First, if you attend to theology, then you will be able to ask in some detail what counts for and against the theological foundations of your ethical stance. In this regard, a host of topics seem important today, among them biological perspectives on human morality. Another matter, now of interest also to the Vatican, is the decentering implications, perhaps especially for some incarnational theologies, of recent cosmological findings and the possibility of life elsewhere.[57] Second, you may compare your own theological vision with the outlooks, worldviews, or comprehensive doctrines that orient other persons and communities, whether these doctrines are Christian, theological, religious, or not. This point touches on comparative religious ethics. But it also seems important to ask what we may learn by comparing our own visions and doctrines with those suggested by classical and recent humanisms, sociobiologists, political ideologies, consumerist cultures, therapeutic perspectives, and so on.

So much, then, for the importance of being your own theologian. What shall we say of the Christian ethicist who downplays theology in order to assure colleagues at college and university that she can make intellectual contributions unsullied by religious sensibilities and convictions? There are, after all, important elements of a Christian ethic that, occasionally and with good reason, may be presented apart from their theological grounds. Moreover, it is not the case that, due to their theologies, Christian ethicists will understand every moral norm and problem wildly differently than others do. Nevertheless, to recall my undergraduate teacher, Van A. Harvey, there is pathos in the attempt to minimize the theological.[58] A Christian ethicist who does so may, in fact, operate in a considerably less critical manner than her more theologically inclined counterparts. She may also find both nonreligious colleagues and Christian ministers wondering whether there is finally anything integral, compelling, or especially interesting in what she has to say. We therefore arrive at a point on which both church and academy may agree: a Christian ethicist without a theology is finally beside the point.

Notes

1. James M. Gustafson, *Can Ethics Be Christian?* (Chicago: University of Chicago Press, 1975), 191.

2. John P. Reeder Jr. "What Is a Religious Ethic?" *Journal of Religious Ethics* 25, no. 3 (25th Anniversary Supplement, 1997): 164, 171–73.

3. James M. Gustafson, *Moral Discernment in the Christian Life: Essays in Theological Ethics*, eds. Theo A. Boer and Paul E. Capetz (Louisville: Westminster John Knox, 2007), 85–97.

4. Thomas Aquinas, *Summa Theologiae*, vol, 1, *Christian Theology*, ed. Thomas Gilby, OP (New York: McGraw-Hill, 1963), Ia, I, 3, 7.

5. Gordon D. Kaufman, *In Face of Mystery: A Constructive Theology* (Cambridge, MA: Harvard University Press, 1993), 3–17.

6. The Latin *doctrina* means teaching and instruction, knowledge imparted by teaching, and the habit produced by instruction. See Charlton T. Lewis and Charles Short, *A Latin Dictionary* (Oxford: Clarendon, 1907), 605. Thus, doctrinal reflections need not be theological or religious.

7. For example, new scholarship about Paul on justification, grace, and law centers on the pastoral challenge of expanding the community of God's people to include non-Jews. See John G. Gager, *Reinventing Paul* (New York: Oxford University Press, 2000).

8. Douglas F. Ottati, "Whose Gospel? Which Culture?" *Insights: A Journal of the Faculty of Austin Seminary* 108, no. 2 (Fall 1993): 41–57.

9. Vigen Guroian reminded me that his Armenian Orthodox tradition, having rejected the Chalcedonian Definition, is officially Monophysite. The reminder did me good, after teaching at a Presbyterian seminary.

10. See James Calvin Davis, ed., *On Religious Liberty: Selections from the Works of Roger Williams* (Cambridge, MA: Belknap Press of Harvard University Press, 2008), 1–45.

11. Rosemary Radford Ruether, *Sexism and God-Talk: Toward a Feminist Theology*, with a new Introduction (Boston: Beacon, 1993).

12. Peter Rideman, *An Account of Our Religion, Doctrine and Faith Given by Peter Rideman of the Brothers Whom Men Call Hutterians* (Rifton, NY: Plough, 1970), 43, 89, 92–93.

13. Ibid., 107, 108, 111–14, 105.

14. John Calvin, *Institutes of the Christian Religion*, ed. John T. McNeill (Louisville, KY: Westminster John Knox, 1960), 4.20.2.

15. Ibid., 4.20.3–4, 6.

16. Ibid., 4.20.8.

17. Ibid., 4.20.11–12.

18. Ibid., 4.20.16, 19.

19. Douglas F. Ottati, *Reforming Protestantism: Christian Commitment in Today's World* (Louisville: Westminster John Knox, 1995), 125–35.

20. John Howard Yoder, *The Original Revolution: Essays on Christian Pacifism* (Scottdale, PA: Herald, 1971), 13–33; and Yoder, *The Politics of Jesus: Vicit Agnus Noster*, 2nd ed. (Grand Rapids, MI: Eerdmans, 1994), 112–33.

21. Stanley Hauerwas, *Against the Nations: War and Survival in a Liberal Society* (Minneapolis: Winston, 1985), 130. Hauerwas distinguishes his position from "the Anabaptist vision" but also claims to be "a high church Mennonite." See Hauerwas, *In Good Company: The Church as Polis* (Notre Dame, IN: University of Notre Dame Press, 1995), 62, 65–78.

22. Abraham Kuyper, *Lectures on Calvinism* (Peabody, MA: Hendrickson, 2008), 77–79, 85, 92.

23. Robin W. Lovin, *Christian Realism and the New Realities* (New York: Cambridge University Press, 2008), 76–81.

24. John W. de Gruchy's claims, "the reformed tradition's world formative impulse" can become a repressive compromise with established institutions. *Liberating Reformed Theology: A South African Contribution to an Ecumenical Debate* (Grand Rapids, MI: Eerdmans, 1991), 18.

25. Lovin, *Christian Realism and the New Realities*, 130.

26. Jeffrey Stout, *Democracy and Tradition* (Princeton, NJ: Princeton University Press, 2004), 6, 87, 280.

27. John Rawls, *Political Liberalism*, exp. ed. (New York: Columbia University Press, 2005), 247–252; Rawls, "The Idea of Public Reason Revisited," *University of Chicago Law Review* 64 (Summer 1997): 772–76, 781–82. K. Roberts Skerrett says Stout, Hauerwas, John Milbank, and Oliver O'Donovan fail to read Rawls' later proposals with care; Skerrett, "Political Liberalism and the Idea of Public Reason: A Response to Jeffrey Stout's *Democracy and Tradition*," *Social Theory and Practice* 31, no. 2 (April 2005): 173–90.

28. Linell Cady notes two narratives of secularization, one dominated by opposition to religion, the other, by increasing pluralism. "Secularism, Secularizing, and Secularization: Reflections on Stout's *Democracy and Tradition*," *Journal of the American Academy of Religion* 73, no. 3 (September 2005): 871–83.

29. Nigel Biggar, "Saving the Secular: The Public Vocation of Moral Theology," *Journal of Religious Ethics* 37, no. 1 (2009): 167–68.

30. James Calvin Davis, *The Moral Theology of Roger Williams* (Louisville: Westminster John Knox, 2004), 93–139.

31. However, Reformed theologians such as Karl Barth and Miroslav Volff, make proposals that move in a different direction. See Douglas F. Ottati, "What Reformed Theology in a Calvinist Key Brings to Conversations about Justice," *Political Theology* 10, no. 3 (2009): 460–62.

32. David Tracy, "How My Mind Has Changed," *Christian Century*, October 10, 1990, 901–4.

33. *Book of Confessions: Study Edition* [Part I of the Constitution of the Presbyterian Church (USA)] (Louisville, KY: Geneva, 1999), 3.20.

34. W. Nijenhuis, *Ecclesia Reformata: Studies on the Reformation* (Leiden: E. J. Brill, 1972), 73–96.

35. This is a point made by Heinrich Bullinger in the Second Helvetic Confession, *Book of Confessions*, 5.010–11.

36. Francois Wendel, *Calvin: Origins and Development of His Religious Thought*, trans. Philip Mairet (Grand Rapids, MI: Baker, 1997), 31.

37. Calvin, *Institutes of the Christian Religion*, 2.2.15. See also Augustine, *Teaching Christianity (De Doctrina Christiana)*, trans. Edmund Hill, OP (Hyde Park, NY: New City), 104; Thomas Aquinas, *The Disputed Questions on Truth*, trans. Robert W. Mulligan, SJ (Chicago: Henry Regnery, 1952), I, I, 8.

38. Calvin, *Institutes of the Christian Religion*, 1.5.2.

39. Jonathan Edwards, *The Works of Jonathan Edwards*, vol. 6, *Scientific and Philosophical Writings*, ed. Wallace E. Anderson (New Haven: Yale University Press, 1980), 145–69, 353.

40. Kuyper, *Lectures on Calvinism*, 116. In *Sacred Theology* (Lafayette, IN: Sovereign Grace, 2001), 261–64, he affirms the liberty of inquiry from the church, even in the case of theology.

41. See my *Hopeful Realism: Reclaiming the Poetry of Theology* (Cleveland: Pilgrim Press, 1999), 69–84.

42. Wilfred Cantwell Smith noted difficulties with common or generic concepts. *Towards a World Theology: Faith and the Comparative History of Religion* (Philadelphia: Westminster Press, 1981), 180–94.

43. Yoder, *Politics of Jesus*, 19–20; Yoder, *The Priestly Kingdom: Social Ethics as Gospel* (Notre Dame: University of Notre Dame Press), 46–79. For an approach that grounds self-criticism Christomorphically, see Joseph Sittler, *The Structure of Christian Ethics* (Louisville: Westminster John Knox, 1998).

44. William Schweiker, *Theological Ethics and Global Dynamics: In the Time of Many Worlds* (Oxford: Blackwell, 2004), 199–219; and David E. Klemm and William Schweiker, *Religion and the Human Future: An Essay on Theological Humanism* (Oxford: Blackwell, 2008).

45. David Kelsey's *Eccentric Existence: A Theological Anthropology*, 2 vol. (Louisville: Westminster John Knox, 2009) focuses on this point.

46. Jonathan Edwards, "A Dissertation Concerning the End for Which God Created the World," *The Works of Jonathan Edwards*, ed. Edward Hickman (Edinburgh: Banner of Truth, 1974), 1:116–21; and *Book of Confessions*, 7.001.

47. Calvin, *Institutes of the Christian Religion*, 1.1.1–2.

48. Ibid., 1.14.22.

49. Ibid., 1.17.1. Calvin's principal example of God working without intermediaries derives from Genesis 1, where God makes light *before* he makes the sun and moon. John Calvin, *Commentaries on the First Book of Moses Called Genesis*, trans. John King (Grand Rapids, MI: Baker, 1998), 82.

50. Calvin, *Institutes of the Christian Religion*, 2.16.2–4.

51. Ibid., 2.8.39–40, 3.7.4–6.

52. Calvin treats objections to his doctrine in ibid., 3.23.

53. Jonathan Edwards, "A Careful and Strict Enquiry into the Prevailing Notions of the Freedom of the Will," in *Works of Jonathan Edwards*, ed. Hickman, 1:3–89.

54. Friedrich Schleiermacher, *The Christian Faith*, ed. H. R. Mackintosh and J. S. Stewart (Philadelphia: Fortress, 1976), #163.

55. Karl Barth, *The Humanity of God*, trans. John Newton Thomas and Thomas Wieser (Richmond, VA: John Knox, 1960), 37–65. "It is when we look at Jesus Christ that we know decisively that God's deity does not exclude, but includes His *humanity*. Would that Calvin had energetically pushed ahead on this point in his Christology, his doctrine of God, his teaching about predestination, and then logically also in his ethics! His Geneva would then not have become such a gloomy affair" (49).

56. Schweiker, *Theological Ethics and Global Dynamics*, 211.

57. Douglas F. Ottati, "Which Way Is Up? An Experiment in Christian Theology and Modern Cosmology," *Interpretation* 59, no. 4 (October 2005): 370–81. The Pontifical Academy of Sciences held a "Study Week on Astrobiology," November 6–10, 2009, www.vatican.va/roman_curia/pontifical_academies/acdscien/own/documents/pasactivities.html.

58. Van A. Harvey, "The Pathos of Liberal Theology," review of *Blessed Rage for Order: The New Pluralism in Theology* by David Tracy, *Journal of Religion* 56 (1976): 382–91.

How Does Christian Ethics Use Its Unique and Distinctive Christian Aspects?

Charles E. Curran

IN THIS ESSAY I RESPOND TO THE QUESTION OF HOW THEOLOGICAL ETHICS
are theological by moving it in a direction that attends to the specifically Christian contribution to ethics. I begin with three somewhat related presuppositions
or questions—on human wisdom, audience(s), and the relationship with other
types of ethics—that indicate how I understand the discipline of Christian ethics.
I follow with a discussion of quandary ethics before moving to a systematic
overview of and approach to Christian ethics. I conclude with a challenge to
raise the distinctive contributions that the Christian tradition makes to the discipline of ethics and its hearers today.

Three Presuppositions

In understanding how theological ethics are theological, we must first examine whether Christian ethics in addition to the scriptures and ecclesial
traditions accepts human sources of moral wisdom and knowledge. This addition has been a traditional issue in Christian ethics. My answer is yes, and is
in accord with the position of many others. This issue has been called the theological aspect of the natural law question. Are there sources of moral wisdom
and knowledge that the Christian shares with all others, or do Christians use
only uniquely Christian sources? The natural law recognizes that human reason reflecting on what God has made can determine how God wants us to live
in this world. The well-known Wesleyan Quadrilateral accepts four sources of
moral wisdom and knowledge, including human sources: scripture, tradition,
reason, and experience.[1]

A critical piece of this inquiry obviously concerns what these human
sources of moral wisdom and knowledge are. Reason (in general), philosophy,
science, and human experience have been recognized by Christian ethicists as
sources of moral wisdom and knowledge. Important further issues concern

what is meant by these different human sources, in what sense they are normative, and how they relate to the uniquely Christian sources of moral wisdom and knowledge.

Notice that the discussion about this issue is itself theological; that is, the discussion gives distinct attention to the relationship of the question to Christian ethics qua Christian—a decidedly theological discourse. Those who recognize human sources of moral wisdom and knowledge ultimately base it on the theological doctrine of creation. God created the world and God created human beings with reason so that human beings with their reason, reflecting on what God has made, can reach conclusions on what God wants us to do in this world.[2] Those who oppose this position also do it on theological grounds. Three theological reasons have been proposed against human sources of moral wisdom and knowledge. First, those who hold to a strict position of the scripture alone do not have room for admitting human sources of moral wisdom and knowledge. However, Jaroslav Pelikan has pointed out that the axiom "Scripture alone" has seldom been taken in an absolutist way.[3] A second theological reason for denying the human sources of moral wisdom and knowledge comes from the destructive force of human sin. How can sinful human reason based on a sin-infested world ever come to true moral wisdom and knowledge?[4] A third argument against human sources of moral wisdom and knowledge is identified especially with the work of Karl Barth, who insisted there can be no two starting points for Christian ethics. We must start only with Christ.[5] I believe there is some truth in these arguments. So, for example, while sin can and does distort human reason, human sources can and do arrive at some true wisdom.

A second presupposition concerns the audience for the discussion. Does Christian ethics address just Christians and the Christian church, or does it also address all people and urge Christians to work with all others for a more just society? The documents of the World Council of Churches and Catholic social teaching as found in papal and Church documents address all people including non-Christians, and call for cooperation of Christians with all others in the work of making a better world.[6] Such an approach obviously coheres with the first presupposition that recognizes the role of human sources of moral wisdom and knowledge.

A third presupposition for my understanding of Christian ethics concerns the relationship between Christian ethics and other types of ethics, especially philosophical ethics. The very terms "Christian ethics" and "theological ethics" indicate that Christian ethics is a species of the discipline of ethics. Ethics is the noun, and theological or Christian is the adjective. From this perspective, all ethics goes about its business seeking to respond to the same basic questions about being and doing but using specific and different sources of moral wisdom and knowledge peculiar to the species. James M. Gustafson has pointed out that all ethics deal with three basic questions—the specific criteria of judgment and acts (duties), the character of the moral self (virtues), and the nature and locus of the good.[7] In my judgment, Christian ethics is a species of ethics all of which deal with the same basic questions and realities. Thus, in Christian ethics as in philosophical ethics there have been different approaches, such as narrative ethics, virtue ethics, deontological ethics, and teleological ethics, and there have often been different conclusions about the specific good.

A word about terminology is in order. The specifically Christian sources such as the Christian scripture and tradition are unique to Christians. No other approach has these same sources. But in my judgment, the material content of Christian morality is not necessarily unique. Many others can and do share such concerns as the commitment to the poor, the need for justice, a call for self-sacrificing love, and the importance of mercy and forgiveness. Thus, the content of Christian ethics is not necessarily unique to Christian ethics but is distinctive because this content is characteristic of the Christian approach.

In keeping with these presuppositions, this chapter will develop in some length two specific aspects of the question about the unique and distinctive aspects of Christian ethics. First, the essay will discuss quandary ethics, where the human sources of moral wisdom and knowledge have played a prominent role and unfortunately at times an almost exclusive role. The next section will develop a systematic overview of Christian ethics, showing how the unique sources and distinctive content of Christian ethics should be used.

Quandary Ethics

One who accepts the role of human sources of moral wisdom and knowledge in Christian ethics recognizes that this role is most prominent in quandary ethics. Quandary ethics deal with concrete, objective human situations. In addition, it is here that human reason, science, and human experience predominate. The many discussions about the use (or lack) of scripture in Christian ethics well illustrate the lesser role of uniquely Christian sources in dealing with quandary ethics. Scripture is more applicable to the more general aspects of Christian ethics such as virtues, values, and dispositions. Since the scriptures were written in a particular and specific time that differs very much from present-day circumstances, scripture does not have that much direct contribution to the discussion of specific actions today. To wit, our discipline has become very conscious of the danger of the illegitimate use of scripture as a prooftext in the discussion of particular actions.[8] Today, Christian ethicists generally recognize that we have paid too much attention to quandary ethics in the past to the neglect of an ethics on being. However, there will always be a place in Christian ethics for a consideration of the morality of particular acts facing Christians and society as a whole, especially when disputes exist about these actions.

At times in exploring quandary ethics, the human sources of moral wisdom and knowledge have been used exclusively, and there has been no place at all for the unique Christian sources. In addition, an emphasis on quandary ethics often leaves little or no place for the distinctive content of Christian ethics. Two examples illustrate this reality.

Catholic moral theology before Vatican II (1962–65) well exemplifies the exclusive use of human reason in quandary ethics. Catholic moral theology employed its theory of natural law to address these issues. From a theological perspective, natural law serves to mediate the eternal law, which is the plan of God's reason for the world. Human reason reflecting on God's creation can discern what God wants us to do. One does not go immediately and directly to God to determine what should be done in this world. However, the neoscholastic understanding of the supernatural and natural orders colored this approach. For the neoscholastic, the natural order concerns life in this world, whereas the supernatural refers to the life of grace. As a result, quandary ethics was not only heavily based on human sources of moral wisdom but, for all practical purposes, since quandary ethics concerned life in this world, it exclusively used these human sources. There was no room for any unique Christian sources. Because the manuals of Catholic moral theology trained confessors to know what acts were sinful, these textbooks reduced all ethics to quandary ethics.[9]

Criticism of this approach came from two different but somewhat overlapping reasons. First, the natural order as such has never existed; it is only a "remainder concept."[10] As a matter of fact, today we are living in an order that involves God's creative action and where God's redeeming action is present as well as the negative aspect of the presence of human sinfulness. Second, Vatican II criticized such an exclusively human approach for not giving enough importance to both sin and grace. Vatican II also recognized that Christian morality cannot be reduced only to quandary ethics.[11]

Even in quandary ethics there is a place for unique Christian sources and some distinctive Christian content. What I call the stance of Christian ethics plays a role even in quandary ethics. The Christian ethicist and the Christian person with this stance look at the world in terms of the fivefold Christian mysteries of creation, sin, incarnation, redemption, and resurrection destiny. While the stance or perspective alone cannot resolve quandaries, it can provide some parameters and attitudes that affect quandary ethics. For example, such a stance with its eschatological understanding recognizes that at times violence might be necessary to defend and protect justice in our world, but the temptation exists to resort to violence too quickly. Such a perspective also supports a theological realism that avoids the extremes of optimism and pessimism about the human condition and recognizes the limits of anyone using human reason. As individuals, groups of any kinds, and nations, we are limited by the very fact that we are particular creatures existing in a particular time and place in which, additionally, we are all affected to some degree or other by human sinfulness. In addition, Christian virtues (e.g., mercy, compassion, justice) and Christian values or principles (e.g., preferential option for the poor, the sanctity and dignity of human life) affect quandary ethics.

A second example of quandary ethics comes from the history of Christian medical and bioethics.[12] For all practical purposes, before the late 1960s Roman Catholics were the only ones interested in medical ethics. Other Christians, philosophers, and medical schools were not interested precisely because it was generally recognized that good ethics and good medicine were the same, since they employed the same basic criterion: what is for the good of the patient? Roman Catholic medical ethics spent much of its time discussing specifically Catholic issues, such as contraception and sterilization, and to its credit also made some important lasting contributions such as the principle that, in a critical care quandary, one is required to use only ordinary and not extraordinary means to preserve life. In its approach to medical ethics, the Roman Catholic tradition concentrated on a quandary ethics based exclusively on natural law.[13]

After the late 1960s the field of bioethics grew and developed in an exponential manner. The primary reason for this tremendous growth came from technological developments in medical practices. For example, the possibility of transplanting one of two paired organs (e.g., kidneys) from one person to another and the growing importance and need for experimentation to develop new medicines and approaches raised recognition that there was no longer only the one person, the patient, to consider. Technological developments in artificial reproduction and other life-enhancing areas created many new problems. These developments reinforced the role of bioethics as dealing with quandaries.

Protestant ethicists soon after started to write in bioethics. Paul Ramsey and James Gustafson were among the earliest and most prominent. In light of growing concerns about these new issues, they too concentrated on quandary ethics. They recognized the predominant role of human reason in this area and the need to speak to all; to their credit, they also insisted on the need to use distinctive Christian aspects. Ramsey employed the biblical concept of covenant to explain the relationship between the physician or researcher and the patient as person.[14] Gustafson developed three theological themes that influence our attitude to human life and biomedical actions: God intends the well-being of creation; God is both the ordering power that preserves and sustains the well-being of creation and the creating power of new possibilities for well-being in events of nature and history; and human beings are finite and sinful.[15] Unfortunately, subsequent Christian bioethicists did not always follow their example.

Beginning with Congress's establishment in 1974 of the National Commission for the Protection of Human Subjects in Biomedical and Behavioral Research, government advisory commissions came into existence to deal with bioethical issues. Starting with President Jimmy Carter, all subsequent presidents have appointed commissions to look into bioethical issues. President Ronald Reagan's advisory commission produced ten book-length studies about with such issues as the definition of death, foregoing life support, informed consent, experimentation, genetic manipulation, and access to health care. Later commissions dealt with cloning and embryonic stem cell research.[16]

Many of these same issues also had legal aspects, and the courts decided cases dealing with the right to forego life support and who could make that decision. Legal bioethics became a huge discipline in its own right. Medical schools also began to teach bioethics with emphasis on the quandary issues that were arising. And hospitals began to have ethics committees to address the problems arising in their institutions.[17]

In these contexts a general impression existed that the introduction of particularistic perspectives such as Christian theology would be inappropriate. The concerns of public policy, legal ethics, and medical school education had to address all people and not appeal to one religious tradition or any religious traditions. The most used textbook in colleges, universities, medical schools, and nursing schools was *Principles of Biomedical Ethics* by Tom L. Beauchamp and James F. Childress, originally published in 1979 with a sixth edition in 2009.[18] Childress himself was trained as a Christian ethicist and still writes from that perspective, but in the *Principles of Biomedical Ethics* he prescinded from any theological considerations and wrote as a philosopher. Other significant authors in the area of bioethics, such as Robert Veatch and Leroy Walters, had also been trained in theological ethics but generally wrote in bioethics only from a philosophical perspective.[19] The need to address public policy and the general public thus argued against using any theological warrants in bioethics.

However, religious thinkers have strongly defended some use of religious language and concepts in the public square. For example, Nigel Biggar and Linda Hogan's recent book brings together many essays defending religious voices in public places.[20] Robin Lovin insists on what he calls unapologetic politics. The unapologetic principle maintains that no context is required to explain itself in terms that reduce it to an instrument of other purposes. Thus, in discussing public issues affecting society, churches and religious ethicists of all types can appeal to their unique and distinctive religious aspects. Although the unapologetic principle states that groups and institutions will not be required to formulate their claims using only human sources of moral wisdom and knowledge, it does not say that they are not allowed to continue to do so. A Christian church, for example, might decide that it would be more effective in a particular case to not appeal to its own unique religious sources. Lovin points out that his understanding applies to public discourse in general but not to the coercive actions in the three different branches of government: executive, legislative, and judicial. The public sphere, however, is much bigger than the governmental sphere.[21]

The important distinction made earlier between unique sources and distinctive content in Christian ethics helps to address this issue of Christians speaking in the public arena. Distinctive Christian content, such as a preferential option for the poor or the role of forgiveness, is also recognized by many non-Christians. I have maintained that there is no unique, specific material content to Christian ethics in the sense that no others can accept a similar material content.[22]

The historical development of Christian bioethics is instructive because it also shows that only later in the development of the discipline did bioethics in general and Christian bioethics in particular involve more than just quandary ethics. Different authors later talked about the role of virtue ethics with regard to the physician herself.[23] The famous Dax case, where doctors saved the life of a severely burned patient who did not want to be treated, well illustrates how bioethics had forgotten about the patient.[24] William F. May, in his 1991 book *The Patient's Ordeal*, points out that bioethics in general and Christian bioethics tended to forget completely about the patient. The patient is dealing with ultimate questions of meaning—the meaning of life itself, of diminishment, suffering, and death. Christian ethics has a very significant role to play in these areas.[25]

To his great credit, Stanley Hauerwas, more than any other Christian ethicist, has recognized problems created by a one-sided emphasis on quandary ethics, has insisted on the role of the unique Christian narrative, and has written about the realities of diminishment, suffering, disabilities, and death. However, Hauerwas generally disagrees with some of the presuppositions I hold about Christian ethicists speaking to all people. Rather, he emphasizes the role of Christian ethics as employing the Christian narrative to speak directly to the church and not to the world.[26] In my judgment, the unique and distinctive aspects of Christian ethics should always be present, even in quandary ethics to some extent, but these aspects become more significant and important as the focus of Christian ethics considers more than quandaries. The following section will develop a systematic overview of all the aspects of Christian ethics.

Systematic Overview

In what follows I summarize my thematic and systematic understanding of Christian ethics and illustrate in a necessarily very brief way the role of the unique and distinctive Christian aspects. My systematic approach to Christian ethics involves five steps—stance, model, subject pole, object pole, and conscience and decision making, which bring the subject and object poles together.[27]

Stance

The stance is the fundamental perspective or horizon with which the Christian ethicist and all Christians envision the reality of our world. This horizon or stance involves the fivefold Christian mysteries of creation, sin, incarnation, redemption, and resurrection destiny. Creation reminds us that all that exists is good but is finite and affected by the second element in the stance, sin. Sin distorts creation but does not destroy it. The mystery of the incarnation underscores some continuing goodness of creation and humankind by the fact that God has joined Godself to the human. The mysteries of redemption and resurrection destiny refer to the tension between the "already" of redemption and the "not yet" of the eschatological fullness. This tension between the already and the not yet calls for the Christian to grow and develop in the moral life, and to try to move the world in which we all live toward eschatological fullness but with the realization that we will always fall far short. Note that the stance, with its acceptance of creation and incarnation, also grounds the recognition that Christian ethics uses the human sources of moral wisdom and knowledge about the world and our place in it. The stance affects to some degree all the other aspects of Christian ethics.

Model

The second step involves the model of Christian ethics, a relationality–responsibility model. Often philosophical ethics speaks of deontology, teleology, relationality, or virtue ethics as normative theories. But this norm-talk comes from a narrow perspective that sees ethics primarily as quandary ethics. Model is a much broader concept than normative theory, and it summarizes the basic understanding of how the moral life operates. Here uniquely Christian sources also coincide with some common human sources as the bases for seeing the moral life in terms of the person's multiple relationships with God, neighbor, world in history and in nature, and self—and the human responsibilities within these relationships. The Trinity reminds us that the divine image of personhood is revealed in relational terms. The basic "love command" in the New Testament involves God, neighbor, and self, and this command also grounds and confirms the relationality model. The relationship to the world of nature together with the creation element of the stance recognizes the ecological aspect of the Christian life as relationally dependent on nature and creation. The understanding of sin touches all these relationships.

Subject Pole

The subject pole of morality, the third step, concerns the person as both subject and agent. As subject, the person makes herself who she is and grows in these multiple relationships, and as agent, the person strives to act in the world. Both the stance and the model contribute to understanding of the subject in terms of a theological anthropology. The human person is a finite, sinful, and graced person who lives in these relationships. The social and relational understanding of the human person stands as a strong criticism of the prominent individualism in the American ethos today.

The subject pole involves both the fundamental commitment of the Christian person as such and the virtues that modify the person as self and agent. The basic commitment is the most important reality in the formation of the person. The New Testament, especially in the Gospels, puts special emphasis on discipleship as describing this fundamental commitment.[28] The basic commitment should permeate and influence all that the person is and does. I see this basic commitment in terms of the four relationships. Like all relationships, the basic commitment cannot be taken for granted but needs to develop and grow. Above all, one needs to become ever more conscious and explicit about the importance and role of this basic commitment to see that it influences all that one is and does and in what ways.

Since this basic commitment is the most important part of the Christian moral life, one would expect Christian ethicists to give great importance to it. But such is not the case. In fact, writings in Christian ethics seldom develop this basic commitment in any depth. Recently Roman Catholic moral theologians have written on the fundamental option or the basic orientation of the Christian person.[29] However, Catholic moral theologians who spent a great deal of time developing fundamental option theory showed comparatively little interest in how this reality serves as the basic orientation of the person directing and influencing the entire moral life. The fundamental option theory was used primarily to explain the reality of mortal sin.[30] The manuals of moral theology tended to identify mortal sin with categorical actions involving grave matter. Mortal sin in this view is a quite frequent occurrence in Christian moral life. But mortal sin as the breaking of our basic love commitment with God cannot be such a frequent occurrence in a Christian life. Mortal sin as the breaking of the fundamental option for God cannot be determined solely on the basis of the external act itself. This emphasis on the fundamental option has made a significant contribution to the understanding of mortal sin, but its primary role in directing and guiding the whole life of the Christian has not received much attention in Catholic moral theology.

In addition to the basic orientation or fundamental option of the person, the subject pole of morality involves the virtues that should characterize the life of the Christian person in terms of both the personal growth of the individual and the actions that the person does. The classical tradition recognized the three theological virtues of faith, hope, and charity, as well as the cardinal moral virtues of prudence, justice, fortitude, and temperance. From the theological perspective, even these moral virtues involved both the gift of God's grace and the human response. I see the virtues in light of the fourfold relationships mentioned earlier. Some virtues, such as the theological virtues as well as creativity and fidelity, involve all four relationships. In the specific relationship to God, for example, the two most important virtues are openness to receive the gift of God, and gratitude and thanksgiving for these gifts. Openness is the fundamental condition to receive the gift of God, rooted in the scriptural understanding of the poor in spirit.[31] Gratitude and thanksgiving for the gifts received from God above all show themselves in worship and praise of God. The virtues in our relationship to God well illustrate how distinctively Christian aspects should also affect our other relationships with neighbor, world, and self, but space constraints prevent any further discussion of the virtues affecting these relationships.

The distinctively Christian aspects have their greatest role to play with regard to the subject pole of ethics. The basic orientation and virtues of the Christian person raise considerations that have often been treated under the heading of spiritual and ascetical theology. All Christians are called to the fullness of love of God and neighbor, and they must strive for continual growth or conversion in their lives. Prayer and the spiritual and corporal works of mercy are important ways of growing in this orientation and in the panoply of Christian virtues. Moreover, the liturgy has a fundamental role in nurturing and developing the Christian life. At its best, the liturgy is also a call to action in personal and social life. Christians should follow the example of Jesus by nourishing one another and by sharing their bread and wine and all they have with those to whom they are committed, and especially with those who are poor or needy. It is fair to say, as a whole and stifled, perhaps, by the demands of quandary ethics, that Christian ethics has not given enough emphasis to these dimensions of the Christian life.

Object Pole

By its very nature, the object pole of Christian ethics does not involve distinctively Christian aspects as much as the subject pole. Nevertheless, these aspects have a significant place in Christian theological ethics. The object pole refers to the values, principles, and norms that guide life in the world. The Christian values of love, mercy, forgiveness, and justice are most significant. These values play a greater role in the personal realm but should affect also the social realm, as illustrated by Donald Shriver's book *An Ethic for Enemies: Forgiveness in Politics*.[32] There are also more specific values and principles, such as the preferential option for the poor and the fact that the goods of creation serve the needs of all God's people. Time constraints prevent any further discussion of the distinctive Christian content with regard to the object pole of ethics.

Conscience

In my systematic approach to Christian ethics, conscience is what brings the subject pole and the object pole together in concrete decision making. Here the distinctively Christian aspects should have a more important place than is often recognized. Scripture and the Christian tradition have developed what has been called the discernment of spirits as a way to determine what is God's will. In the New Testament, the Holy Spirit is closely connected with determining the will of God for our life and actions. The New Testament also recognizes other spirits, whose influence can be good or bad.[33] Subsequent commentators on the Christian life, such as Ignatius of Loyola and Francis de Sales, have written much about the discernment of spirits.[34] It is true that in earlier times people spoke much more about the role of these spirits (e.g., angels and demons), whereas today we would tend to see them primarily as natural causes, such as our own inspirations and feelings. But what the earlier spiritual writers have said about the discernment of spirits and the discernment of the Holy Spirit can be applied to our understanding of conscience today.

What are the criteria that spiritual writers have used to determine the discernment of spirits? An obvious criterion is the fact that by their fruits you will know them. Good spirits produce good fruits, whereas bad spirits result in bad fruits. Ignatius of Loyola and Francis de Sales also emphasize interior peace as a criterion for discerning spirits and the will of God. They recognize there is danger of a false peace but, in keeping with an old axiom, possible abuse does not take away legitimate use. The recognition of the role of interior peace in the discernment of spirits and the will of God coheres with what human experience as well as philosophy and psychology have taught about the peace of a good conscience. With regard to subsequent conscience (after the act has been done), people often refer to the remorse of a bad conscience. The criterion of a good-conscience decision is peace and joy. Thus, even in the understanding of the very specific reality of conscience and decision making, the distinctively Christian aspects of spiritual discernment make a very important contribution and cohere with the recognition from other human sources that true joy and peace are the best criterion of a good-conscience decision.

A Concluding Comment

I have indicated how, in my systematic approach to Christian ethics, the unique and distinctive Christian dimensions should come into play. In the process, especially in the area of the subject pole of morality, it seems we Christian ethicists have not given enough importance to the fundamental commitment to God, the virtues of Christian discipleship, and Christian prayer—important Christian aspects that could (should) bear upon our ethics. But why are these aspects relatively underdeveloped?

A clue in answering this question came to me in writing my book on the history of Catholic moral theology in the United States. Only in 1995 did the first slim volume appear in the United States that discussed the relationship between moral theology and spirituality. Mark O'Keefe, teaching at St. Meinrad Seminary in Indiana, is the author.[35] After that time, writers dealing with these aspects also came from seminaries and theologates.[36] College and university professors to this day have written comparatively little on this aspect, and university presses have not published in this area. This fact raises the question, Why? The reason might very well be that the standards used for academic excellence and advancement in colleges and universities do not consider such topics as areas that are truly academic and scientific.

I want to be very careful and nuanced here. On the whole, the development of Christian ethics in the last half century in the United States has been phenomenal, precisely because of its location in the halls of US higher education. Look at the history of our own society. We began a little more than fifty years ago as essentially the society of male, white teachers of social ethics in Protestant seminaries. We have changed greatly over fifty years, and our discipline has a breadth and a depth that is beyond the imagination of our founding fathers (literally, fathers is not an improper use of exclusive language). On the whole, I have no doubt that the college and university setting has been most beneficial for our discipline. But I have also come to the conclusion that the criteria for academic recognition and advancement have been a factor in our collective failure to give enough importance to the unique and distinctive Christian aspects of the discipline. Theology in the eyes of some is a very soft discipline and not rigorously academic. This is the conclusion I have reached and one of the reasons for the question of this essay, "How does Christian ethics use its unique and distinctive Christian aspects?" What do you think?

Notes

1. In reality, the term "Wesleyan Quadrilateral" does not come from John Wesley, but from Albert Outler. See Ted A. Campbell, "The Wesleyan Quadrilateral: A Modern Methodist Myth," in *Theology in the United Methodist Church*, ed. Thomas G. Langford (Nashville: Kingswood, 1990), 127–82. For the acceptance of the Wesleyan Quadrilateral by some evangelicals, see Donald A. D. Thorsun, *The Wesleyan Quadrilateral: Scripture, Tradition, Reason, and Experience as a Model of Evangelical Theology* (Grand Rapids, MI: Zondervan, 1990).

2. Josef Fuchs, *Natural Law: A Theological Investigation*, trans. Helmut Reckter and John A. Dowling (New York: Sheed and Ward, 1965).

3. Jaroslav Pelikan, *The Vindication of Tradition* (New Haven, CT: Yale University Press, 1984).

4. Helmut Thielicke, *Theological Ethics*, vol. 1, *Foundations*, ed. William H. Lazareth (Philadelphia: Fortress, 1966), 398.

5. Henry Chavannes, *L'analogie entre Dieu et le monde selon saint Thomas d'Aquin et selon Karl Barth* (Paris: Cerf, 1969).

6. A. J. van der Bent, *Christian Response in a World Crisis: A Brief History of the WCC's Commission of the Churches on International Affairs* (Geneva: World Council of Churches, 1986); and Kenneth R. Himes, ed., *Modern Catholic Social Teaching* (Washington, DC: Georgetown University Press, 2004).

7. James M. Gustafson, *Christ and the Moral Life* (New York: Harper & Row, 1968), 3.

8. A recent book from the Congregation of the Doctrine of the Faith of the Vatican recognizes the problem of prooftexting in moral theology; see Pontifical Biblical Commission, *Bible and Morality: Biblical Roots of Christian Conduct* (Città del Vaticano: Editrice Vaticana, 2008).

9. See, for example, Mark E. Graham, *Josef Fuchs on Natural Law* (Washington, DC: Georgetown University Press, 2002).

10. For Karl Rahner's understanding of nature as a remainder concept, see Anne Carr, "Theology and Experience in the Thought of Karl Rahner," *Journal of Religion* 53 (1973): 363–64.

11. For my analysis of Vatican II's contribution to moral theology, see Charles E. Curran, *Catholic Moral Theology in the United States: A History* (Washington, DC: Georgetown University Press, 2008), 131–44.

12. Jennifer K. Walter and Eran P. Klein, eds., *The Story of Bioethics: From Seminal Works to Contemporary Explorations* (Washington, DC: Georgetown University Press, 2003).

13. Gerald A. Kelly, *Medico-Moral Problems* (St. Louis: Catholic Hospital Association, 1958).

14. Paul Ramsey, *The Patient as Person* (New Haven, CT: Yale University Press, 1970), xii–xiii and throughout.

15. James M. Gustafson, *The Contributions of Theology to Medical Ethics*, Pere Marquette Theology Lecture (Milwaukee: Marquette University Press, 1975).

16. "Former Bioethics Commissions," Presidential Commission for the Study of Bioethical Issues website, www.bioethics.gov/commissions.

17. Renee C. Fox and Judith P. Swazey, *Observing Bioethics* (New York: Oxford University Press, 2008).

18. Tom L. Beauchamp and James F. Childress, *Principles of Biomedical Ethics*, 6th ed. (New York: Oxford University Press, 2009).

19. For the latest of Veatch's many writings, see Robert M. Veatch, Patient, *Heal Thyself: How the New Medicine Puts the Patient in Charge* (New York: Oxford University Press, 2009); and Veatch, *Disruptive Dialogue: Medical Ethics and the Collapse of Physician-Humanist Conversation* (New York: Oxford University Press, 2005). Leroy Walters's most important contribution has been his work as editor and coeditor of the *Bibliography of Bioethics*, 35 vols. (Detroit: Gale Research, 1975–2009).

20. Nigel Biggar and Linda Hogan, eds., *Religious Voices in Public Places* (Oxford: Oxford University Press, 2009).

21. Robin W. Lovin, *Christian Realism and the New Realities* (New York: Cambridge University Press, 2008), 117–51.

22. Charles E. Curran, "What Is Distinctive and Unique about Christian Ethics and Christian Morality," in *Toward an American Catholic Moral Theology* (Notre Dame, IN: University of Notre Dame Press, 1987), 52–64.

23. James F. Drane, *Becoming a Good Doctor: The Place of Virtue and Character in Medical Ethics* (Kansas City, MO: Sheed and Ward, 1988); and Edmund D. Pellegrino and David C. Thomasma, *The Christian Virtues in Medical Practice* (Washington, DC: Georgetown University Press, 1996).

24. Lonnie D. Kliever, ed., *Dax's Case: Essays in Medical Ethics and Human Meaning* (Dallas: Southern Methodist University Press, 1989).

25. William F. May, *The Patient's Ordeal* (Bloomington: Indiana University Press, 1991).

26. For an overview of Hauerwas's many writings in Christian bioethics, see Stephen E. Lammers, "On Stanley Hauerwas: Theology, Medical Ethics, and the Church," in *Theological Voices and Medical Ethics*, ed. Allen Verhey and Stephen E. Lammers, 57–77 (Grand Rapids, MI: Eerdmans, 1993). The journal *Christian Bioethics: Non-Ecumenical Studies in Medical Morality* often publishes articles taking approaches somewhat similar to Hauerwas.

27. Charles E. Curran, *The Catholic Moral Tradition Today: A Synthesis* (Washington, DC, Georgetown University Press, 1999).

28. See Dietrich Bonhoeffer, *Cost of Discipleship*, 2nd ed., trans. R. H. Fuller (New York: MacMillan, 1959).

29. For examples of this approach to fundamental option, see Brian F. Linnane, "Rahner's Fundamental Option and Virtue Ethics," in *Philosophy & Theology* 15, no. 1 (2003): 229–54; and Jean Porter, "Moral Language and the Language of Grace: The Fundamental Option and the Virtue of Charity," *Philosophy & Theology* 10 no. 1 (1997): 169–98.

30. Timothy E. O'Connell, *Principles for a Catholic Morality* (New York: Seabury, 1978), 45–82. O'Connell, in what was basically the first new textbook in Catholic moral theology in the United States after Vatican II, relies heavily here on Karl Rahner and Josef Fuchs. I personally develop the fundamental option in light of the relationality–responsibility approach and have problems with the Rahnerian approach.

31. Albert Gelin, *The Poor of Yahweh* (Collegeville, MN: Liturgical, 1964).

32. Donald Shriver, *An Ethic for Enemies: Forgiveness in Politics* (New York: Oxford University Press, 1995).

33. Jacques Guillet, Gustave Bardy, François Vandenbroucke, Joseph Pegon, and Henri Martin, *Discernment of Spirits*, trans. Sister Innocentia Richards (Collegeville, MN: Liturgical, 1970). This book is the authorized English translation of the lengthy article in the *Dictionnaire de Spiritualité*.

34. Jules J. Toner, *A Commentary on St. Ignatius: Rules for the Discernment of Spirits* (St. Louis: Institute of Jesuit Sources, 1982); Toner, *Discerning God's Will: Ignatius of Loyola's Teaching on Christian Decision Making* (St. Louis: Institute of Jesuit Sources, 1991); and Richard M. Gula, *Moral Discernment* (New York: Paulist, 1997).

35. Mark O'Keefe, *Becoming Good, Becoming Holy: On the Relationship of Christian Ethics and Spirituality* (New York: Paulist, 1995).

36. Curran, *Catholic Moral Theology in the United States*, 141–44.

The Ethical Complexity of Abraham Lincoln: Is There Something for Religious Ethicists to Learn?

Lloyd Steffen

ABRAHAM LINCOLN'S UNORTHODOX RELIGIOUS VIEWS CONNECTED TO AN ethical stance that is not reducible to any single overarching philosophical theory. By attending to virtue cultivation, a rational utilitarianism, and a divinely grounded natural law commitment to human equality, Lincoln devised a principled yet flexible ethic that addressed the complexity of the moral life. Despite apparent philosophical difficulties, Lincoln's "hybrid ethic" nonetheless coheres to reveal familiar features of ordinary moral thinking while illuminating moral judgments in the face of dilemmas. As such, it is worthy of attention by ethicists, who have much to learn from the humility Lincoln expressed in connecting religious sources to ethical meaning.

Introduction

Abraham Lincoln may be the most written about nonreligious figure in world history. The Library of Congress counts more than fourteen thousand volumes dedicated explicitly to Lincoln, and in recent years even more room had to be made on library shelves for the scores of new studies and interpretations published in anticipation of the two hundredth anniversary of Lincoln's birth, which took place in 2009. Best known among these new studies is Doris Kearns Goodwin's *Team of Rivals*—a favorite, as we were informed by his press spokespersons, of President Barack Obama.[1]

Lincoln continues to compel the interest of historians and scholars, but he fascinates beyond such professional audiences. His story, complete with references to his moral character, is so central to the American mythos that it can show up in the most unlikely of places, as this short summary of his biography illustrates: "Before he became the sixteenth President, Abraham Lincoln led a fascinating life growing up in the harsh environment of frontier America. But despite the hardships, his perseverance and dedication to serving his fellow citizens resulted in many vital contributions to his country. As president during one of the most critical times in the nation's history, his character and values learned as a boy enabled him to preserve the union, as well as his place in history as a great American (Cracker Jack prize)."[2]

This Cracker Jack summary reminds us that Lincoln's values and character were critical to the person he was and became, and this claim, simple as it is, is not in dispute. But given all that we have learned about Lincoln's life, and given some of the new scholarship that has come forth in recent years, we can say that the story of Lincoln's ethics, if we may call it that, is not really so simple as our mythmakers would have it. Lincoln's ethic, despite its clarity as an expression of practical reason and despite what proved to be its functionality in Lincoln's life, is, as a theoretical matter, rather complex. That complexity is most evident in its refusal to honor the antagonisms bequeathed by Enlightenment thinkers to moral theory—the antagonism between duty-bound, deontological ethics versus consequentialist utilitarianism, and between an ethics of action versus one focused on virtue and character development. Lincoln's ethic is not monolithic or exclusivist; it is not systematic but synthetic. It is a hybrid ethic that includes duty, principles, and practical attention to consequences; it is an ethic concerned with realism, right action, and responsibility; and it is concerned with goodness, personal virtue, and character formation.

I want to consider three characteristics of this hybrid ethic: its commitment to character development and the cultivation of virtue; its unmistakable consequentialism; and its avowal of bedrock principles that Lincoln himself believed were God-given and nonnegotiable. This ethic is challenging as a philosophical position, but even more complications are added because this ethic was also shaped by attention to theological matters, especially the idea of divine purposes, which he claimed not to understand.[3] The intersection of moral thought with political realities and with theological reflection adds yet other layers of complexity to his moral thought.

In what follows, I offer what I think to be the relevance of this reflection on divine purposes for those of us who continue to ponder questions of moral meaning in a theological context. First, I turn to the Lincoln ethic, beginning with some general comments about the role of reason, then to the ethic's component parts. Second, I consider the content of that ethic.

Lincoln's Ethic—The Basics

By referring to "Lincoln's ethic" I do not mean to suggest that Lincoln ever presented a complete and coherent moral theory, much less grasped his own ethical stance in a systematic way. He was not a philosopher in our understanding of the term (though I am reluctant to say he was not a theologian). Neither did he consciously subscribe to any particular ethical theory although he fashioned an ethical stance deeply reflective of Enlightenment values. Lincoln's ethic is Enlightenment bound and reason driven, yet I want to suggest it also has a premodern feel to it, especially regarding pre-Enlightenment natural law thinking. Lincoln's principled yet flexible ethic seems akin in many respects to the ethical stance of Cicero: the Cicero who would write about virtues in a book on duties; the Cicero who would take his deeply held principles into the political arena to finagle with the intricacies of power relationships; the Cicero who would resort to calculating consequences in the effort to advance beyond concern with mere personal advancement the high-minded moral end of a common good conformed to natural justice.[4]

Enlightenment Reason

With reason and self-discipline value constants, Lincoln's ethical thought exudes confidence in the power of reason to steer the course of human events toward the end of a civil and just society dedicated to liberty, human equality, and self-government. Historian Allen Guelzo has written that Lincoln "remained a Victorian child of the Enlightenment, of Paine and Burns and Mill."[5] Fred Kaplan, in his masterful analysis of Lincoln's writing, notes that Lincoln "found in his Enlightenment models and in Shakespeare the affirmation of his tested but sustained faith in man's reasoning faculty as his highest and in reason's power to advance good works."[6]

A lover of poetry, Lincoln also demonstrated a natural analytical ability, an aptitude toward mathematics, and a technical problem-solving ability we would today associate with engineering. Lincoln demonstrated left-brain creativity, inventing—though never actually using—a floatation device designed to lift up boats stranded on shoals. He received a patent for this, the only president ever to hold one. But it was in the law that Lincoln found a profession that suited his rationalistic temperament. Richard Cardewine writes, "Lincoln's preference for swaying opinion by reasoned argument rather than by feeding prejudice remained a constant of his political career."[7] And he found a political home temperamentally suited to his analytical cast of mind in the Whig Party, which endorsed an orderly plan of economic development that itself reflected a moral rationalism. In an age when Jacksonian Democrats "valorized passion over reason," attracting revivalist Methodists and Baptists, the "sober, industrious, thrifty people" who made up the Whig Party faithful presented themselves as logical, systematic, organized and programmatic—in short, rational and, not insignificantly, averse to passion.[8]

Lincoln looked to the nation's founders as paragons of both virtue and reasonableness. In his first public speaking engagement, the January 1838 Lyceum speech in Springfield, Illinois, Lincoln reflected on George Washington and the Revolution, noting that the post-Revolution generation, Lincoln's own, must sustain the "temple of liberty" on the foundations of reason. "Passion has helped us; but can do so no more. It will in future be our enemy. Reason, cold, calculating, unimpassioned reason, must furnish all the materials for our future support and defence. Let those materials be molded into *general intelligence, sound morality* and, in particular, *a reverence for the Constitution and laws*."[9]

Sound morality and reverence for law were fused in Lincoln's mind, and both were to be sustained and cultivated by reason—cold, calculating, and unimpassioned. In Lincoln's mind, passion in the body politic was equivalent to the breakdown of law, and mob violence represented defiance not only of law but of reason itself. It could only be countered, Lincoln averred in the Lyceum speech, with a "reverence for the laws," which the young Lincoln held must "become the *political religion* of the nation."[10] This religion of reverence for law was reason-based, staunchly opposed to unreflective passion, and inclusive of all people: "Let the old and the young, the rich and the poor, the grave and the gay, of all sexes and tongues, and colors and conditions sacrifice unceasingly upon its altars."[11] In those words Lincoln shared his vision not only of a self-governing, liberty-loving polis but of a moral community sustained by cold, calculating, unimpassioned reason.

Given Lincoln's known capacity for tenderheartedness, it is strange to hear him use the language "cold" and "calculating" to talk about the material support for sound morality. But there can be no doubt that his ethical views rested on confidence in the power of the rational faculty, which he brought to the "slavery debate." With slavery an even more heated topic in Lincoln's day than abortion has been in ours, and with Lincoln himself quite passionate in his expressed opposition to slavery, Lincoln nonetheless entered the political arena offering a cooling, rational voice with respect to policy options. So he dissociated himself from the abolitionists not because he hated slavery any less than they did but because abolitionists believed a government that condoned slavery was illicit, a position that demonstrated the very lack of reverence for the rule of law he abhorred. Yet he would pave a path to the White House by opposing efforts to allow slavery to spread beyond the states where Lincoln argued the nation's founders had placed it to set it on a course toward ultimate extinction. His best calculation about how to settle the crisis unleashed by the 1854 Kansas-Nebraska Act (the 9/11 event of the 1850s) was to leave slavery where it was, oppose the Kansas-Nebraska bill, and make no changes politically, so that progress toward the morally commendable end of eliminating slavery might be achieved peacefully and, dare we say it, reasonably, with the American experiment in self-government preserved.

Lincoln's commitment to rational inquiry carried over into religion, which he subjected to the same analytical, critical, and skeptical use of reason that he applied to everything else. As a youth he mocked preachers, and he grew to maturity repudiating Christian supernaturalism when it took fire as "enthusiasm." He playfully remarked, "When I hear a man preach I like to see him act as if he were fighting bees!"[12] But he sometimes got in trouble. When running for the Illinois state legislature, he was accused of being an unbelieving scoffer, an "infidel." He was forced to respond in a flyer, which is fascinating for what it does not say as much as for what it does: "That I am not a member of a Christian Church, is true; but I have never denied the truth of the Scriptures; and I have never spoken with intentional disrespect of religion in general, or of a denomination of Christianity in particular. . . . I do not think I could myself be brought to support a man for office, whom I knew to be an open enemy of, and scoffer at, religion."[13]

However, he did subject the Bible to a kind of legal inquiry, testing it against the rules of evidence and taking a certain intellectual delight in exposing its contradictions. In his twenties he wrote a manifesto criticizing Christian supernaturalism and the Bible as divine revelation. Shocked by its contents, friends seized the document and for fear of the harm it might bring its author threw it in a fire.[14] His earliest law partner, John Stuart, thought Lincoln's unorthodoxy bordered on atheism and remarked that Lincoln "went further against Christian beliefs—and doctrines & principles than any man I ever heard: he shocked me—Lincoln always denied that Jesus was the . . . son of God as understood and maintained by the Christian world."[15] Lincoln, however, was no atheist. He did believe in a creator who operated in the world "according to the maxims of justice and rationality in his dealings with humankind," as Cardewine rightly says.[16] Lincoln subjected the religious practices and interpretations he encountered to critical analysis, and in the end sought to discern the reason within religion, perhaps wanting a religion that was finally reasonable. As the years passed, he found himself intellectually stifled though continually preoccupied with what could be known and grasped of so great a mystery as the divine will and eternal justice. His reflections on these questions, whether in private (i.e., his "Meditation on the Divine Will") or in public (i.e., his second inaugural), are theological statements of the utmost seriousness and worthy of studied consideration.

Kaplan has written that, for the young Lincoln, "Reason, logic and experience seemed the best guides. 'He did not seem to think that to be of much value which could not be proven or rather demonstrated,' a friend, Joseph Gillespie, recalled."[17] And Douglas Wilson has commented: "In a predominantly religious culture in a highly romantic and sentimental age, Lincoln's intellectual efforts, like his politics, were against the grain, taking the form of resistance to the pressures of conformity and pointing him in the direction of skepticism and rationality. . . . Lincoln was casting his lot with the rationalism of the Enlightenment and the skeptical spirit of the eighteenth century. As he was to indicate in many ways in the years ahead, he thought of himself as committed to the cause of reason."[18]

Natural Law Reason

Lincoln's confidence in reason extended to what we might call "natural law" thinking. John Finnis has written that "a sound theory of natural law is one that explicitly . . . undertakes a critique of practical viewpoints, in order to distinguish the practically unreasonable from the practically reasonable, and thus to differentiate the really important from that which is unimportant. . . . A theory of natural law claims to be able to identify conditions and principles of right-mindedness, of good and proper order among [persons] and in individual conduct."[19] Were we to test Lincoln's many pronouncements on the wrongness of slavery against this view, we would conclude rather easily that Lincoln avowed an ethic consistent with this version of natural law. He distinguished the practically unreasonable from the practically reasonable, identifying conditions and principles of right-mindedness as a nation faced its responsibility to present before the world its founding principle—that all are created equal and endowed by their creator with inalienable rights. This principle was a "self-evident" truth accessible by natural reason. Lincoln reasoned that slavery mocked the self-evident truth at the heart of the American experiment, and allowing slavery to expand into the territories threatened the very possibility of a free people sustaining democratic self-government.

A natural law ethic posits that human beings are able to access the meaning of justice, even the reality of a God, or in Jefferson's words, a creator, through the natural endowment of reason. God is even the source or guarantor of this natural capacity. Lincoln appealed to a sense of natural justice to press his case that slavery is a "monstrous injustice," although he befuddles us with qualifications that blacks are not his social or political equal, evidence for some that he was a white supremacist. It is worth noting, however, that his sparring partner, Stephen Douglas, race-baited Lincoln in the 1858 Illinois senate debates, denying the humanity of the Negro and accusing Lincoln of supporting miscegenation in Illinois, a state with highly restrictive "black laws."[20] Lincoln was put on the defensive, but he always tried to get the issue back to human equality and the fundamental dignity that slavery denied persons by depriving them of the fruits of their own labor. In Peoria, Illinois, Lincoln said that the issue comes down to

> whether the Negro is *not* or *is* a man. If he is not a man, why in that case, he who is a man may, as a matter of self-government, do just what he pleases with him. But if the Negro *is* a man, is it not to that extent, a total destruction of self-government, to say that he too shall not govern himself? . . .If the Negro is a *man*, why then ancient faith teaches me that "all men are created equal"; and that there can be no more right in connection with one man's making a slave of another. . . . What I do say is that no man is good enough to govern another man, *without that other's consent*. . . . Now the relation of masters and

slaves is, *pro tanto*, a total violation of the principle [of consent of the governed] but [a master] governs the slave by a set of rules altogether different from those which he prescribes for himself. Allow *all* the governed an equal voice in the government, and that, and that only is self-government.[21]

Lincoln then exposes the hypocrisy of the slavery defender, noting how much even slaveholders hate the slave trader, "You despise him utterly. You do not recognize him as a friend, or even as an honest man. Your children must not play with his." People avoid shaking hands with the slave trader "instinctively shrinking from the snaky contact. . . . Now why is this? You do not so treat the man who deals in corn or cattle or tobacco."[22] Lincoln was appealing to a sense of natural justice and reminding defenders of slavery that they knew in their heart of hearts that slavery was a "vast moral evil"—how could they not?

Lincoln's political opposition to the extension of slavery into the Kansas and Nebraska territories allowed him to clarify the moral meaning of slavery itself. He never denied the fundamental humanity of those in bondage. On the contrary, he affirmed their natural right to liberty, to happiness, and to the fruits of their labor. He affirmed a radical equality of persons and sought a civil society that embodied that equality. These commitments led him to advocate women's suffrage as early as 1836,[23] and endorsing Negro suffrage in his last public speech led one in his audience, John Wilkes Booth, to resolve at that moment to kill Lincoln.

In his public statements, Lincoln consistently appealed to foundational principles of human equality, believing that human beings bore a natural God-given sense of justice that even slaveholders, who refused to let their children play with the children of slave traders, could not deny. Guelzo has written that in this debate over the moral meaning of slavery, Lincoln "needed a morality with which to embarrass popular sovereignty's appeal to selfishness—not the chilly morality of duty, but the morality of natural law, even of natural theology. And so, for the first time, Lincoln began to speak . . . in terms of certain natural moral relations, which slavery violated. 'I think that if anything can be proved by natural theology, it is that slavery is morally wrong.'"[24]

Lincoln's appeal to a natural religion appeared in an 1864 story Lincoln himself wrote and published in a Washington, DC, newspaper under the title "The President's Last, Shortest and Best Speech." Two wives of imprisoned Confederate soldiers came begging their release. Lincoln writes:

On Saturday the President ordered the release of the prisoners, and then said to this lady: "You say you husband is a religious man. Tell him when you meet him that I say I am not much of a judge of religion, but that in my opinion, the religion that sets men to rebel and fight against their government, because, as they think, that government does not sufficiently help some men to eat their bread on the sweat of *other* men's faces, is not the sort of religion upon which people can get to heaven."[25]

The appeal here is to a natural law understanding of a basic injustice that reason can see out of its own native endowment. A religion that is not on the side of justice and human equality is folly, and Lincoln believed it a moral duty to oppose such a religion. Although he distinguished the practically reasonable from the practically unreasonable throughout his public career, Lincoln never veered from condemning slavery as a fundamental injustice. He would support his case by appealing to a sense of natural justice that even a natural theology would embrace. To oppose the injustice of slavery and the hypocrisy it entailed as it threatened to untie the national bonds of unity set forth in the Declaration of Independence was, he believed, a moral duty.

Virtue, Consequences, and Principles: Ethical Content

Lincoln's ethic divides into three distinct component parts—virtue, consequences, and dutied principles. These parts correspond to his commitment to prudence, realism, and responsibility.

Virtue

Lincoln's virtues are as American as a box of Cracker Jack. Lincoln, an ambitious man, actually revealed his core motivation in his first campaign document: "I have no other ambition so great as that of being truly esteemed of my fellow men, by rendering myself worthy of their esteem."[26] He hungered for the approval, even the admiration of others, and he wanted to be remembered for having lived, an ambition that was realized in his own mind (rightly) when he signed the Emancipation Proclamation. To earn such esteem, Lincoln tended to how he lived and comported himself. He was honest in his dealings with others, although some have argued that what appeared to be honesty was actually people's reactions to his independent ways. He was tenderhearted; modest, although enormously confident in his own intellectual powers; an autodidact who worked hard to make himself plainly understood; he was patient, perhaps to a fault with his children; he did not hold grudges; he could be self-sacrificing; he was a jokester gifted with a wonderful sense of humor, although his stories have not survived because so many were off-color; and his own lifelong suicidal depressions instilled in him a deep sympathy for the sufferings of others.[27] He avoided self-righteousness and moralizing and did not like it in others; he endorsed the Whig virtues of soberness, industriousness, and thrift. He had a sense of honor, which may have been a factor in his marriage proposal to Mary Todd, and he once came close to fighting a duel; he avoided hunting, tobacco, and liquor but claimed no virtue in these behaviors, noting that virtue should not be attributed to one who does not feel a temptation. He liked people and they him; he was generous, forgiving, and aware of his limitations.

William Miller has argued that prudence was a central virtue in Lincoln's moral repertoire, for it was a bridge to the intellectual virtues. Writes Miller, the "prudent person . . . used his powers of observation and reasoning to take careful account of the real and concrete situation, the particular situation, not simply in order protect his own skin . . . but in order continually to adapt the appropriate moral claims and purposes . . . to the real world."[28] By this measure, Lincoln embodied prudential wisdom.

Lincoln's imperfections have been duly noted by scholars, including such matters as his anger, his troubled marriage, a certain secretiveness, and melancholy gloominess. He demonstrated a lack of filial piety, being an estranged son who refused to visit his dying father or attend the funeral.[29] What we can say is that from his youth he had been filled with virtue maxims from the Bible, Shakespeare, John Bunyan, Aesop, and Thomas Dilworth's *Speller*, so that Lincoln came to believe that the upbuilding of character was essential for earning the esteem of others. He exemplified in his professional career the American virtues of working hard and making the most of the opportunity for the self-improvement that only liberty could make available. For one who believed that people should be free to get ahead by the application of effort, Lincoln made the cultivation of virtue the first pillar of his ethic, a prescription for all.

Utilitarian-Consequentialist

Lincoln was a realist given to making decisions based on a best calculation of foreseen consequences. American Whigs had shown enthusiasm for the liberal utilitarianism of Jeremy Bentham, and Lincoln read and admired the writings of John Stuart Mill. Guelzo discusses "the utilitarian cast of Lincoln's legal thinking," noting that "people were motivated by selfishness, as Bentham and Mill had warned, and the only avenue that offered any semblance of escape from the domain of selfishness was [for Lincoln] the triumph of 'reason' and 'all-conquering mind.'"[30] Lincoln had avowed a fatalism and a "Doctrine of Necessity" much akin to Mill's "philosophical necessity," holding that people do not choose freely but act in line with the conditioning and constraints of necessity and in response to motives (a very Benthamite notion). Although it potentially subverted human responsibility, this fatalism seemed to make Lincoln sympathetic to people and the difficult situations in which they found themselves. "In the case of Brutus and Caesar," Lincoln was said to have argued, "the former was forced by laws and conditions over which he had no control to kill the latter, and vice versa."[31]

That Lincoln would urge action based on his best calculation of rationally anticipated results is evident from a speech he gave in New England during the election of 1848. Lincoln urged voters not to support the free soil, antislavery candidate, Martin Van Buren, because he could not win. Lincoln argued that votes wasted on Van Buren would allow a proslavery Democrat to be elected. He then commended the Whig candidate, Zachary Taylor, a slaveholder. In the face of ideological purists loathe to support Taylor, Lincoln claimed that it is not always clear what our duty is, and if it were always clear, he argued, "we should have no use for judgment; we might as well be made without intelligence; and when divine or human law does not clearly point out what our duty is, we have no means of finding out what it is [except] by using our most intelligent judgment of the consequences."[32] This may be his clearest statement on the integration of consequentialist thinking into his ethic.

As president he would exercise what Richard Caldewine has called a "cold statistical ruthlessness" in contemplating the long-range acceptability of even heavy Union losses. After the Union defeat at Fredericksburg, Lincoln observed that despite the losses of two Union for every Confederate soldier, "if the same battle were to be fought over again, every day, through a week of days, with the same relative results, the army under Lee would be wiped out to its last man, but the Army of the Potomac would still be a mighty host [and] the war would be over."[33] This tolerance for Union losses is a consequentialist realism that certainly affected Lincoln's willingness to refuse a negotiated end to hostilities. He foresaw a Union victory due to Federal forces simply outlasting their opponents. Lincoln's ability to make flexible yet reasoned decisions based on consequences when duty was unclear represents yet another pillar in Lincoln's ethical stance.

Principles and Duties

Of course, if one's duty were clear and unhampered by ambiguities, then we ought to "dare to do our duty as we understand it" or, in the language of the second inaugural, "as God gives us to see the right." In addition to his consequentialism, Lincoln was highly principled but also "temperamentally distrustful of absolutism, the pretensions to superior sanctity, and the pharisaism of those religionists who pressed him toward more radical action against the south."[34] That said, Lincoln acknowledged that an issue of natural justice such as slavery did not admit of compromise, for to be wrong on such an issue is to be "wholly wrong."[35] Lincoln would say "I am inflexible. I am for no compromise" on any action that would perpetuate or extend slavery.[36] In Lincoln's view, "slavery is founded in the selfishness of man's nature—opposition to it in his love of justice." These two principles, he said, were "in eternal antagonism."[37] Lincoln recognized the role that principles played in guiding action, and it was critical that on the issues where moral clarity was available and duty clear, principles should rule the day.

Lincoln is not known to have read Kant, although his law partner, Billy Herndon, did, so Kant's ideas may have been familiar to Lincoln. Regardless of a direct tie to Kant, Lincoln clearly endorsed a responsibility ethic that acknowledged a duty to observe what in Kant would have articulated as two principles: respect for persons and universalizability.

Lincoln respected persons in the abstract, in virtue of their fundamental humanity. In the debate at Alton, Illinois, he invoked the word "dehumanize" to discuss the "evil" of making the Negro property and nothing but property.[38] He refused to demean those who lacked political rights, including women and slaves. He also demonstrated respect in his personal dealings. Frederick Douglass, for instance, said of Lincoln, "I was impressed with his entire freedom from popular prejudice against the colored race. He was the first great man that I talked with in the United States freely, who in no single instance reminded me of the difference between himself and myself, of the difference of color. . . . I account partially for his kindness to me because of the similarity with which I had fought my way up, we both starting at the lowest round of the ladder."[39]

Lincoln invoked the principle of universalizability with some frequency, as in his famous statement, "As I would not be a slave so I would not be a master [and] whenever I hear any one arguing for slavery I feel a strong impulse to see it tried on him personally."[40] He was capable of putting himself in the shoes of others, as when he said, "When Southern people tell us they are no more responsible for the origin of slavery than we, I acknowledge the fact,"[41] noting that "they are just what we would be in their situation."[42] Responsibility for slavery was shared by all, North and South, he maintained in his Peoria speech, and he would reiterate this point in his second inaugural. He invoked universalizability in working out an argument about race and color, as a note found in his papers demonstrated: "If A. can prove, however conclusively, that he may, of right, enslave B.—why may not B. snatch the same argument, and prove equally, that he may enslave A?—You say A. is white, and B. is black. It is color, then; the lighter, having the right to enslave the darker? Take care. By this rule, you are to be slave to the first man you meet, with a fairer skin than your own."[43]

Slavery offends against natural justice, and, in accordance with a principle of universalizability, Lincoln would conclude that slavery was wrong and that his God-given duty was to oppose it. Conversely, he also understood his duty as president to be first to preserve and defend the Union, and he acknowledged he would do so even at the cost of allowing slavery to continue. Duties can conflict. Lincoln employed practical reason to sort out his duties, but he clearly welcomed the opportunity created by the necessities of the war to issue the Emancipation Proclamation, which allowed him to meet both his Constitutional duty and his moral obligations on the slavery issue for the first time at the same time.[44] Principles and duties tied to responsibility constitute the third leg of Lincoln's ethic.

Lincoln's ethic, then, was a hybrid fashioned by practical reason. Unlike Enlightenment moral theories that would place an Uppercase Duty in a position of mutual exclusion over against an Uppercase Consequentialism, Lincoln evaded an ethic expressive of Uppercase Moral Realities, fashioning instead a lowercase ethic that brought principles, duties, virtues, and consequences all into play. This ethic is, at least in the face of the Enlightenment heritage, a distinctive way to reconcile the resources of moral thought with the practicalities of living the moral life and dealing with moral problems. As I suggested earlier, coming at ethics this way is akin to Cicero and has more to do with pre-Enlightenment natural law than with the Enlightenment ethics with which we are today so familiar.

Implications for Religious Ethics

The Lincoln legacy is to be found in the practical transformation effected by the Thirteenth, Fourteenth, and Fifteenth Amendments, which turned the legal direction of the country toward an ever-increasing expansion of political inclusiveness. Lincoln re-created the nation at Gettysburg, declaring the founding principle of the nation to be the "four score and seven years ago" Declaration of Independence notion of human equality, not the Constitution, which was a flawed instrument of practical governance in obvious need of correction. So what has this to do with religious ethics, and do religious ethicists have anything to learn from Lincoln?

Lincoln's political and ethical thought bear the imprint of religion. Despite his problems with the Christianity of his day and his natural bent toward skepticism, he nonetheless avowed a notion of divine Providence and grounded his bedrock belief in human equality in the divine will. He did possess a natural theology of sorts, moving away from impersonal process terms such as necessity to talk about Providence, God, and even Father in Heaven as he aged.[45] Lincoln's honest confrontation with transcendence was a dynamic engagement, and he understood the divine will to be beyond human knowing. His youthful skepticism was no doubt altered and chastened when, as president, he had to confront the tragedies of war and what must have been his own agony about his role in the deaths of six hundred thousand Americans. His "not knowing," once of a piece with intellectual skepticism, became toward the end of his life a "not knowing" born of a heartfelt humility.

Two theological reflections are worth a brief consideration. The first, "Mediation on the Divine Will," written probably in 1862, captures Lincoln's thinking: "The will of God prevails. . . . In the present civil war it is quite possible that God's purpose is something different from the purpose of either. I am almost ready to say this is probably true—that God wills this contest, and wills that it shall not yet end."[46]

The Second Inaugural Address reiterates this musing on the ineluctable mystery of the divine will. Lincoln noted that the parties to the conflict read the same Bible and pray to the same God, "and each involves His aid against the other. . . . It may seem strange that any men should dare to ask a just God's assistance in wringing their bread from other men's faces; but let us judge not that we be not judged. The prayers of both could not be answered; that of neither has been answered fully."[47]

The terrible toll of the war pressed on Lincoln and on Americans in general, and Lincoln sought in this speech to understand the larger meaning of the war and why "God wills that it continue." Lincoln's reflections here are not moral inquiries but questions about transcendent purposes beyond even a president's pay grade. But Lincoln does not assume Job's stance and call God's justice into question; rather, he accedes to the proposition that all were responsible for the war, and that if God's will is that war should continue "until every drop of blood drawn with the lash shall be paid with another drawn by the sword," then, he says in his second inaugural, "the judgments of the Lord are true and righteous altogether."

But not understandable. The second inaugural attempts to locate the meaning of the war in a theological frame, but Lincoln does not claim to understand the logic of the divine position; it is not a reasonable position but a given, the meaning of which is beyond our ability to fathom. Lincoln moves away from that position, unable to resolve the ultimate meaning of the war, certain though he is that ending slavery is just. With resolve, he turns toward the peace sure to come. Turning to those better angels of our nature that first flitted on the scene at the first inaugural, Lincoln invokes the language of "malice toward none; charity for all." "With firmness in the right as God gives us to see the right," he pledges help to those afflicted by the war—the widow and orphans, and calls for a just and lasting peace. What framed this vision of a peace without malice—surely Lincoln knew that malice would be a profound motivating factor in Reconstruction—and charity for all—surely Lincoln knew that charity was not uppermost on the minds of those about to become victors—was something beyond what reason could deliver through rational ethics. The ethic he appeals to at the end of the inaugural is infused with transcendent religious meaning. By asking for God's assistance in the effort to see what is right, he is looking beyond a reason-based Enlightenment ethics to an ethic of love and nonjudgmental reconciliation. This is an ethic new to Lincoln in many ways, for it is interpretable as a religious ethic, specifically a Christian ethic of love and forgiveness.

Lincoln knew he was facing difficulties in the Reconstruction, and subsequent history bore out the extent to which the post–Civil War era would be filled with recrimination, continued subjugation and oppression of blacks, and creation of a postslavery racial divide in the United States that is still with us, despite all the progress. What is fascinating is Lincoln's insight that, despite his inability to understand the whys and wherefores of the divine plan as that plan was working its way out in the struggle at the time he delivered the second inaugural, he still made an ethical turn. This turn was not simply to an acknowledgement that a divine justice may be working its way out (who can know?) but to an ethic that would help all Americans approach the hard days ahead with an eye toward peace, with an eye toward only those guidelines, known from the Gospel stories Lincoln knew so well, that would assure peace—with malice toward none, with charity for all.

For those who do ethics in a religious context, three lessons may be taken from this examination of Lincoln's ethic. First, Lincoln refused to be dominated by a theory. He unfettered practical reason, allowing it full range to analyze and discern, evaluate and guide—in short, to live and breathe—as he sought to work through the moral controversies of his day. His hybrid ethic, while it is undoubtedly a source of consternation for any strict Kantian or any strict Utilitarian, conformed to a vision of goodness and functioned as an operational means for reconciling ethical thought with action. His reliance on reason as a God-given endowment and the foundation for affirming human equality allowed him to connect a reason-based ethic with one that was also grounded in a religious source. On this view, Lincoln could be said to hold to a natural law interpretive schema, with nothing in natural law denying such a reason-centered, God-grounded connection.

Second, Lincoln reminds us of reason's limitations and the profound obstacles that await those seeking to grasp the ways of Providence. The enthusiastic skepticism of a very bright youth finally gave way to a burdened national leader's realization that transcendent things were beyond human grasp, at which point Lincoln, with some nobleness of spirit, stood before it in what I think was genuine humility. That is, I believe, a profound lesson, especially for monotheists who talk a good game when it comes to humility but who too often play the game poorly. Lincoln yearned to understand the divine will, yet he knew such understanding was not to be his, or anyone else's. I suspect that is why he never joined a church—too much certainty there about things that could not be known. Lincoln, I think, really believed we cannot penetrate the deeper mysteries tied to transcendent matters, so he turned to the ethical teachings he found in scripture, looking ahead to the practical need for civil behavior rather than settling for comforting beliefs that would always remain speculative. When he received the gift of a Bible in 1864, he wrote a thank you note saying "it is the best gift God has given to man. All the good the savior gave to the world was communicated through this book. But for it we could not know right from wrong."[48] This comment is thoroughly ethical in its theological meaning; it is action-related, not doctrinal.

What is central for Lincoln in the Bible is the ethical material. When he wrote "all the good the Savior gave the world was communicated through the book," "all the good" meant all those things we must do to realize the good, including malice toward none, charity for all. The Bible's ethics lessons were not lost on Lincoln, and it is not speculation on the divine will that is crucial. In this view he is rather consistent his life long. He may have yearned for reasoned understanding, but in the end he would settle for peace and the practical means for achieving it.

In a recent book, Death-of-God theologian William Hamilton argues that Lincoln was one of three great American theological minds of the nineteenth century, along with Herman Melville and Emily Dickinson. He notes that Lincoln was recapturing Calvinist insights later in life, even in the second inaugural. Then, in a confessional mode, Hamilton writes this:

> Forgiveness in the Second Inaugural transcends all the nicely calculated (and real) differences between North and South. It is we who must transmute the sober claims of justice raised by slavery and the war into something like love. If forgiveness was once God's business, it has now become ours. He [Lincoln] is the kind of Christian I hope to be, or to become. Influenced by his Christian inheritance, yet deeply critical of what many have made of it, he managed to use both secular and religious language to express the faith he ended up with. "Charity to all."[49]

That is the final insight—that charity is the need and the ethical requirement laid upon us. Charity is something we must do. It is our duty, it is a calculable good, and it should be in our attitude and character. The obligation to charity may be from God or inspired by God; it may be from reason; it may arise as the result of our simply being unable to fathom the deeper sense of things, perhaps even those things Lincoln experienced as we all do, though he in a more dramatic form and as a major player on the stage of history. For, as president, Lincoln experienced the heartache of loss and disappointment, the tragedies of war and injustice, the weariness of struggle, all of which he countered with the constancy of good friends, ennobling intellectual companions (such as Shakespeare), and the sense that he was working the arc of history toward greater justice and inclusion. But the second inaugural ends with the need to express charity, to seek justice and show mercy, and to envision a "just peace." That seems a good and vital message for ethicists working in a religious context to heed. Of course we do not need Lincoln to get to it, but his journey to this understanding is certainly wrapped in a compelling story, one still worthy of our attention today.

Notes

1. Doris Kearns Goodwin, *Team of Rivals: The Political Genius of Abraham Lincoln* (New York: Simon and Schuster, 2005).

2. This little summary is the text on the inside of a small paper assembly project with Lincoln's image on it I received as my prize in a Cracker Jack box. I think that it was on someone's mind to remind a potential prize recipient, most likely a young person, perhaps at a picnic or ball game, that there are certain values you can have even as a young person that will stand you in good stead and open the door to greatness—and Abraham Lincoln is proof of that.

3. Lincoln's most prominent reflection on the inability of human beings to grasp the divine will was his second inaugural statement: "The Almighty has His own purposes."

4. Cicero argues that to live in accordance with natural law is justice since "justice comes from nature." *The Republic and The Laws*, Jonathan Powell, ed., Niall Rudd, trans. (Oxford: Oxford University Press, 1998), 108.

5. Allen C. Guelzo, *Abraham Lincoln: Redeemer President* (Grand Rapids: Eerdemans, 1999), 314.

6. Fred Kaplan, *Lincoln: The Biography of a Writer* (New York: HarperCollins, 2008), 43.

7. Richard Cardewine, *Lincoln: A Life of Purpose and Power* (New York: Alfred A. Knopf, 2006), 48.

8. Guelzo, *Abraham Lincoln*, 61.

9. Quoted in Paul M. Angle and Earl Schecnk Miers, eds., *The Living Lincoln: The Man and His Times, in His Own Words* (New York: Fall River Press, 1992), 26–27. All italics in Lincoln's quotes are Lincoln's own.

10. Ibid., 23.

11. Ibid.

12. Quoted in Cardewine, *Lincoln*, 34.

13. Quoted in John C. Waugh, *One Man Great Enough: Abraham Lincoln's Road to the Civil War* (Orlando: Harcourt, 2007), 148.

14. Cardewine, *Lincoln*, 35; and Douglas L. Wilson, *Honor's Voice: The Transformation of Abraham Lincoln* (New York: Alfred A. Knopf, 1998), 84.

15. Quoted in Cardewine, *Lincoln*, 36.

16. Ibid.

17. Kaplan, *Lincoln*, 30–31.

18. Wilson, *Honor's Voice*, 85.

19. John Finnis, *Natural Law and Natural Rights* (Oxford, Clarendon Press, 1980), 16.

20. Illinois was almost admitted into the Union as a slave state, but when it was not the legislature passed "black laws," which placed heavy indenture restrictions on Illinois' small black population. See Cardewine, *Lincoln*, 20.

21. Quoted in Angle and Miers, *Living Lincoln*, 169–70.

22. Ibid., 168–69.

23. Ibid., 11.

24. Guelzo, *Abraham Lincoln*, 188.

25. Quoted in ibid., 634.

26. Ibid., 9.

27. See Joshua Wolf Shenk, *Lincoln's Melancholy: How Depression Challenged a President and Fueled His Greatness* (Boston: Houghton Mifflin: 2005).

28. William Lee Miller, *Lincoln's Virtues: An Ethical Biography* (New York: Alfred A. Knopf, 2002), 223.

29. Ibid., 41.

30. Guelzo, *Abraham Lincoln*, 370–71.

31. Quoted in ibid., 118.

32. Abraham Lincoln, "Speech at Worchester, Massachusetts, September 12, 1848," in *Collected Works of Abraham Lincoln*, vol. 2, ed. Roy P. Basler (New Brunswick, NJ: Rutgers University Press, 1953), 3–4.

33. Quoted in Caldewine, *Lincoln*, 252.

34. Cardewine, *Lincoln*, 247.

35. Miller, *Lincoln's Virtues*, 204.

36. Quoted in ibid., 435.

37. Ibid., 263.

38. Lincoln, *Collected Works of Abraham Lincoln*, vol. 3, ed. Roy P. Basler (New Brunswick, NJ: Rutgers University Press, 1953), 304.

39. Quoted in Michael Burlingame, *The Inner World of Abraham Lincoln* (Urbana: University of Illinois Press, 1994), 36.

40. Ibid.

41. Ibid.

42. Quoted in Angle and Miers, *Living Lincoln*, 161.

43. Lincoln, "Fragment on Slavery [April 1, 1854]," in *Collected Works* 2:223–23.

44. Lincoln felt that he was on shaky Constitutional ground for the Emancipation Proclamation, which is why he pushed hard for passage of the Thirteenth Amendment, which unambiguously ended slavery in the United States.

45. Richard Cardewine, "Lincoln's Religion," in *Our Lincoln: New Perspectives on Lincoln and His World*, ed. Eric Foner, 223–48 (New York: W. W. Norton, 2008).

46. Quoted in Angle and Miers, *Living Lincoln*, 449.

47. Ibid., 639.

48. Ibid., 618–19.

49. William Hamilton, *Essays and Other Things* (Philadelphia: Xlibris, 2010), 28, 29.

Christ and Culture Revisited: Contributions from the Recent Russian Orthodox Debate

John P. Burgess

WESTERN SCHOLARS HAVE POINTED OUT BOTH THE USEFULNESS AND limitations of H. Richard Niebuhr's *Christ and Culture*. This essay relates Niebuhr's five types to discussions of church and culture in contemporary Russian Orthodoxy. I propose a sixth type, Christ in culture, that best illuminates the Church's current program of *votserkovlenie* ("in-churching"). To its Russian representatives, "Christ in culture" enabled the Christian faith to survive communist efforts to destroy the Church, and this cultural legacy continues to define Russia's national identity today. The Church's task, therefore, is not to convert Russians but rather to call them back to their historic self-understanding by means of historical commemoration, religious education, and social outreach. The essay critically evaluates this program of in-churching and the possibilities of a Christ-in-culture type for understanding distinctive features of historically Christian cultures in both East and West.

It goes without saying that H. Richard Niebuhr's *Christ and Culture* is a classic of American Christian social ethics.[1] While scholars in recent years have criticized Niebuhr's typology, it continues to assist many readers in recognizing and understanding key ways in which Christians past and present have responded to their culture.[2] Here I argue that Niebuhr's five types—Christ against culture, the Christ of culture, Christ above culture, Christ and culture in paradox, and Christ, the transformer of culture—while illuminating aspects of the contemporary Russian Orthodox discussion of Christ and culture, miss some of its most important features. I therefore propose the usefulness of a sixth type, what I call Christ in culture. The Christ-in-culture type draws our attention to ways in which Christian theological and ethical values become embedded in a culture and continue to inform a culture, even when that culture no longer understands itself to be explicitly Christian. The representatives of Christ in culture may call for a culture's transformation, but this transformation is less a movement to a new identity than a return to a historic identity that has made a continuing witness to the temporal and eternal ends of the gospel.

I believe that a Christ-in-culture type, though particularly relevant to Orthodoxy in postcommunist Russia, also illuminates aspects of church and culture in the West that scholars might otherwise neglect. Attention to this type therefore opens up new lines of scholarly reflection about church and culture in both West and East.

The essay unfolds in four moves: (1) a brief overview of the social situation of the Russian Orthodox Church today; (2) an examination of Niebuhr's types, especially the Christ of culture and Christ above culture, and how they illuminate contemporary Russian Orthodoxy or fall short; (3) a case for a Christ-*in*-culture type; and (4) an evaluation of the theological possibilities and limitations of the Christ-in-culture type, also in relation to cultural contexts beyond contemporary Russia.

The Social Situation of the Russian Orthodox Church Today

The Russian Orthodox Church, like other Christian churches, experienced brutal repression under the Soviet regime.[3] On the eve of the 1917 Revolution, the Russian Orthodox Church had 75,000 houses of worship and more than 1,000 monasteries. By 1941 only 150–300 churches remained, and of the 100 monasteries still active, only 2 were in the territory of Russia. As many as 100,000 priests, monks, nuns, and other church leaders were killed during those years. Just in the 1930s, 80–85 percent of all priests were arrested, and most died in prison or were executed.

After the Nazis invaded the Soviet Union in 1941, Stalin abruptly changed course. Scholars still debate his motivations.[4] Perhaps he felt that despite his efforts to eradicate it, Orthodox Christianity continued to sit so deeply in the national psyche that the Church could help him to motivate popular resistance to Hitler. Perhaps he simply wanted to win Allied political and military support by demonstrating that the USSR also guaranteed freedom of religion. In any case, Stalin allowed the Church to elect a patriarch and to reopen several thousand parishes.

The reprieve of the oppression of religion was short-lived. With Stalin's death (1953), Khrushchev unleashed a new antireligious campaign. If Stalin had employed sheer terror, Khrushchev focused more on ideological education, a scientific atheism that dismissed religion as a pitiful remnant of a capitalistic society. Association with the Church brought professional and personal hardship, such as denial of a university education and disqualification from many kinds of work. The state again closed churches but moved especially vigorously against the remaining monasteries.

Years of political stagnation followed in which the Church secured its existence at the price of publicly supporting Soviet policies and submitting to the control of the KGB. Only with the rise of Gorbachev did the government slowly loosen its grip on the Church. By 1989, as the communist Eastern Bloc began to dissolve, the Orthodox Church had seven thousand parishes (although more than half were outside of the Russian Federation, especially in Ukraine) and twenty-two monasteries.

Today the Orthodox faithful believe that nothing less than a miraculous rebirth of the Church has taken place. More than thirty thousand parishes and eight hundred monasteries exist. In Moscow alone, the number of active churches has jumped from forty-two to nearly nine hundred, 70–80 percent of all Russians identify themselves as Orthodox, and the Church has won political favor, material wealth, and social prominence.[5]

Against this backdrop a vigorous debate about the relation of Orthodox Christianity to contemporary Russian society has taken place. Three basic positions have emerged. The first emphasizes a Western model of freedom of religion and separation of church and state, both of which the Russian Constitution guarantees (although within limits, giving Russia's so-called historic religions legal privileges not available to smaller sects).[6] The Church should represent its values to the larger society through the give and take of democratic political processes, without insisting that it alone has the truth.

The second position builds on Slavophile ideas of the nineteenth century, contrasting Russian values of social solidarity and religious piety with Western individualism, market competition, and godlessness. Some who hold this position call for the restoration of the czar and a rejection of the global marketplace. A few extremists even honor Stalin as a saint because he saved the nation from the Nazis and turned it into a great world power. Apocalyptic ideas sometimes enter into this thinking too. The end of time is near, and a great battle has already begun between an Orthodox East and a morally decadent West, which is spreading its corrupting influence in Russia through drugs, sexual promiscuity, and excessive material consumption.[7]

Proponents of both of these positions are relatively small in number (although the second generates more attention and passion than the first and represents more of a threat to the Church hierarchy). A third position has come to predominate: that although church and state are constitutionally separate, they must cooperate to renew the nation's historic religious identity, which is primarily Orthodox.[8] Some who hold this position speak of the traditional Orthodox teaching of a symphonia between church and state. The state gives the church the social space in which to inculcate moral values of social utility, including patriotism. The church supports the state as long as it honors the church and allows it to promulgate its teachings and practices. Together, although in separate realms, church and state work for the good of the nation.

Examined more closely, however, the notion of symphonia is misleading in the contemporary Russian situation. Traditionally, the czar confessed the Orthodox faith and served as its personal protector. An extensive legal apparatus ensured that the rhythms of Orthodox practice dominated public life. Other forms of Christianity had no legal standing. Today's Russian Orthodox Church affirms the constitutional separation of church and state, remembering that symphonia in practice led again and again to state domination of the Church, even to the point of persecution.

With the election of Patriarch Kirill in 2009, the Church further advanced its vision of Christianity and culture. The key term has become *votserkovlenie*, literally, the "in-churching" of Russian society. Kirill has argued that Russia's identity and social values rest on Orthodox Christian foundations.[9] Russian culture is essentially Orthodox in character. The way in which Russians think and make sense of their lives is deeply rooted in a Christian worldview, whether they are aware of it or not. The mission of the Church is not to convert secularized Russians to Christianity but rather to show them that they are in some sense already Christian by virtue of being Russian.

The program of votserkovlenie has become all the more urgent in Kirill's eyes, given the vast ignorance of Orthodox teaching and practice in contemporary Russian society. While the Church has rebuilt a great deal of its physical infrastructure and reestablished itself as a social entity, fewer than 5 percent of Russian Orthodox regularly attend church, and even fewer observe basic church practices, such as the Great Fast (Lent). Since the fall of communism, the Church has won people's formal affiliation. Now it is time to win back their hearts.[10]

The program of votserkovlenie is multifaceted.[11] One aspect is education. The Church has called for the public schools to offer instruction in the "foundations of Orthodox culture." Most parishes have established Sunday Schools for children and lecture series for adults. Orthodox radio and television programs aim at a popular audience. Orthodox publishing houses release a torrent of books, magazines, and DVDs to introduce people to the basics of Orthodoxy. St. Tikhon's Orthodox University in Moscow, recently accredited by the state, trains a new generation of public leaders to represent Orthodox values in society.

A second aspect of votserkovlenie is memorializing the victims of Stalinism and communism. More than a thousand new martyrs of the twentieth century have been canonized and placed into the church calendar. New churches and shrines stand on the sites of former gulags and killing fields. Church museums and publications remind contemporary Russians of these tragic events and admonish them never to let them happen again. Russian society owes the Church a historical debt to help revive it today.[12]

A third aspect of votserkovlenie is outreach to society's weak and needy. The Russian Orthodox Church has been at the forefront of developing diaconal ministries, such as hospices, drug rehabilitation programs, orphanages, and feeding programs. In integrating physical care with prayer and worship, the Church demonstrates how Christian values should inform society's response to those at its margins.[13]

In each case—education, memorializing of the martyrs, and care for society's weak and needy—the Church draws on its narratives, symbols, and rituals to offer Russians a new identity in the wake of the fall of communism.[14] The state has often supported these efforts financially and politically, as though seeking a civil religion to promote social solidarity and national pride. Upon his inauguration in 2008, President Dmitry Medvedev received Patriarch Aleksii II's blessing and an icon of the Vladimir Mother of God. Both Medvedev and Prime Minister Vladimir Putin attended the enthronement of Patriarch Kirill the following year.

Niebuhr's Types and Contemporary Russian Orthodoxy

Niebuhr's typology can help us to understand distinctive features of these Russian developments. As James Gustafson has demonstrated, Niebuhr sought to identify a logical range of ideal types informed by a deep familiarity with historical sources.[15] His types are heuristic devices that help us to see basic tendencies in Christian social thought. Niebuhr was influenced by Ernst Troeltsch's typology in *The Social Teaching of the Christian Churches* but felt that Troeltsch's two major types (the sect type and the church type) set up an unfortunate binary opposition and neglected nuances in other positions.[16] Niebuhr therefore expanded on Troeltsch's typology while never insisting that his five types exhausted the possibilities.

As Gustafson notes, Niebuhr's goal was to help us to recognize and to sympathetically understand different ways in which Christians have related to their culture. The types did not function as explanations (one could not say that Tertullian or Tolstoy adopted his position *because* he was devoted to the notion of Christ against culture). Nor were they a taxonomical scheme (one could not say that Aquinas fit only into the Christ-above-culture type, or Augustine into the Christ-transforming-culture type). Some scholars have accused Niebuhr of failing to be consistent with his own purposes.[17] But Gustafson's admonitions still hold. We should not use the types to reduce complex historical phenomena to banal oversimplifications. Rather, we should use them to see better the dominant features of the Christian tradition as a whole.

Niebuhr, like most Protestant scholars until recently, neglected Orthodoxy.[18] While he knew basic patristic resources, his deep reading of the Christian tradition seems to have been limited to Western classics. This fact, however, does not invalidate the usefulness of his typology for examining Orthodoxy. Because the types function as a set of logical possibilities, they can illuminate, as

Gustafson has again noted, a wide range of religious (and not only Western or even Christian) responses to culture.

My brief comments on the renewal of Orthodoxy in Russia are themselves informed by Niebuhr's typology. Christ against culture helps us to recognize features of those Orthodox circles that oppose East and West, a Christian Russia, and a godless, market-driven Europe and America. Similarly, Christ and culture in paradox helps illuminate the position of those Orthodox who insist on a strict separation of church and state yet call on the church to actively participate in democratic politics.[19] Russian Orthodoxy, like other historical movements, cannot be reduced to one type or the other. Rather, all five types illuminate aspects of its complex life today.

Orthodox scholar Vigen Guroian has argued that Orthodox social ethics is consistently transformationist or conversionist.[20] Initially, however, two of Niebuhr's other types seem more applicable to contemporary Russian Orthodoxy in relation to its program of votserkovlenie: the Christ of culture and Christ above culture.

The Christ-of-culture type illuminates Orthodoxy's tendency to equate national (or ethnic) and religious identity, a tendency that continues in Russia to this day.[21] The Orthodox Church acknowledges that the Russian Federation includes people groups historically associated with other traditions, especially Islam, Buddhism, and Judaism, while emphasizing that ethnic Russians have historically been Orthodox.

Even though Protestants and Catholics have been present in Russia for centuries, they first came as immigrants from Western and Central Europe. For this reason, the Orthodox often regard Russians who have become Protestant or Catholic as having abandoned something essential about their ethnic identity. Protestants or Catholics in Russia may deserve constitutional protections, but to the Orthodox they nevertheless appear to be steered and financed from abroad. In the 1990s the Russian Orthodox Church was especially upset about Western Protestant evangelicals who sent missionaries to Russia as though it were not already a Christian (Orthodox) nation. The Church subsequently pushed for, and won, state legislation that restricted foreign evangelists' activities.

The Christ-of-culture type further illuminates traditional Orthodox notions of a symphonia between church and state. Because the Russian nation is essentially Orthodox, it is right, some would argue, for state leaders to confess the Orthodox faith, and to protect the Orthodox Church and promote its activity and influence in society. While a strict symphonia is legally impossible in today's Russia, some of its arrangements can and should continue, as when the Church offers state leaders God's blessing, or when the state helps finance Church restoration and building projects.

The Christ-of-culture type also helps illuminate aspects of Patriarch Kirill's program of votserkovlenie. Kirill assumes that Russians are at heart Orthodox.

While he acknowledges that Russia has become more pluralistic religiously and that every citizen has a right to freedom of religion, he nevertheless believes that most Russians will choose to associate with the Orthodox Church because it is part of their historic identity. The Church has the responsibility to remind Russians of their Orthodox roots. The Bolshevist repudiation of religion was a tragic assault not only on the Church but also on the Russian people. Orthodoxy represents the best historic values of Russian society: honest work, social solidarity, national pride, and the cultivation of beauty.[22]

For some Western observers, the Russian Orthodox tendency toward the Christ of culture is further confirmed by its historic tendency to refrain from publicly criticizing state injustices. Whenever in the past the Church did raise a voice of protest, the state quickly repressed it.[23] Czars deposed patriarchs who fell out of their favor. Peter the Great abolished the Holy Synod and turned the Church into a department of state. Soviet persecution forced Church leaders to compromise the Church and even the faith in order to ensure the Church's survival.

Given this history, a Church culture of public silence or guarded public statements has evolved. Today, too, the Church hierarchy avoids public displays of displeasure with state policies on urgent social questions of the day, such as human rights, where Russia has a spotty record. On the contrary, the Church in its official documents has defined human rights largely in terms of individuals' responsibilities to the commune (the nation) rather than in terms of restrictions on the state in order to protect individual freedoms.[24] As Niebuhr noted, a church that thinks in terms of the Christ of culture easily ends up accommodating itself to dominant cultural values rather than informing them.

But the Christ-of-culture type, while bringing some things into focus, also misses important features of contemporary Russian Orthodoxy. The Christ-and-culture type puts the focus too much on Orthodoxy as part of Russians' ethnic identity and neglects that the Church is interested in something more. It offers people not only a social identity but also the possibility of eternal salvation. For this reason, some Western observers have suggested that the Christ-above-culture type more usefully illuminates Russian Orthodoxy than does the Christ-of-culture type.[25]

Niebuhr, drawing on the thought of Thomas Aquinas, conceived of the Christ-above-culture type as delineating two stages of Christian existence.[26] At one stage Christians are members of society. Scripture confirms and clarifies the natural law that is accessible to human reason and upon which society bases its laws. At a second stage Christians are members of the church, which proclaims a gospel of radical transformation. God's supernatural grace enables people to die to an old life of sin and to live rightly before God. They fulfill not only social but also religious obligations. They use the things of this world in order to pursue not only temporal but also eternal ends.

While the Russian Orthodox Church has often been suspicious of Western scholasticism and has emphasized that theology is best experienced in the liturgy rather than in the abstract systems of theological thought, the Christ-above-culture type does helpfully lift up key features of contemporary Russian Orthodox life. When Kirill calls for popular religious education, he is concerned that Russians not only know their religious heritage but also come to be more fully integrated into the sacramental life of the Church. The memorializing of the martyrs of the twentieth century asks Russians not only to remember the state's assaults on their ethnic and religious identity (and to commit themselves to resisting such attacks in the future) but also to enter into a spirituality of suffering that the Orthodox hold to be essential to sanctification and theosis.[27]

Similarly, the Church's diaconal ministries are concerned not only with people's physical needs but also with their spiritual well-being. To receive the Church's care is also to receive its invitation to participate in the liturgical and sacramental life of the Church in order to receive new life in Jesus Christ.[28]

The hierarchy of the Russian Orthodox Church today does not seek the legal establishment of the church that characterized prerevolutionary Russia. While some Orthodox nostalgically long for a golden age of the past, many Church leaders acknowledge that the Orthodoxy of the nineteenth century was hopelessly compromised by its wealth and social prominence and had lost the hearts of the people. The October Revolution succeeded so quickly only because so many Russians had already abandoned the Church and were not truly captured by its vision of life in God. The rise of communism was God's judgment on a church that had accommodated itself to social expediency rather then representing the gospel.

The Church today, therefore, while participating vigorously in social life, must above all point people to divine salvation. Without awareness of their eternal destiny, people will not be able truly to fulfill their social responsibilities. Perhaps for this reason, monasteries have again become so central to the life of the Russian Orthodox Church, for they have special responsibility to cultivate the Church's spiritual vision in the midst of the wider culture.[29]

Niebuhr noted the inherent instability of the Christ-above-culture position and how historically its representatives have inevitably reduced the dynamic relationship of Christ and culture to static institutional arrangements between church and state. The Christ-above-culture type seems inevitably to devolve into a Christ-of-culture position.[30]

These dangers clearly face the Russian Orthodox Church today. Social developments in Russia belie the assumption that the country is essentially Orthodox or that an Orthodox vision of life before God will permeate the wider culture if the Church promotes votserkovlenie. Western-style assumptions about social pluralism and the individual's freedom to choose his or her own lifestyle increasingly make inroads into the Russian mentality as the nation participates in the global marketplace. The Church finds itself challenged to rethink its relation to Russian society.

Christ in Culture

The Christ-of-culture and Christ-above-culture types illuminate important aspects of contemporary Russian Orthodoxy. At one point, however, they fail. Kirill's program of votserkovlenie proceeds from the conviction that aspects of the gospel are embedded in Russian culture itself. The Christ-of-culture type illuminates the way in which the Church regards Orthodoxy as an essential part of Russian ethnic identity. The Christ-above-culture type illuminates the way in which the Church sets forth a political program and a vision of humans' eternal ends that goes beyond anything that the state can legislate. Neither of these two types, however, adequately points out the ways in which, in an Orthodox understanding, Russian culture itself proclaims both the temporal and eternal dimensions of the gospel.

Kirill had staked out this position long before his ascension to the patriarchate and while he was still head of the Church's Department of External Relations. In an important speech on gospel and culture at a World Council of Churches conference in 1996, Kirill argued that once a culture has been transformed by the gospel, it unwittingly becomes the bearer of the gospel.[31] During the Soviet era, a time when the voice of the Church could hardly be heard publicly, the gospel lived on in the nation's cultural inheritance, such as church architecture and icons, even though the communists regarded them as mere museum pieces. The Church's message was also "preserved in songs, proverbs, and sayings, even though people forgot completely where they had come from," such as the Russian word for Sunday, *voskresen'e*, which is a version of the word for resurrection, *voskresenie*.

Kirill recalls the Soviet tour guides who unintentionally proclaimed the gospel, even to groups of party members, whenever they explained the design of an Orthodox church or the subject matter of an icon. Schoolchildren who were assigned Dostoyevsky encountered the spiritual message of Father Zossima (a message based on sayings of St. Isaac the Syrian, whose spiritual poetry has entered Russian Orthodox hymnody). In an interesting turnabout of logic, if for some Orthodox the success of the October Revolution demonstrated the Church's spiritual bankruptcy, for Kirill the equally stunning and sudden fall of communism in 1991 has now demonstrated the utter failure of the more than seventy years of official state atheism to destroy the gospel that was embedded in Russian society.[32]

Since becoming patriarch, Kirill has continued to advance versions of this argument. Because Russian culture has been shaped by Christian values, it has also implicitly assisted the Church in communicating Christianity's vision of humanity's eternal destiny. This cultural heritage is not narrowly Russian but rather is shared with other Slavic peoples, especially Ukrainians and Byelorussians. The same saints, icons, and rhythms of the church calendar unite them in a common spiritual vision, despite their ethnic and national differences, which have become all the more apparent since the breakup of the Soviet Union.[33]

Just as a deep reading of the Christian tradition informed Niebuhr's typology, even though the typology itself was a heuristic device and not a taxonomy, so too a deep reading of the Russian Orthodox tradition leads someone like Kirill to the position that I am calling Christ in culture. Russians are who they are today only by virtue of the gospel, whose transforming power has become embedded in aspects of their culture. Not only the Church but also the culture bear and transmit the gospel's temporal and eternal values. Russian culture was not always Christian, but once it experienced Christianization, it became a continuing witness to the gospel.

Even those Russians today who know little or nothing about Orthodox faith or practice have been quietly shaped by this cultural heritage. The Church does not have to convert them from one identity to another. Rather, its task is to help them to become more aware of their inherited identity and to grow more deeply into it by entering into the Church's life as fully as possible—first through baptism, then through participating in the liturgy, receiving the eucharist, and observing the rhythms of the Church year. Most Russian Orthodox leaders do not share typical Protestant laments about people who are only nominally Christian because they do not know enough about the gospel to make a credible confession of the gospel. From the Orthodox perspective, a person who affirms his or her cultural identity is already in some sense on the way to the Church and ready to be baptized and incorporated formally into it.

Kirill's program of votserkovlenie therefore reaches into every area of social life not to Christianize it but to lift up the Christian values already inherent to it and to relate it again to the Church's life (to "in-church" it). In a way reminiscent of Pope John Paul II, Kirill, an equally charismatic speaker, has not hesitated to speak at mass youth rallies, send representatives to biker meetings, and promote Church contact with young Russians who call themselves doubters.[34] The Church seeks to reestablish a presence in all of society because all of society needs to know that it has already been shaped implicitly by the gospel.

Evaluating the Christ-in-Culture Type

After reviewing each type, Niebuhr offered a theological evaluation of its strengths and weaknesses. Niebuhr's aim, again, was not to declare one of the types finally superior to the others but rather to deepen our understanding of how each of them points to enduring tendencies and tensions within the Christian faith. A Christ-in-culture type potentially complements Niebuhr's five and helps us to understand traits of Christian responses to culture that the other types do not. While I would need to draw on a wider reading of the Christian tradition to demonstrate the usefulness of a Christ-in-culture type than I can do within the limitations of this essay, I here make some tentative judgments.

The Christ-in-culture type strongly affirms that God the Creator is also God the Redeemer. This God enters into time and leads it toward its ultimate redemption beyond time. The redemptive work of Christ is not limited to the transformation of the inner self of the believer or even to the gathering of a community of faith that seeks to live out Jesus' way of life. Rather, this work is evident in all of nature and culture. The Christ-in-culture type emphasizes that God became human flesh in Jesus Christ and that the resurrected Christ continues to be active and present among us. The world, therefore, is more than a neutral backdrop to God's relations with humanity. Nature and culture show forth the glory of God, especially to those who have eyes to see, and even to those whose vision has grown dull.

The writings of American Orthodox theologian Alexander Schmemann capture well the sense of wonder that inheres in the Christ-in-culture type. Especially in his journals, Schmemann describes moments in which the world around him awakens him to God's glory.[35] There is no rigid difference for him between the world of nature and the world of culture, or between God's creative and redemptive work. Humans constantly interact with both nature and culture, and both can become revelatory of God, especially when they touch us with their beauty. For Schmemann, a memory of walking down a street in Paris on a rainy autumn morning many years ago suddenly becomes a moment of reverie in which he becomes aware again that life is a divine gift before which he stands humbled and amazed. Such moments represent for him the very redemption of time that God has achieved through Christ's life, death, and resurrection.

The close connection between creation and redemption is paralleled by that between the kingdom of God that is already here and the kingdom that is yet to come.[36] Unlike the Christ-of-culture type, which tends to reduce the kingdom either to a this-worldly social project or to an inner spiritual kingdom of personal enlightenment, and unlike the Christ-above culture type, which tends to regard this world as, at best, a preparation for the world to come, the Christ-in-culture type maintains a dynamic tension between the already and the not yet.

To be sure, the kingdom is fulfilled only beyond this world. No ultimate resolution of the deep contradictions of human life and history takes place in our time and space. Yet the kingdom is already breaking into our world. Epiphanies constantly take place. It is the work of the liturgy both to usher us into the kingdom that is already in our midst and to help us to become more aware of it, as incomplete and imperfect as it is, when we return to the world around us.

Kirill, however, moves beyond Schmemann's attention to personal experiences of nature and culture's transparency to the divine glory. Kirill's program of votserkovlenie is premised on the conviction that specific aspects of Russian culture were transformed by the gospel in the past and continue to offer witness to the gospel in the present, even if many Russians have forgotten their Christian cultural roots. By interpreting and commemorating this heritage, educating people in it, and demonstrating its power to offer them new life in the midst of their physical and spiritual brokenness, the Church calls people into the Christian life and therefore back into their true cultural identity.

The Christ-in-culture type has similarities to Niebuhr's type of Christ, the transformer of culture. Representatives of both types emphasize the capacity of the gospel to permeate culture and lift it up to "adoration and glorification of the One who draws [people] to himself."[37] Both emphasize that the Son "has entered into a human culture that has never been without his ordering action."[38] They also agree that cultural transformation is impossible without conversion of the individual from self-centeredness to Christ-centeredness.

Nevertheless, there are important differences between the two types. In explicating the Christ-transforming-culture type, Niebuhr emphasizes that God's redemptive work calls culture into a new identity. A representative of Christ in culture, such as Kirill, argues that God calls a culture back to its historic identity. Niebuhr believes that culture must be redeemed from a gospel that comes to it from outside of itself. Kirill, by contrast, declares that aspects of Russian culture already embody the gospel. Niebuhr understands cultural transformation first in terms of the transformed individual who reframes his or her social relationships in light of the gospel. Kirill sees a dynamic relationship that begins from the culture and flows back into it: what is already transformed in Russian culture proclaims the gospel to the individual, and, in response, the transformed individual preserves, protects, and promotes this cultural inheritance.[39]

It is striking that John Paul II and now Benedict XVI have sometimes spoken this way about European culture in general. Europe cannot be Europe unless it remembers and affirms its Christian roots.[40] Even Karl Barth, hardly a prime example of the Christ-in-culture position, could assert that Sunday as Sabbath came to be embedded in European culture in a way that indirectly expressed the liberating message of the gospel.[41]

The Christ-in-culture type may be especially applicable to European cultures that were shaped for centuries by Christian teachings and practices. I have often wondered, for example, at the effort people make in small German villages to maintain their church buildings, even if they rarely attend Sunday services. From one point of view, they are simply preserving their heritage. The village does not seem complete to them without its famous church from an earlier period of their history. Some church leaders, however, would make an additional point that the Christ-in-culture type helps us to understand. They would say that German culture cannot be German without also giving the gospel a voice, even if in this quiet and seemingly innocuous way. One might also draw parallels to specifically religious rituals, such as baptism and marriage, which continue to define many European cultures, despite apparent secularity.[42]

Even a society such as the United States, which has always been more pluralistic religiously and ideologically than either Germany or Russia, vigorously debates how much a Christian (or Judeo-Christian) heritage has shaped essential aspects of national life.[43] Scholars investigate to what extent a commitment to democracy or human rights or pluralism has Christian roots and, therefore, to some extent continues to bear witness to specifically Christian values, even if no longer directly in the name of the church.

Similarly, ethicist Max Stackhouse has argued in recent writings that modernization and globalization have deep Christian roots.[44] He even asserts that they are a manifestation of divine grace in human culture. If they are not to become distorted or destructive, the church must develop a public theology that interprets them to the wider society as specifically religious phenomena. To use Kirill's term, modernization and globalization and its leading representatives must be "in-churched."

Our job here is not to judge the correctness of the positions that Stackhouse, Kirill, Schmemann, or others take on very different aspects of Christ and culture but to see how a Christ-in-culture type helps us better to understand key features of their thought. I do wish to indicate, however, areas in which a Christ-in-culture approach will look problematic to its critics.

The Christ-in-culture type seems to perform a sleight of hand. It asserts that there is something essentially Christian in a people, even if they have forgotten it or are unaware of it. Like Socrates who believed that even a slave boy could give the correct answer to a difficult mathematical problem if only his interlocutor asked him the right questions, representatives of the Christ-in-culture type sometimes assert that the church just has to make people aware of a Christian identity that is already theirs. Russians really are Orthodox, whether they know it or not.

Such assumptions, however, fail to take history seriously enough (a charge that Niebuhr also directed against the Christ-above-culture type). It is one thing to assert that a culture or certain cultural phenomena (whether art and architecture, or democracy, or human rights) have Christian roots. That is a historical question, and people should care about its resolution if they are to understand their past and how it has shaped them. It is quite another thing, however, to assert that cultural phenomena once shaped by the gospel continue to set forth the gospel today. That is a theological question and not easily resolvable.

Protestants, Catholics, and Orthodox alike affirm that the gospel involves an existential encounter with the God who reveals the divine self in Jesus Christ. While the gospel includes the rehearsal of a story and the explication of a set of moral values, and while this story and these values may embed themselves in a culture, the gospel always involves something more. It calls a person to be reoriented, to turn away from selfish self-centeredness toward God and others, in love, trust, and service.

While Protestants, Catholics, and Orthodox likewise believe that God has called a church into being to set forth the gospel through Word and sacrament and life together, they also agree that God remains free to call people to relationship with the divine self in other ways, outside of the church and its worship. The heavens proclaim the glory of God, and so too can the great historical achievements of a Christian culture.

But here legitimate questions arise. The witness that a culture once made to the gospel can also grow quiet and even be obscured, even when the church attempts to remind people of it.

Cultures are dynamic. They are continually recontextualizing the meaning of the past. A cathedral that a medieval European understood to point to the transcendent God may, generations later, simply represent a magnificent engineering feat. An icon that once invited worshippers to encounter Christ and the saints as alive and present to them may later be appreciated primarily as a human artifact that offers insight into the values and concerns of a long past era. Similarly, the notion of human rights, even if historically indebted to the gospel, can receive approbation without committing anyone to the gospel.

If the Christ-in-culture type easily fails to acknowledge how history "bears all its sons away," it also tends to focus only on the positive achievements of the Christian heritage. It lifts up the beauty, righteousness, and truth that the gospel has contributed to culture but underplays distortions of the gospel that have also embedded themselves in a culture. The representatives of Christ in culture are more apt to speak of Gothic architecture than medieval feudalism, of human rights than slavery, and of divine transfiguration of this world than humans' self-serving projections about the divine realm. Niebuhr pointed out that the Christ-of-culture and Christ-above-culture types did not illuminate human sin as strongly as the other types, and this neglect also seems to be the case with the Christ-in-culture type.

Moreover, representatives of the Christ-in-culture type tend to downplay their sinful motivations in finding Christ in culture. A church that claims to know that a culture's true identity is in Christ is easily tempted to be a church that claims excessive worldly power and honor for itself. The confidence that God has entered into time and space leads to the assumption that the institutional church should enjoy material prosperity as a sign of divine and social favor. To its critics, the Russian Orthodox Church, having endured unimaginable suffering in the twentieth century, is now a church of unspeakable wealth and political power. They argue that this church regularly misuses its wealth and power to silence dissident voices from within that proclaim a different, more demanding gospel.[45]

Of further concern is how the Church should relate to other voices in society as a whole. The program of votserkovlenie often puts Russian Protestants and Catholics at a social disadvantage and inflames suspicions that they are "Western."[46] In a similar vein, Kirill has argued that Western missionary activities are dangerous because they attempt to "refashion [Russian] culture in the Western mode."[47] In regard to religious education in the public schools, the Orthodox are willing to make space for Russia's other historic religions, which are associated with other ethnic groups. However, the only form of Christian education will be Orthodox.[48] Even the Church's way of commemorating the past or providing social services can displace alternative points of view, as when the state returns historic sites to the Church that have been managed for years as museums or public institutions.[49] To its critics, the program of "in-churching" must be countered by a Christian public theology that challenges the Church to hear and value other, critical voices in a pluralistic society.

In contemporary Russia, representatives of the Christ-in-culture type tend to frame society in terms of two actors: the church and the state. The Church, especially through its hierarchs, should provide society with Christian spiritual and moral values; the state should provide for social order. This approach allows little to no space in postcommunist Russia for a civil society in which a variety of interest groups can organize themselves, publicly debate spiritual and social values, and learn the art of democratic procedure that so many Western Christians value in their societies.[50] Many Russian Orthodox instinctively associate "freedom" and "democracy" with chaos, and "pluralism" with ethical relativism. A strong church and a strong state seem to them to be the best guarantors of social stability and cultural vitality.[51]

A Christ-in-culture type cannot account for these tendencies anymore than Niebuhr's types can explain the contributions of the Western church to democracy. But we may wager this conclusion: just as Russian Orthodoxy might help Western Christians to become more aware of the ways in which the gospel can become embedded in a culture, so too Western Christianity might help Russian Orthodoxy to become more aware of how Christ and culture can fruitfully interact in a wide variety of ways. Niebuhr's typology challenges all of us to see and understand more appreciatively just how rich the gospel is and just how much we still have to learn, if we are faithfully to relate the Christ in whom we believe to the cultures in which we live.

Notes

Much of the information on which this essay is based has come from the author's regular trips to Russia over the last seven years and popular Russian Orthodox journals and websites. Of particular value are *Foma*, a popular Orthodox journal directed to "doubters"; *Neskuchnii Sad*, which reviews various aspects of Orthodox life and promotes the Church's diaconal work; the website maintained by the Sretenskii Monastery in Moscow (www.pravoslavie.ru/), which promotes popular Orthodox education; the web page of a significant Orthodox radio station in St. Petersburg (http://grad-petrov.ru/); and three websites that regularly post news and analyses of Orthodox church life from a wide variety of church and secular sources (www .interfax-religion.com/; http://religare.ru/index.html; and www.blagovest-info.ru/index.php/).

1. H. Richard Niebuhr, *Christ and Culture* (New York: Harper and Brothers, 1951).

2. For a good review of the critical literature, see John G. Stackhouse Jr., *Making the Best of It: Following Christ in the Real World* (New York: Oxford University Press, 2008), 22–42.

3. My account of the recent history of the Russian Orthodox Church is particularly indebted to Hans-Christian Dietrich, *"Wohin sollen wir gehen . . ." Der Weg der Christen durch die sowjetische Religionsverfolgung* (Erlangen: Martin-Luther Verlag, 2007). See also Nathaniel David, *A Long Walk to Church: A Contemporary History of Russian Orthodoxy* (Boulder, CO: Westview Press: 2003); and Dimitry Pospielovsky, "Russian Orthodox Church," in *The Encyclopedia of Christianity*, ed. Erwin Fahlbusch and Geoffrey Bromiley (Grand Rapids, MI: Eerdmans, 2005), 4:767–81.

4. See Dietrich, *"Wohin sollen wir gehen,"* 169–81; and Davis, *Long Walk*, 18–19.

5. See Davis, *Long Walk*, 126; "Russian Church Monasteries Increased Thirty-Six Fold, Parishes and Clergy—More than Fourfold under Alexy II," *Interfax* (January 27, 2009), www.interfax-religion.com/?act=news&div=5632; Vserossiiskii Tsentr Izucheniya Obshchestvennogo Mnenniya (All-Russian Center for the Study of Social Opinion), Press Release No. 938 (April 21, 2008); and John Garrard and Carol Garrard, *Russian Orthodoxy Resurgent: Faith and Power in the New Russia* (Princeton, NJ: Princeton University Press, 2008), 242–54. Within the borders of the Russian Federation, the number of churches has increased from two thousand to more than thirteen thousand. See Serge Schmemann, "Soul of Russia," *National Geographic Magazine* 215, no. 4 (April 2009): 112–37.

6. For the legal situation, see John Witte Jr.'s, introduction to *Proselytism and Orthodoxy in Russia*, ed. John Witte Jr. and Michael Bourdeaux (Maryknoll, NY: Orbis, 1999), 1–27.

7. See Irina Papkova, "The Freezing of Historical Memory? The Post-Soviet ROC and the Council of 1917," in *Religion, Morality, and Community in Post-Soviet Societies*, ed. Mark D. Steinberg and Catherine Wanner (Washington, DC: Woodrow Wilson Press, 2008); and Schmemann, "Soul of Russia," 112–37.

8. The present patriarch, Kirill, has advanced a version of this position, as reflected in "The Basis of the Social Concept of the Russian Orthodox Church" (2000), of which he was the principal author; see www.mospat.ru/en/documents/social-concepts/. For various angles on church–state cooperation for the sake of renewing Orthodox Russia, see Garrard and Garrard, *Russian Orthodoxy Resurgent*; Schmemann, "Soul of Russia," 112–37; Clifford Levy, "At Expense of All Others, Putin Picks a Church," *New York Times*, April 24, 2008, www.nytimes.com/2008/04/24/world/europe/24church.html; and William Yoder, "Head Start or Crisis? The Russian Longing for the Christian State," Press Release #11-06, Russian Evangelical Alliance, April 18, 2011.

9. See "Address by His Holiness Patriarch Kirill of Moscow and All Russia after His Enthronement at the Cathedral of Christ the Saviour on 1 February 2009," Russian Ortho-

dox Church website, www.mospat.ru/archive/en/44057.htm. For insightful reflections on Kirill's program of in-churching, see Leonid Sevastyanov and Robert Moynihan, "Kirill's Vision of a Great Russia," *Moscow Times*, January 29, 2009, www.themoscowtimes.com/opinion/article/kirills-vision-of-a-great-russia/374013.html.

10. See John P. Burgess, "Orthodox Resurgence: Civil Religion in Russia," *Christian Century* 126, no. 12 (June 16, 2009): 25–28.

11. See John P. Burgess, "Monasticism as a Force for Religious and Cultural Renewal in Post-Communist Russia," *Journal of Religion in Europe* 4, no. 2 (2011): 1–20. See also Bishop Hilarion Alfeyev, *Orthodox Witness Today* (Geneva: WCC Publications, 2006), 112–24. Upon becoming patriarch, Kirill appointed Hilarion as chairman of the Church's Department of External Church Relations.

12. See John P. Burgess, "Community of Prayer, Historical Museum, or Recreational Playground? Challenges to the Revival of the Monastic Community at Solovki, Russia," *International Journal for the Study of the Christian Church* 7, no. 3 (August 2007): 194–209.

13. See Kirill, "Basis of the Social Concept."

14. See Garrard and Garrard, *Russian Orthodoxy Resurgent*.

15. James M. Gustafson, "Preface: An Appreciative Interpretation," in *Christ and Culture*, H. Richard Niebuhr (San Francisco: HarperSanFrancisco, 2001), xxi–xxxv.

16. Ernst Troeltsch, *The Social Teaching of the Christian Churches* (London: Allen und Unwin, 1931).

17. See Stackhouse, *Making the Best of It*, 34.

18. Typical of the Protestant blind spot to Orthodoxy is Martin Marty's *Pilgrims in Their Own Land: 500 Years of Religion in America* (New York: Penguin, 1985). Of its more than five hundred pages, only two are devoted to Orthodoxy in America.

19. John Stackhouse argues that Niebuhr's Christ and culture in paradox best illuminates the situation of Christian witness to the world under the conditions of democratic, pluralistic societies. See Stackhouse, *Making the Best of It*.

20. See Vigen Guroian, *Incarnate Love: Essays in Orthodox Ethics* (Notre Dame, IN: University of Notre Dame Press, 1987), 24. I am thankful to Professor Perry Hamalis of North Central College for making me aware of this reference.

21. For the association of Orthodoxy and the Christ-of-culture type, see Stackhouse, *Making the Best of It*, 24.

22. See Kirill, "Basis of the Social Concept."

23. Wallace Daniel reviews the growing subjection of the Russian Church to the state in his book *The Orthodox Church and Civil Society in Russia* (College Station: Texas A & M Press, 2006), 14–23. Other historians argue that the Byzantine concept of symphonia had fatal flaws from the beginning, resulting in state domination of the Church. See Alexander Schmemann, *The Historical Road of Eastern Orthodoxy* (New York: Holt, Rinehart and Winston, 1963), 151–53. See also Roy R. Robson, *Solovki: The Story of Russia Told through Its Most Remarkable Islands* (New Haven, CT: Yale University Press, 2004), 41–53, 132–45; and Pospielovsky, "Russian Orthodox Church," 767–81.

24. See "The Russian Orthodox Church's Basic Teaching on Human Dignity, Freedom and Rights," Russian Orthodox Church website (2008), www.mospat.ru/en/documents/dignity-freedom-rights/. For a careful critique of the document, see Marina Shishova, "Geistliche und politische Dimensionen des Verständnisses von Würde, Freiheit und

Menschenrechten in der Russisch-Orthodoxen Kirche," *Ökumenische Rundschau* 59, no. 3 (2010): 346–62.

25. See Robin Lovin, "Faith for a Change: Christ and Culture in Russia," *Christian Century* 121, no. 4 (February 24, 2004): 8–9.

26. Niebuhr, *Christ and Culture*, 120–41.

27. For general comments on the place of suffering in the Orthodox understanding of the Christian life, see Thomas Hopko, *The Orthodox Faith*, vol. 4, *Spirituality* (New York: Orthodox Church in America), 180–83. For the special place of kenotic suffering in Russian Orthodox spirituality, see George P. Fedotov, *A Treasury of Russian Spirituality* (New York: Sheed & Ward, 1948), 11–14; and the writings of Fyodor Dostoyevsky, especially *The Brothers Karamazov* (1880; repr., New York: Bantam Dell, 2003). A recent example of this spirituality of suffering is Alexander Bouteneff and Vera Bouteneff, trans., *Father Arseny, 1893–1973: Priest, Prisoner, Spiritual Father* (Crestwood, NY: St. Vladimir's Seminary Press, 1998).

28. An interesting example is a model drug-rehabilitation program that an Orthodox monk has developed in a rural parish. Eight recovering addicts live with a small group of monks for up to a year, working in the monastery garden, helping with construction projects, participating in daily prayer and the liturgy, and learning church doctrine. See "Dolzhna li Tserkov' pomogat' 'plokhim'?" ("Should the Church Help 'Bad People'?"), *Neskuchnii Sad* (April 2009): 12–13; and Hegumen Mefodii and Elena Ri'dalevskaya, *Ni umru, no zhiv budu* (I Will Not Die but Will Live) (St. Petersburg, Russia: Statis', 2006).

29. For a valuable discussion of the renewed significance of monasteries in the Russian Orthodox Church, see Scott M. Kenworthy, *The Heart of Russia: Trinity-Sergius, Monasticism, and Society after 1825* (New York: Oxford University Press, and Washington, DC: Woodrow Wilson Press, 2010).

30. Niebuhr, *Christ and Culture*, 146.

31. Metropolitan Kirill (Gundyaev), "Gospel and Culture," in *Proselytism and Orthodoxy in Russia*, ed. John Witte Jr. and Michael Bourdeaux (Maryknoll, NY: Orbis, 1999), 68–74.

32. Russian sociologist Aleksandr Shchipkov argues that "religion did not suddenly emerge during the years of perestroika, but had always been the sole spiritual antidote to Marxism during the Soviet era." See Shchipkov, "Religious Relations in Russia after 1917," in *Proselytism and Orthodoxy in Russia*, ed. John Witte Jr. and Michael Bourdeaux (Maryknoll, NY: Orbis, 1999), 78–92.

33. See Kirill, "Etot Mip Priduman Ne Nami" ("We Did Not Invent This World"), *Foma* 82, no. 2 (February 2010): 70–73.

34. For the pope's activities and the theological vision behind them, see George Weigel, *Witness to Hope: The Biography of John Paul II* (New York: Doubleday, 2010); and Weigel, *The End and the Beginning: John Paul II* (New York: Doubleday, 2010).

35. See Alexander Schmemann, *The Journals, 1973–1983* (Crestwood, NY: St. Vladimir's Seminary Press, 2000).

36. Guroian makes similar claims in *Incarnate Love*, 25. See also Schmemann, *Journals*, 11: "Eternal life is not what begins after temporal life; it is the eternal presence of the totality of life." Schmemann works out these ideas more fully in his book *For the Life of the World* (Crestwood, NY: St. Vladimir's Seminary Press, 1973). Thomas Hopko has written that Alexander Schmemann's entire theology revolves around the idea of the kingdom of God as momentarily and fragmentarily present. See Hopko, "The Legacy of Fr. Alexander Schmemann: Theological Education for Pastoral Ministry," *St. Vladimir's Theological Quarterly* 53, no. 2–3 (2009): 339.

37. Niebuhr, *Christ and Culture*, 196.

38. Ibid., 193.

39. Theologian Tex Sample also makes a case for a Christ-in-culture type, arguing that Christ precedes us in the world wherever we find redemptive, transformative, and liberating power at work in people's lives, whether they are Christian or not. Kirill, by contrast, finds Christ in cultural institutions that make direct witness to the gospel story of Jesus Christ and his work of salvation. See Tex Sample, *US Lifestyles and Mainline Churches* (Louisville, KY: Westminster John Knox, 1990), 149–54.

40. See Weigel, *End and Beginning*, 335–41.

41. Karl Barth, *Church Dogmatics III.4* (Edinburgh: T & T Clark, 1961), 559. Also, see *Church Dogmatics IV.3.2* (Edinburgh: T & T Clark, 1962), where Barth refers to the "little lights"— aspects of culture, including other religions—that indirectly reflect the gospel. My thanks to Wolf Krötke of the Humboldt Universität (Berlin, Germany) for making me aware of this dimension of Barth's thought. See Krötke, "Impulse für eine Theologie der Religionen," in Wolf Krötke, *Barmen—Barth—Bonhoeffer: Beiträge zu einer zeitgemässen christozentrischen Theologie* (Bielefeld: Luther-Verlag, 2009), 269–89.

42. Typical is a recent discussion in Germany about secularized Germans tourists and whether they represent a missionary opportunity for the church when they want to visit interesting churches and monasteries. See the editorial, "Offen für Urlauber," *Mecklenburgische und Pommersche Kirchenzeitung* (October 24, 2010): 1.

43. See, for example, Robert Bellah, Richard Madsen, William M. Sullivan, Ann Swidler, and Steven M. Tipton, *Habits of the Heart: Individualism and Commitment in American Life* (Berkeley: University of California Press, 1985); and Robert Bellah, Richard Madsen, William M. Sullivan, Ann Swidler, and Steven M. Tipton, *The Good Society* (New York: Knopf, 1991). For a discussion of the Christian roots of human rights thinking, see Max L. Stackhouse, *Creeds, Society, and Human Rights* (Grand Rapids, MI: Eerdmans, 1984); and Nicholas Wolterstorff, *Justice: Rights and Wrongs* (Princeton, NJ: Princeton University Press, 2010).

44. See Max L. Stackhouse's presidential address to the American Theological Society (April 3, 2009), "Framing the Global Ethic," *Theology Today* 66, no. 4 (January 2010): 415–29. Also, see his *God and Globalization*, vol. 4, *Globalization and Grace* (New York: Continuum, 2007).

45. Daniel, *Orthodox Church*, 74–108, traces the difficulties that priest Georgii Kochetkov had with Church officials when he began directly criticizing social and political conditions in Russia, in his preaching.

46. Levy, "At Expense of All Others."

47. Kirill, "Gospel and Culture," 74.

48. For recent discussion of these issues, see Valeria Posashko, "OPK: Kak v svetskoi shkole rasskasyvayut o Boge," *Foma* 82, no. 2 (February 2010): 41–45; and the special issue on religious education in public schools, in *Voda Zhivaya* 128, no. 10 (2010). Parents would also have the option of enrolling their children in a general course on world religions and ethics.

49. See Fred Weir, "Moscow Turns Ownership of Public Monasteries over to Orthodox Church," *Christian Science Monitor*, May 27, 2010, www.csmonitor.com/World/Europe/2010/0527/Moscow-turns-ownership-of-public-monasteries-over-to-Orthodox-Church.

50. In a recent paper at a conference in Moscow (St. Tikhon's Orthodox University, November 22, 2010), German Protestant theologian Michael Welker argued that Christians will

welcome the "structured pluralism" that is the basis of civil society and of the search for truth. See also Wendy McDowell, "Welker and Tanner Bring Cutting-Edge Scholarship to HDS," *Harvard Divinity School*, March 20, 2002, http://www.hds.harvard.edu/news-events/2011/02/07/welker-and-tanner-bring-cutting-edge-scholarshipnbspto-hds. For an important study of the emergence of the notion of civil society, see Dominique Colas, *Civil Society and Fanaticism*, trans. Amy Jacobs (Stanford, CA: Stanford University Press, 1997).

51. Note, however, Wallace Daniel's argument that the Russian Orthodox Church has the potential to contribute to formation of a civil society. See Daniel, *Orthodox Church*.

The Election of Israel and the Politics of Jesus: Revisiting John Howard Yoder's *The Jewish–Christian Schism Revisited*

Tommy Givens

IN *THE JEWISH–CHRISTIAN SCHISM REVISITED*, JOHN HOWARD YODER gives an account of the Jewishness of the politics of Jesus and Pauline Christianity. He rightly claims that irresponsible historiography has presented early Christianity as a departure from the Jewish ways of its time, reading the later schism into the New Testament and belying the Jewishness of Christian ethics. He contends that living in the faithfully Jewish ways of Jeremiah, Jesus, and Paul, as many Jewish communities did up to the time of Jesus and many non-Christian Jewish communities and free churches have done since, is what it means to be the people of God. After an appreciative exposition of Yoder's account and a brief articulation of its theological and ethical stakes, I argue that the biblical witness to the election of Israel (neglected in his account) troubles his understanding of the people of God as presupposed and conveyed by his revisionist historiography of the Jewish–Christian schism.

The Argument of Yoder's *The Jewish–Christian Schism Revisited*

In *The Jewish–Christian Schism Revisited*, John Howard Yoder further develops an important insight that already emerged in *The Politics of Jesus*, namely, that Christians have been unfaithful to Jesus to the extent that they have forgotten or denied that Jesus was Jewish—not Jewish simply in some mythically ethnic sense but Jewish in his politics.[1] Yoder claims that Christianity did not depart from being Jewish with Jesus or even Paul but with the likes of Justin Martyr and Constantine.[2] It is thus the dejudaization of Christianity that has tended to relocate the drama of the faith from history to the heart and from politics to souls. It is the same dejudaization of Christianity that has allowed it to justify violence instead of discerning and imitating the nonviolence of Jesus as presented throughout the New Testament. The Christian church's claim to surpass or supersede Judaism, then, is not a properly Christian claim but has constituted a betrayal of Christianity. Consequently, in both *The Politics of Jesus* and *The Jewish–Christian Schism Revisited*, Yoder attempts to exhibit the New Testament's claim to Judaism rather than to overcoming Judaism and implies that much of the church's history has been a fall from Judaism rather than its "fulfillment."[3]

But in *The Jewish–Christian Schism Revisited*, Yoder goes much further in detailing Christianity's fall from Judaism than he did in *The Politics of Jesus*. He does so with some revisionist historiography of the Jewish–Christian schism, or "the parting of the ways."[4] He recognizes that predominant Christian self-understandings have not been historically responsible in telling the story of the Jewish–Christian schism. Instead, these self-understandings have assumed the rigid and timeless, anti-Jewish, "Christian" terms of the apparent outcome of the schism, and then have projected them, with various theopolitical interests, into the times and places of Jesus and Paul and the earliest Christian churches. Besides minimizing the ethical import of the Jewishness of Jesus and New Testament Christianity, such Christian self-understandings effectively preempt any engagement with the ambiguous and extended period of time from Jesus to the emergence of two separate "religions" called Christianity and Judaism centuries later. This is to understand Judaism and Christianity as distinct "systems, existing primordially in a 'normative' form," such that the history of the schism can only be one of Judaism and Christianity becoming what they timelessly and essentially are in mutual opposition.[5]

This standard anti-Jewish historiography of the Jewish–Christian schism has typically traded in a series of questionable historical assertions that imply the inadequacy of ancient Jewish life. The function of these assertions is to present Christianity as the supersession, fulfillment, or perfection of imperfect Jewish hopes and ways. According to Yoder, they typically include some variation of the following three claims. The first claim is that, prior to Jesus, the Jewish people was limited and particular (i.e., "of the flesh") whereas the Christian people of God is unlimited and universal (i.e., "of the spirit"). More specifically, the Jewish people was ethnocentric and legalistic whereas the Christian people of God is ethnically diverse (or ethnically superior[6]) and justified by faith. The second claim is that the Jewish people refused the transcendence of God and God's written word, instead construing God's purpose as concentrated on itself and identifying God's authority with its own human traditions and hierarchies, whereas Christianity witnesses to God's concern for all and abides strictly by the transcendent authority of scripture as delivered by the Holy Spirit. The third claim alleges that the Jewish people expected and pursued with violence a political kingdom of God on earth whereas the Christian people of God recognizes that the kingdom of God cannot be won by violence because it is a spiritual kingdom rather than another earthly one. By implication, if the people of God must resort to violence, it is only to secure the material conditions for spiritual goods, not to establish the kingdom of God on earth.[7]

Yoder observes that in telling the sort of story of the Jewish–Christian difference that these assertions imply, which often passes as simply *the* story of Christianity, Christian discourse has typically presented these inadequacies as characteristic of, if not essential to, Judaism. Accordingly, it has credited Jewish opposition to Jesus and his disciples with embodying such inadequacies, and Jesus and the teaching of the New Testament with correcting them and thereby rejecting Judaism. To be sure, Jesus was born into a Jewish community, as were his early disciples such as Paul, but they supposedly went against the grain of "Jews in general" or "normative Judaism," which explains why most Jews rejected Christianity. On the traditional Christian account that Yoder means to revise, then, the Jewish–Christian schism was about the Jewish rejection of Jesus and of the orthodox Christian faith, while the inadequacies of Jewish thinking and practice constitute the Jewish foil of the glory of Christianity.[8]

Revising Christian Understandings of Jewish Life since Jeremiah

Yoder argues that the Christian characterizations of Jewish life before, during, and after the life of Jesus are simply historically wrong. Besides defining what it means to be Christian with a false Jewish foil, they also serve to hide the corruption of the politics of mainstream Christianity. In response to the first claim, Yoder notes that from the time of Jeremiah and in response to the God-ordained reality of dispersion, the Jewish community was multiethnic and cosmopolitan.[9] It had been welcoming proselytes from among the Gentiles and seeking the peace of the cities wherever it lived for centuries before the mission of the Apostle Paul.[10] In fact, Constantinian Christianity became parochial, chauvinist, and protectionist because its "universality" was no more than the limits and particularity of Roman universalism.[11] Yoder insists that the concern of Jewish communities with rigorous obedience to the covenant law was not a matter of earning God's favor or keeping Gentiles out; it was a matter of communal and personal training for Jews as well as Gentile adoptees. It characterized a way of life in which faithfulness to the God of Israel was ethically concrete and politically possible in diasporic conditions anywhere, as we see in Jewish *halakhah* such as the Sermon on the Mount.[12] It was later Christianity that rendered the concrete demands of covenant faithfulness secondary in favor of doctrinal purity and political control; its "justification by faith" was not so much a matter of humility before God or welcoming Gentiles as it was of blunting the edge of God's commands.[13]

As for the supposed Jewish refusal of transcendence and its corollary scriptural authority, Yoder maintains that Jewish communities did not construe God's purpose as limited to themselves, and they did not replace the divine authority of Torah with their own human traditions or hierarchies. As a dispersed people they were more world-conscious than Roman Christianity and less apt to locate the most high God on their own turf in order to make him the enemy of their enemies.[14] As indicated already, they had been adopting Gentiles into the Jewish way of life for centuries before the time of Jesus and Paul. With respect to the function of scripture, Yoder claims that Torah was regarded as supreme in each local Jewish community and mediated by diffuse intellectual institutions and figures whose authority was derived from the text of Torah, which anyone could read anywhere.[15] Rather than turning to a centralized hierarchy, they relied on interlocking local networks of public social process and actual scriptural study to clarify the force of scripture's commands, inform Jewish identity, and promote Jewish unity under the rule of Torah.[16] Among Jews after exile, according to Yoder, God was thus more coherently transcendent by means of God's written word than in Constantinian Christianity, which forsook the authority of scripture by privileging institutional stability and theological speculation by an episcopal center over the unfettered authority of the scriptural words of the uncentralizable God.[17] The supposed transcendence of God's word and Spirit in later Christianity in fact functioned as the immanence of divine authority in corruptible ecclesiastical structures that co-opted the scriptural text, which was supposedly inscrutable to the masses.[18]

And finally, against the third claim, Yoder contends vigorously that Jesus and New Testament Christianity did not have to correct any broad Jewish tendency to seek the kingdom of the God of Israel by violence; they simply continued the nonviolent modes of authority and the embrace of the politics of diaspora that had characterized the Jewish people for centuries under the influence of Jeremiah.[19] Jesus and his disciples were not opposed by "Jews in general" or by "normative Judaism" but by elites based in Jerusalem rather than in the Diaspora.[20] Unlike Jewish authorities such as Johanan ben Zakkai, these elites refused to learn the hard ethical lessons culled from the Maccabean lapse into the pre-exilic ways of territorial kingdom in the land of Judah.[21] Again, it was later Christianity that went the way of Jerusalem elites and against rabbinic Jewish wisdom in setting aside the nonviolent ethos of diasporic Jewish life in favor of alliances with Gentile lords, territorial political sovereignty, and centralized coercive power. The supposed limits imposed on violence by mainstream Christianity's spiritual and heart-centered understanding of the kingdom of God in fact served to prop up its politics of violent control.

In sum, Yoder argues in *The Jewish–Christian Schism Revisited* that the standard Christian understanding of the Jewish–Christian difference has constructed a Jewish straw man. In so doing, it has concealed mainstream Christianity's corruption of the Jewish politics of Jesus and the New Testament.[22]

Revising Christian Understandings of the Jewish–Christian Schism

Yoder's picture of late Second Temple Jewish life suggests that Jesus and the New Testament did not correct Jewish ways but on the whole continued and deepened them.[23] Consequently, although a crucified Messiah and Pauline adoption of Gentiles were indeed scandalous and cause for some discord, the Jewish–Christian schism cannot be neatly attributed to anything as historically naked as Jewish "unbelief" in Jesus as Messiah or Jewish rejection of Christian hospitality of Gentiles.[24] Such attributions are a classic case of what Yoder names as a historical determinism, wherein the supposedly timeless difference between Judaism and Christianity leads historians to "look in earlier texts for explanations of the later polarizations."[25] Yoder observes that, historically, the schism was in fact the avoidable outcome of a contingent series of developments, none of which necessitated the next or sealed the fate of later generations.[26] While there were certainly cases of something like local synagogue splits in the first century, the large-scale bifurcation of the Judaeo-Christian community into "the Jews" and "the Church" was not comprehensive or widely observable until much later.[27] And what many Jews resisted among Christians, according to Yoder, was not any unadorned doctrinal claim about Jesus or the unqualified participation of Gentiles in Christian community. They resisted excessive Christian identification with idolatrous Gentile ways and refusal to be trained by Torah.[28] Such Jewish communities came to associate Jesus' messiahship and prevalent Christian ways of embracing Gentiles with capitulation to idolatry, covenant unfaithfulness, the wrong kind of political authority, and an increasingly pagan way of life. Christianity, therefore, did not lose its Jewishness by its early confession that Jesus is Messiah or by welcoming Gentiles committed to Jesus' Jewish *halakhah*; Christianity lost its Jewishness much later, after gradual corruption and capitulation by forsaking the witness of scripture and the particular ethos of Jeremiah, Jesus, and Paul.[29] Thus, Yoder's revisionist historiography deprives prevalent Christian self-understandings of their historically false Jewish foil and urges Christians to recover the Jewish ways of Jesus as we find them throughout the New Testament and in the witness of both free church and Jewish communities since.[30] Accordingly, Yoder describes the purpose of his revisionist historiography as "theological, interpreting the notion of 'theology' especially in the ethical and pastoral modes."[31]

Historical and Ethical Representation in Yoder's Method

In offering his revisionist account of Second Temple Jewish life and the Jewish–Christian schism, Yoder does not deny that historical exceptions to his generalizations can be identified or that certain Jewish communities opposed and persecuted certain early Jewish Christians. He claims that such opposition was local and sporadic rather than systematic, and exceptions to non-Christian Jewish tolerance and nonviolence were historically just that—exceptions.[32] He insists that the Jewish ways he has described under the heading "Jeremianic" are in fact representative of the way things typically were among later Second Temple Jewish communities, including those who became Christian.[33] These ways were simply the politics of serving the God of Israel, who had sown his people across the known world and exposed the unfaithfulness of clutching at political control, of regarding equality with God as something to be grasped. These ways were what it meant to be Jewish.

Yoder's account raises a number of historical, exegetical, and other theological questions. To what extent is his picture of Jeremianic Judaism in fact representative of Jewish life in diasporic conditions and at the time of Jesus and early Christianity? Do not passages such as Galatians 3:28—that in the oneness of Messiah there is no longer Jew nor Greek—upset Yoder's claims about the continuity between Second Temple Jewish life and the New Testament? Why do even Jesus' disciples have such a hard time understanding and trusting him in the Gospels if he was simply continuing and deepening late Second Temple Jewish ways? Were Jesus and New Testament Christianity simply "more of the same" diasporic Jewish way of life they inherited, as Yoder says, or was there something crucially new to the Christian gospel about the kingdom of the God of Israel?[34] Wasn't there something fundamentally new to the apocalypse of God's righteousness in Jesus—to a crucified Messiah, the resurrection of only that one man, and the Pentecostal Spirit of that resurrection?

But where would answers to such questions lead? To some competing, generalized description better than Yoder's of what represents Jewishness or yet another argument about how Jewish New Testament Christianity is or isn't? While I am sympathetic with much of Yoder's picture of Second Temple Jewish life, his grounds for revising the standard Christian story of the Jewish–Christian schism, and his case for Christian nonviolence, I question the whole imaginary of identity implicit in his ethically rich account of the Jewish–Christian schism. It is an imaginary in which, because the people of the God of Israel is particular, its identity can be represented or circumscribed. I question both the possibility and the ethics of specifying historically or ethically what represents the people of the God of Israel and then predicating the identity and calling of the people of that God on that representation. In other words, I question the possibility of circumscribing the identity of the people of God in the past or present such that particular persons or communities qualify or do not qualify as members, whether Jewish or Christian, by virtue of some available criterion of authenticity.

The Stakes of Representing the People of the God of Israel

Before questioning the soundness and ethics of Yoder's account, I should ask what seems to move Yoder to specify what represents being the people of the

God of Israel or to somehow circumscribe that identity such that true Christians (or Jews) are compelled to identify or not identify with certain communities or persons of the past or present. Yoder understands that the God of Israel is not any old god. Nor will this God settle for creation to be any old way. The God of Israel is the God who, by God's word, loves, reveals, commands, and delivers, all with eschatological purpose. That God's self-revelation, according to Yoder's understanding of scripture and history, has not been primarily to disclose theoretical truths to be believed or to heal persons one at a time. The God of Israel has chosen to form a holy people by God's word and to be uniquely present in and through that people by that word to heal the world of violence and death.[35] Thus, God issued a covenant call and promised to keep calling until the world's healing is complete. The resulting people, on Yoder's account, is composed of those who have heeded God's call in obedience. That people of God, Yoder argues, came to be a suffering servant, an unlikely savior that nevertheless has borne all creation's promise in its wandering, peaceful, and costly way of life.[36] God's revelation and calling reached their fullness in sending Jesus, whose resurrection revealed one crucified Jew to be not the first stone but the cornerstone of this people of faith, stretching from Abraham to the present. The people of God is therefore not any old people. It is not ethically or politically neutral or at bottom ancestral or creedal. It is the people that faithfully witnesses to the healing, peacemaking presence of the God of Israel.

To ask who the people of the God of Israel was and is, then, is to ask how that people lives. There is, for Yoder, no ethically neutral reserve in its identity. For if the people of God can live any old way and remain the people of God, then the God of Israel is just any old god and neither that god nor that people holds any promise. Yoder of course recognizes that mainstream Christianity has understood that being Christian demands something particular. But Christian communities have made the mistake of identifying the particularity of the people of God that corresponds to the particularity of that God with something other than the political ways of Jesus. They have reduced what it means to be Christian to a mere spirituality, or what people supposedly believe, or the rites people have undergone, or the standing of people vis-à-vis a centralized institution that defines Christianness. This reductionism has not only settled for being violent as just the way things have to be politically; it has also empowered such violence with the mystique of Christian religion.

But the God of Israel we meet through scripture, Yoder observes, has not revealed a mere spirituality or propositions to be believed, or rites to be undergone, or an institutional standing to be acquired and maintained. Yoder claims that only an anti-Jewish "religion" could know such a god as the God of Israel and represent or circumscribe the people of God that way.[37] The God of Israel has revealed covenant commands to be obeyed, a Messiah to be followed, and a scriptural story of the people of God that teaches and empowers its hearers and readers to be politically faithful. Notice, then, that the

Christian mistake, according to Yoder, has not been to identify something that represents the people of God or to circumscribe that people somehow as those who are truly the people of God. The mainstream Christian mistake has been what it has identified as representative or circumscriptive. Spirituality, beliefs, standard rites, and limited institutional structure have their place, but these must not relativize the commands of covenant obedience or reduce their scope to something prepolitical, much less something nonpolitical. What represents or circumscribes the people of the God of Israel is the faithful way that people live as a people, the way they love their neighbors, especially when these neighbors are enemies. To refuse that peacemaking politics is to cease to be the people of God.[38]

Yoder claims that that peacemaking politics was what Jeremiah was about, that many Jews actually lived by that politics in recognizing diaspora not only as punishment but also as calling, and that Jesus and Paul and the rest of New Testament Christianity continued and deepened this Jewish politics of faith, as have many non-Christian Jews since.[39] Yoder claims that those ancients or moderns who refused the Jeremianic way, be they the first century Jerusalem elite or David Ben-Gurion, were simply not Jewish in any thick, representative sense of the term.[40] Moreover, he claims that Jesus and the New Testament churches are Jewish such that to be Christian—to be faithful—is to be Jewish.[41] The Constantinian Christian counterparts to the Jerusalem elite or David Ben-Gurion fail to qualify as the people of God for the same reason these latter do: they have not lived Jewishly.

Critique of Yoder's Account of the Peoplehood of Israel

The basis of my critique of Yoder's account is manyfold but at its heart is this: the ground of the people of God, according to scripture, is not the people's faithfulness but God's election, and Jesus himself—God's elect one—did not disown Israel's unfaithful but loved them as his very self. Jesus' nonviolent solidarity with Israel's unfaithful is crucial to his life, death, and resurrection as Israel's Messiah and the one Christians confess as Lord. "He was numbered with transgressors" (Lk 22:37; Is 53:12). Thus, while faithfulness is indeed the culmination of God's election, it is not the condition of it, and faithfulness to the living God who continuously elects his people into being consists in a certain kind of solidarity with the unfaithful, not disowning them as not truly the people of God.

Yoder's hermeneutic, however, whether as historiography or Christian theological ethics, cannot help but disown the unfaithful as not part of the people of God, or, at the very least, as unrepresentative of the people of God. Yet as we find throughout the Bible, in both the Tanakh and the New Testament, the people of God includes both faithful and unfaithful, and its membership is always both. The people of God is thus held together and distinguishable in the world by something deeper than and prior to the faithfulness of its member communities and persons; it is held together and distinguished by God's election. Yoder is rightly concerned to describe the particularity of the people of God who is holy and to do so in a way that challenges Christian anti-Jewishness and reforms what it means to be Christian. But describing the particularity of the people of God simply must attend to how God's election has formed that people in time, how the people is made not of being right but of being forgiven. Conceiving who the people of God is and is not in terms of faithfulness and unfaithfulness keeps Yoder from fully carrying out his own program of peace because he must disown and finally forget the unfaithful rather than bear patiently with them and embrace them as his own by virtue of God's irrevocable election.[42] This claim about the solidarity of the faithful and the unfaithful leaves me with the problem of what difference God's revelation or Jesus really makes, and how the way the people of God live has anything to do with who they are—that is, how the people of God is holy as God is holy. I outline a way of addressing that problem at the end of the essay as a conclusion to my sketch of the Christian ethics of God's election of Israel.

The Problem with Representing the People of the God of Israel

As we have seen, Yoder turns the standard anti-Jewishness of Christianity directly on its head, as Christianity has typically understood Jewishness as the timeless measure of what being Christian is not, or at least a measure of what it outgrew. For Yoder, Jewishness became in exile the measure of what being truly Christian is, and this politics is what we find in its fullness in Jesus and the way of the cross. Paul was therefore not the Hellenizer of Judaism but the Judaizer of Gentiles because he led them into this politics of diasporic faithfulness to the God of Israel, that is, into the politics of the cross.[43] Yet this representation or circumscription of Jewishness is the problem. We can neither simply endorse Yoder's historical or ethical generalizations nor challenge his claims with similar generalizations of our own. The identity of the people of God is underdetermined by historiography or ethical analysis so long as these are understood as capable of representing or circumscribing the people. This underdetermination obtains even if we must insist with Yoder that (because God is not any old god or a timeless god but the God of the people of Israel) the people of God is indeed determined both historically and ethically. With his way of turning Christian anti-Jewishness on its head, Yoder cannot escape a vicious, closed circle in which competing claims to authenticity as the people of God employ a weapon of pure identity against one another. We may like what Yoder counts authentic or representative more than what traditional Christian accounts do, the way he draws a "Jewish" circle around the true people of God. But whether for or against the Jews, employing this weapon assumes that the identity of the people of God can be circumscribed, represented, and then wielded. This is to claim a total view of the people of God and to assume responsibility for identifying and maintaining its borders. On Yoder's understanding, the "true" people of God must decide who truly belongs and who does not, and it is responsible for enacting the difference: the people of the God of Israel is fundamentally self-constituted.[44]

Before we dismiss this understanding of the people of God as intolerant or illiberal, we should note that many Christians find its basic logic quite compelling. We do not want any old claim that certain people belong to the people of God past or present to count as truly being part of the people of God. We wince at accounts of God's heteronomous election of a people or of persons precisely because they appear to leave that people or those persons ethically unaccountable. Surely the people of God must be meaningfully different! We are happy only for God to elect those who elect God. We want to insist that among the many incompatible claims to be the people of the God of Israel past and present, some are false claims, and some are true ones. Hitler may have been baptized in the triune name of God, but surely he does not count as Christian! Surely we are in possession of some standard, however minimal, whereby those we despise and those who dishonor the name "Jew" or "Christian" or the name of God can be counted as excluded. Otherwise, being the people of God does not seem to mean anything substantive at all, and there is apparently no hope in it.[45]

What we cannot deny, however, is that the name of the God of Israel has been despised and dishonored for a time by the unfaithful, and yet the unfaithful have not been disowned, even if some are remembered by scripture or tradition as utterly contemptible. What we cannot deny is that Jesus purposefully died the death of an accursed man, as among those cut off from Israel. That death led to resurrection. That solidarity of the Christ with all Israel rather than just faithful Israel, says the New Testament, forgives Israel's sins (e.g., Mt 1:21; Lk 1:68; Acts 5:31; Rom 11:27; 2 Cor 5:14–15; Heb 8:8–13; 1 John 2:2) and draws Gentiles to Zion to learn the law of the God of Israel (Is 2:1–4; Rom 10:1–21; Gal 5:13–6:2). Thus, in 1 Corinthians 10, Paul urges non-Jewish Christians in Corinth to remain faithful to the God of Israel and to resist idolatry, not by disowning the unfaithful Israelite generation who wandered the wilderness and succumbed to idolatry but by remembering them as ancestors and learning from their example.[46] In Romans, non-Jewish Christian readers are likewise urged not to arrogantly disown Jews who openly oppose them but to know them as beloved sisters and brothers: "With respect to the gospel, they are enemies because of you, but with respect to election, they are beloved because of the ancestors" (11:28).[47] The people of the God of Israel does not command a total view of itself so that it can be represented or circumscribed to the effect of excluding enemies of the past or present. It is simply not an entity possessed of some timeless and intrinsic purity vis-à-vis who it is not but an impure, moving body of struggle, contestation, and reconciliation over time. The people of God is therefore not self-constituted. It is not constituted by human faithfulness to the exclusion of unfaithfulness. It is constituted by God's faithfully holding human faithfulness and unfaithfulness together with forgiveness, and this constitution is the work of God's election, the work of the Word of God.[48]

The Particularity and Ethics of Election

So what difference does God's revelation or Jesus really make, and how does the way people live have anything to do with who they are? How is the people of God holy as God is holy? How can we understand the difference between the people of the God of Israel and the rest of the world? To ask such questions is, according to Jeremiah, to ask about the difference between day and night (33:25–26), the most basic difference to the unfolding of the world over the course of time. Yet it is much easier to say that there is a difference between day and night than to say when exactly it is, and neither one is what it is independent of the other. That should warn us against trying to represent or circumscribe who the people of God is and to exclude those we despise. For such is to pretend to be in control of day and night, of who the people of the God of Israel is, which is determined materially by that God over time. It is not determined by what we imagine or declare. But refusing the futility of representing or circumscribing the people of God does not leave anyone unaccountable or preclude our participation in God's determination of this people. How, then, does God materially determine over time who the people of God is?

In addressing this question, it must first be observed that not all ways of being the people of the God of Israel endure. The Bible reminds us that God has a way of making certain ways of living as the people of God difficult to sustain while maintaining and invigorating others. Thus, some people throughout Israel's history were destroyed such that their future in Israel was left uncertain or eventually cut off altogether. Some Israelite communities were assimilated over generations into surrounding Gentile communities, whether before exile or afterward, their "biological" descendents eventually losing all memory of their Israelite past, as in the cases of the ten tribes of the Northern Kingdom. Some left legacies of shame and derision, or they left no legacy at all, their memory blotted out as time wore on.[49] Others were not cut off and managed to sustain the remembrance of their Israelite past. Still others were adopted into Israel from among the Gentiles and so received that Israelite past as their own (e.g., Ex 12:47–49). But it is finally God as the author of Israel's history, not any temporary human figure or court, not even death by itself, who has finally, materially, and gradually woven certain human strands out of Israel's future and others into it. The course of Israel's living history can therefore not be reduced to any dead law such as ethnicity that hides from historical scrutiny the contingent conditions that have availed for continuity and collective memory across generations, including those contingent conditions that have availed for procreation.[50] Those who in retrospect were on their way out (e.g., the ten tribes of the Northern Kingdom of Israel) do not need historians or ethicists to preempt God's writing them out of the story or out of the people. Quite the contrary: even if their example as part of the people of God has come down to us as primarily negative, they must be remembered as ancestors so long as there is the slightest trace of them. Correlatively, those who have found themselves opposing "us" in the name of the God of Israel in our time must be engaged as beloved sisters and brothers. For what has led "them" even to contend with "us" in the name of that God and not some other?

As many have rightly insisted, God's election cannot and does not trivialize the human response. Nor is it just a way of saying that some people elect God, that God chooses as God's own only those who choose God. If the revelation of the God of Israel in time, that is, in the flesh, is to be taken seriously, election means that the identity of the people of God is not an honorary status that can be removed from a particular person or community, whether by their own unfaithfulness or by some temporary human judge. Election means that the people of the God of Israel is stuck with being who it is, and yet it is blessed to be that people. In the Bible we see that unfaithfulness only makes being the people of God a curse inside of a promise, a curse that bodes suffering, sometimes even the extinction of a whole line or even of whole tribes, but finally the reformation of the covenant people and blessing not only for some but for all.[51]

Thus, being irrevocably the people of the God of Israel does not preclude ethical accountability, as Yoder understandably fears. Being that people is often much more dangerous and depressing than not being the people of God, because the God of Israel is particularly stubborn about not leaving those living under God's name alone. Consequently, it is not theologically (or historically) superfluous that unfaithful persons or communities have managed to pass as Israelite or Jewish or Christian in our memory or in our present. Nor is it immaterial how they have been remembered or the sort of ethical claim their memory makes on us. Such is the presence of Israel's checkered past, the work of the God of Israel that continuously forms the people of that God through time. We are only kicking against the goads and kidding ourselves if we claim to know that the unfaithful really are not part of the people of God according to some criterion available to us. Worse, we fail to learn from their example when we do not perceive how we share in their unfaithfulness. Thus, more important than the difference between historical faithfulness and un-faithfulness within Israel is the difference between the part of Israel that has been remembered at all and the rest. The former difference between faithfulness and unfaithfulness is derived from the latter difference between being remembered and being blotted out.[52] Correspondingly, more determinative than what we perceive as the difference between faithfulness and unfaithfulness in our time is the difference between those who somehow call on the name of the God of Israel and those who do not even bother.[53] Again, the former difference is materially derived from the latter. To be chosen by the God of Israel is not, in the first place, to get that God right, whether ethically, doctrinally, or otherwise, although ethics and doctrine do matter given that some ethical and doctrinal ways of being that people have proven difficult to sustain over generations. To be chosen by the God of Israel is to have been seized in time and space by God as among those God claims as already God's own by covenant, and so to have been compelled by God to live in response to that claim, to find the name of that God on the lips, even if it is to curse him. It is only because the God of Israel has done that—that is, seized people and made that claim on them as his people—that to be faithful to that God is even possible.[54]

So even when some in the people of God live unfaithfully in the past or present, they are not living in just any old way. They are living in response to the call of the God of Israel. They are still different from those who have eluded or lost any occasion to bother with the God of Israel because they find themselves in the body in and through which the Creator's name will be vindicated and the creation redeemed. Thus, in facing the sprawling and unwieldy diversity of the Jewish past, Yoder is right to resist the relativism of those who insist that historiographical truthfulness about Jewishness is impossible, that is, that there was no such thing as Jewishness, nothing real that held diverse Jews together as Jews. He is right to resist sociological accounts that claim to be ethically or politically neutral. While overwhelmingly complex, ancient Jewish existence was indeed more (ethically or politically) certain ways than other ways. It is possible to tell a story of the ancient Jewish community, and it is also possible to get it wrong. Some generalizations are indeed better than others.[55] This is what Yoder means when he says that "Jewishness was not vague."[56] Being the people of the God of Israel did and does have to do with how that people lives.

Where Yoder has gone wrong is in drawing a circle around those he sees as measuring up to the political demands of the God of Israel and pronouncing that only those are the people of God, lest those demands not be taken seriously. Where he has gone wrong is in attempting to specify who truly represents the God of Israel and identifying those representatives as the faithful. To be the people of God is not in the first place to be a faithful people. It is to have been chosen by God as the people in whom God's faithfulness is revealed, both in judgment of unfaithfulness in that people and in vindication of faithfulness in that same people. In this way God is known as holy, and so the covenant people is not commanded to protect God's holiness as if it could be undermined but to observe it. By observing God's holiness rather than anticipating or co-opting it, the people is holy as God is holy.[57]

Consequently, neither Yoder nor we should play the game of disowning those in the past or present who strike us as unfaithful to God's revelation and nevertheless have come to be known in one way or another as among the people of the God of Israel. We should not play the game of declaring an end to our covenantal solidarity with those who seem to have forsaken the ways of covenant faithfulness. That game continues the anti-Jewish imagination of Christianity, even if its players mean to be radically pro-Jewish, as Yoder means to be. The discipline enjoined upon us is not that of pretending to shape the people of God by pronouncing the good guys in the people of God and the bad guys out—and of course always identifying ourselves with the good guys. It is not to command a total view of the people of God. It is not to preempt or settle with some decision of our own the ongoing struggle, contestation, and reconciliation that make up the life of the people of the God of Israel through time. The decision of who the people of God is is not ours to make but God's, and one in which we participate by response. If we claim a total view of the people of God, we may find ourselves fighting against an incomprehensible God, who characteristically addresses the covenant people in and through those who seem to threaten its integrity (Acts 5:39). Thus, we cannot disown those with whom we have a dispute about how to be the people of the God of Israel, however wrong they may seem, for God has already claimed them in making them part of the dispute. The discipline enjoined upon us is therefore to respond faithfully to the claims to be the people of God with which we are in fact presented, to discourage their unfaithfulness, and to encourage their faithfulness. This discipline will never be a matter of applying some dead and timeless criterion with recourse to ethical or doctrinal generalizations and abstractions about the identity of the people of God. It is instead a matter of acute judgment in time in response to the living Word of God as it has given shape to and moved among the living people of God, the scribal task of being discipled by the kingdom of heaven so as to draw from the community's treasure of memory both new things and old things (Mt 13:52).

In making those acute judgments, Christians must take their lead from Jesus, who followed those before him such as Isaiah in knowing Israel's sins only as his own (Is 6:5). Thus Jesus joined his people in the baptism of repentance at the Jordan. Thus he set his face to go to Jerusalem rather than somewhere else apparently more promising, even when that road of solidarity led to the cross. "He who knew no sin became sin that we might become the righteousness of God in him" (2 Cor 5:21). Dying as he did, instead of starting over with a "faithful" people, was the faithfulness that culminated in resurrection and the forgiveness of Israel's sins, the light that has been drawing Gentiles to Zion to grow with those already seized by the God of Israel into one people of covenant peace. A faithful politics, then, does not presumptuously exclude those we perceive as unfaithful but refuses to abandon them as alien. Let us call this politics "the catholicity of Jesus." The catholicity of Jesus responds to and is the culmination of the election of Israel; it is the way of the one Christians confess as the incarnation of the election of Israel, the incarnation of God's loving choice to hold friend and enemy together in one people in forgiveness, remembrance, and hope. A Christian understanding of election without this catholicity of Jesus cannot overcome a hiatus between God's elect people and God's elect one, that is, the Christ.

Notes

1. John Howard Yoder, *The Politics of Jesus: Vicit Agnus Noster*, 2nd ed. (Grand Rapids, MI: Eerdmans, 2003), 108–9.

2. John Howard Yoder, *The Jewish–Christian Schism Revisited*, ed. Michael G. Cartwright and Peter Ochs (Grand Rapids, MI: Eerdmans, 2003), 81. Hereafter, *JCSR*.

3. Yoder's remark in *JCSR* sums it up: "the 'Fall' of Christianity consisted in the loss of certain elements of the Jewish heritage" (121).

4. For a description of the sense in which his historiography is revisionist and its debt to radical reformation Christianity, see *JCSR*, 43–46.

5. *JCSR*, 69; see also 46–47.

6. Christian people were considered ethnically superior in much modern European scholarship, which is exemplified in this respect (rather than excepted) by the Aryan Jesus of modern German scholarship. See Susannah Heschel, *The Aryan Jesus: Christian Theologians and the Bible in Nazi Germany* (Princeton, NJ: Princeton University Press, 2008).

7. Here I have attempted to synthesize Yoder's various characterizations of mainstream Christianity's conventional understanding of ancient Jewish life, which are scattered throughout *JCSR*, especially pages 69–70, 73, 93–95, 140–41, 148, 150–51, 155, 160, 171.

8. Ibid., 46–47.

9. Ibid., 58, 73, 79.

10. Ibid., 50, 96, 195. On the ancient history of Jewish proselytism, see Shaye J. D. Cohen, *The Beginnings of Jewishness: Boundaries, Varieties, Uncertainties* (Berkeley: University of California Press, 1999). See also Louis H. Feldman, *Jew and Gentile in the Ancient World: Attitudes and Interactions from Alexander to Justinian* (Princeton, NJ: Princeton University Press, 1993).

11. *JCSR*, 73.

12. Ibid., 74–75, 110, 152, 187.

13. Ibid., 140. See p. 54 for Yoder's claim that with Justin the schism becomes "doctrinal." Daniel Boyarin makes the same claim in *Border Lines: The Partition of Judaeo-Christianity* (Philadelphia: University of Pennsylvania Press, 2004), 4, 28. Boyarin is following Alain Le Boulluec, *La notion d'herésie dans la littérature grecque, IIe — IIIe siècle* (Paris: Études Augustiniennes, 1985).

14. *JCSR*, 73, 79, 152, 163.

15. Ibid., 48. Here Yoder describes the "rabbinic" authority that coalesced at Yavneh, taking that authority to be simply illustrative of what constituted Jewish authority before and after Yavneh in diasporic Judaism. On the significance of Yavneh for the formation of Judaism, see Shaye J. D. Cohen, "The Significance of Yavneh: Pharisees, Rabbis, and the End of Jewish Sectarianism," *Hebrew Union College Annual* 55 (1984): 27–53.

16. *JCSR*, 78, 109–10, 187.

17. Ibid., 78, 81.

18. Ibid., 109.

19. Ibid., 33, 71, 152, 170–71. Elsewhere Yoder notes with regret that he did not learn of the Jewishness of early Christianity's nonviolence until relatively late in his career. See Yoder, *Nevertheless: Varieties and Shortcomings of Religious Pacifism* (Scottdale, PA: Herald Press, 1992), 122.

20. Ibid., 47–52.

21. Ibid., 71, 83, 114, 152, 155, 171. Johanan ben Zakkai, perhaps a pupil of the great rabbi Hillel, an anti-Sadducean Jewish sage, and an important figure in the postwar renewal of Judaism, opposed the 66–70 CE Jewish war against Rome and called for peace.

22. Ibid., 72–75.

23. Ibid., 171. Beyond his own undocumented reading of primary material in *JCSR*, Yoder cites as sources for his picture of Second Temple and rabbinic Jewish life Steven S. Schwarzschild (to whom *JCSR* is dedicated), Charles Primus, Jacob Neusner, David Novak, H. J. Schoeps, Elijah Benamozegh, Ephraim Urbach, Everett Gendler, Daniel Smith-Christopher, Robert Wilken, and Reuven Kimelman.

24. Ibid., 133.

25. Ibid., 46.

26. Ibid., 44.

27. Ibid., 51, 56-57, 61, 117, 152. See Boyarin, *Border Lines* for an echo of this claim and an account of the gradual divergence. Key to Boyarin's account is the Jewish and Christian construction of communal identity in increasing opposition to one another, particularly through a novel discourse of orthodoxy and heresy (see esp. 2, 4–7, 11, 15).

28. Ibid., 155.

29. Ibid., 81, 121, 162–63.

30. Ibid., 75–87, 105–17.

31. Ibid., 62.

32. Ibid., 51–58. Yoder suggests here that Christian historiography, which blows early Jewish persecution of Christians out of proportion, is probably distorted by much later tensions. He also deals with the significance of the Jewish anathemas. For a historically better account of the anathemas, see Joel Marcus, "*Birkat-Ha-Minim* Revisited," *New Testament Studies* 55 (2009): 523–51.

33. *JCSR*, 114–15.

34. Ibid., 152.

35. See, e.g., Yoder, *The Priestly Kingdom: Social Ethics as Gospel* (Notre Dame: University of Notre Dame Press, 1984), 138: "From Genesis to Apocalypse, the meaning of history had been carried by the people of God as people, as community." See also, Yoder, *The Original Revolution: Essays on Christian Pacifism* (Scottdale, PA: Herald Press, 1972), 24, 28–29, 31, 101; and Yoder, *For the Nations: Essays Evangelical and Public* (Grand Rapids, MI: Eerdmans, 1997), 83, 85–86, 177.

36. *JCSR*, 152.

37. Ibid., 73–74.

38. Yoder, *Original Revolution*, 28-31; and Yoder, *For the Nations*, 233–36.

39. *JCSR*, 170, 183–84.

40. Ibid., 115.

41. Ibid., 140.

42. Yoder insists on the dignity of those excluded, but he has given up the Bible's way of naming the ongoing covenant union of the faithful and the unfaithful. For Yoder, the unfaithful effectively become indistinguishable from those who have never participated in the covenant community. The result is a denial of the covenant community's participation in the unfaithfulness of the excluded and inadequate patience in ongoing internal disputes.

43. Ibid., 95.

44. The result is a finally voluntarist foundation of peoplehood (whatever the claim to embody God's decree or to be true to history). Yoder has replaced the conventional self-assertion of Christian supersessionism and moved the crucial shift back to the beginning of Israel's exile and the community of "Jeremianic Judaism."

45. Even a Jewish scholar as deeply committed to scriptural teaching about election as David Novak concedes that "Jews can stray so far from the Torah that for all intents and purposes, they—and even more so their children and grandchildren—do indeed forfeit their election and its privileges" (David Novak, *The Election of Israel: The Idea of a Chosen People* [Cambridge: Cambridge University Press, 1995], 246). Yoder is obviously not supersessionist in the sense of holding the Christian church to have replaced the Jews as the people of God. But he does hold to what some term supersessionism today. Yoder's problem with traditional Christian supersessionism is not that it is supersessionist but that its supersessionism is not Jewish.

46. "I do not want you to be unaware, brothers and sisters, that our ancestors were all under the cloud." (1 Cor. 10:1ff).

47. In making this argument for the ethical import of the election of Israel, I am indebted to Jacob Taubes, *The Political Theology of Paul*, trans. Dana Hollander (Stanford, CA: Stanford University Press, 2004); and to Steven Schwarzschild, "On the Theology of Jewish Survival," in *Judaism and Ethics* (New York: Ktav Publishing House, 1970), 289–314. *JCSR* is dedicated to Schwarzschild, with whom Yoder corresponded extensively.

48. In developing this critique of Yoder, I have learned much from the editorial introduction, commentary, and conclusion of *JCSR* by Michael Cartwright and Peter Ochs. In making the claim that the people of the God of Israel does not command a total view of itself, I have drawn on Cartwright's reference to Dietrich Bonhoeffer's understanding of Christianity as having "no overview of itself" (*JCSR*, 212). Cartwright notes that in making this observation about Bonhoeffer, he is drawing on the fine work of David F. Ford, *Self and Salvation: Being Transformed* (Cambridge: Cambridge University Press, 1999), esp. 241–65.

49. They may also seem to have gotten off scot-free while the righteous have suffered, as the psalmist complains.

50. See Amy Jill Levine, "To All the Gentiles: A Jewish Perspective on the Great Commission," *Review and Expositor* 103 (Winter 2006): 141, where she describes as problematic "equating Judaism with ethnicity": "It reduces religious practice to an accident of birth, and it ignores the role of the proselyte to Judaism."

51. Here I mean to say that supersessionism is materially and ontologically nonsensical.

52. There is no neat correspondence between unfaithfulness and dying an ugly death or God's election and those who "survive." The murder of Jews in the Shoah no more indicates their unfaithfulness or rejection than does the crucifixion of Jesus. It is through remembrance that faithfulness and unfaithfulness can be distinguished and the hope of resurrection has emerged.

53. Understanding the history of Israel or the church in this way might ease the apologetic pressure that informs so much Jewish and Christian historiography. The identity or integrity of the people of God does not depend upon establishing its virtue in the past; rather, present virtue is increased by the honesty of current generations about the inadequacy of their ancestors and therefore themselves, as we see in the Tanakh as well as the New Testament.

54. Here the contrast of my understanding with Yoder's can be made clearer (see, Yoder *For the Nations*, 223). While not denying the difference between obedience and rebellion, I deny it is the fundamental duality that Yoder claims it is. Rather, the obedient and disobedient are in solidarity within the covenant community. The memory and hope that comes from this solidarity is constitutive of covenant faithfulness and empowers the covenant community to love its enemies.

55. *JCSR*, 113. This precludes a voluntaristic theological historiography wherein claims about Jewishness (or Christianness) are not contingent upon historiographical truthfulness because history is so diverse as to exert no pressure on, say, Christology or ethics; that is, there is supposedly no Jewish or Christian "story," only disparate data whose "theological" construal as any kind of "whole" is historically arbitrary or willed and not for that reason problematic. This attitude cannot help but promote Christian ignorance of Judaism and the violence that has often accompanied it. Politically peaceful conflict rather than segregated competing views (in governance or scholarly method) is an alternative to violent enmity (cf. Yoder's critique of Krister Stendahl on *JCSR*, 156).

56. *JCSR*, 58. By "vague," Yoder does not mean ambiguous, which he happily admits that Jewishness was. He means totally indeterminate; there was a real difference between being Jewish and being not Jewish.

57. Yoder does not neglect election altogether, and at times he leans in the right ethical direction with it (see *JCSR*, 191; cf. *For the Nations*, 86). Yoder also appeals to the election of the people of God in "Why Ecclesiology Is Social Ethics," in *The Royal Priesthood: Essays Ecclesiastical and Ecumenical*, ed. Michael G. Cartwright (Grand Rapids, MI: Eerdmans, 1994), 115. As Yoder clarifies, the "Abraham–Jesus story" Is a story of the rise of a faithful people rather than a Constantinian people, whereas the biblical story of the elect people, of Abraham to Jesus, includes in the covenant community the likes of Saul and Jeroboam, a people constituted by God's election rather than its own faithfulness. Thanks to Mark Nation for reminding me of Yoder's discussion of election in this final essay.

"I Was in Prison and You Visited Me": A Sacramental Approach to Rehabilitative and Restorative Criminal Justice

Amy Levad

ROMAN CATHOLIC ETHICISTS AND THEOLOGIANS HAVE REMAINED RELA-
tively silent about crises in US criminal justice systems, with two exceptions.
The US Conference of Catholic Bishops published a document in 2000 calling
for rehabilitative and restorative approaches to crime. Historian Andrew Skotnicki has criticized the bishops for ignoring traditional Catholic models of punishment—monastic and ecclesiastical prisons. This essay challenges Skotnicki
and bolsters the bishops' argument by proposing that the sacraments, especially the Eucharist and Penance, provide a stronger basis in Catholicism for
responding to crime and the crises in US criminal justice systems in ways that
foster rehabilitation and restore justice while also reforming broken systems
and promoting social justice.

The State of the Conversation: Christian Responses to Criminal Justice Crises

Criminal justice systems in the United States are in crisis. Currently more than 7.3 million adults in the United States are under some form of supervision by state, local, or federal criminal justice systems, including probation, jail, prison, and parole.[1] At midyear 2009, nearly 1.6 million of these people were in prison, and nearly 800,000 were in jail.[2] These numbers represent a gross increase in the rate of incarceration in the United States over the last several decades. In 1980 the rate of incarceration in prisons was 139 people per 100,000 US residents. Over thirty years, this rate has increased by more than 360 percent; it was 504 people per 100,000 US residents in 2008.[3] Although the United States has less than 5 percent of the world's population, it holds nearly 25 percent of the world's incarcerated people.[4] The United States incarcerates its residents at higher rates than any other nation.[5] In short, we have more people locked up in the United States and at higher rates than at any other time in our history and than any other nation.

While these numbers are troubling enough to raise serious questions about our criminal justice systems, discrepancies related to race and ethnicity among prison and jail populations add greater urgency to addressing this crisis. Racial and ethnic minority populations are incarcerated at astounding rates in comparison with whites. The incarceration rate of black non-Hispanic men is six times that of the incarceration rate of white non-Hispanic men and nearly three times that of Hispanic men.[6] Although about 93 percent of people in state and federal prisons in 2009 were men, in recent years the incarceration rate of women has increased twice as quickly as that of men. While women are incarcerated at a much lower rate than men, the population of incarcerated women reflects similar racial and ethnic disparities as the male inmate population.[7] Increasing incarceration has hit racial and ethnic minority populations in the United States especially hard.

In addition to racial and ethnic disparities, criminal justice systems in the United States are also marred by disparities related to the socioeconomic status of inmates. Measures of the socioeconomic status of people in jail or prison are difficult to find; a person's income and wealth are not noted upon incarceration as are his or her sex and race. One of the best measures of socioeconomic status of prison and jail inmates is whether they need publicly financed counsel, and the most recent data recording this statistic are from more than a decade ago.[8] In 1998 about two-thirds of federal felony defendants required public defense. In 1996 more than four-fifths of felony defendants in the 75 most populous counties in the United States required public defense. While conviction rates did not vary according to whether defendants had privately or publicly financed counsel, defendants with public defense were incarcerated at higher rates and for longer sentences than those with private defense. Criminal justice systems not only disproportionately incarcerate racial and ethnic minorities; they also tend to hold high numbers of poor people behind bars as well.

Together, these data suggest that as the reach of criminal justice systems in the United States continues to expand, these systems grip certain groups of people in our society—especially racial and ethnic minorities and socioeconomically disadvantaged people, and increasingly, women—more tightly than other groups. As these systems have grown, however, they have not necessarily decreased crime, made our communities safer, or resulted in the return of offenders prepared to be fully integrated members of society again.[9] Due to the repeated failure of these systems to realize their purported goals not only over the last several decades but at least over the last two centuries, the "overall direction and basic legitimacy" of modern punishments, especially incarceration, has come under question.[10]

In recent years, Christian ethicists and theologians have entered into the conversation about crises in US criminal justice systems, offering reflections on how Christian beliefs, values, and practices could offer alternative ideologies and practices of criminal justice, which then might support substantial institutional and social reform. Protestant voices have predominated with contributions from such scholars as Lee Griffith, Christopher Marshall, Timothy Gorringe, Richard Snyder, Mark Lewis Taylor, and James Samuel Logan.[11] One limitation of this conversation, however, is the lack of Catholic participants— excepting two significant voices. On the one hand, the US Conference of Catholic Bishops (USCCB) published a document in 2000 titled "Responsibility, Rehabilitation, and Restoration: A Catholic Perspective on Crime and Criminal Justice," which advocated for rehabilitative and restorative reforms for criminal justice systems in the United States.[12] On the other hand, Catholic historian Andrew Skotnicki has been an adamant detractor from the bishops' proposal, criticizing them for not fully understanding debates within contemporary criminology and for failing to draw adequately upon Catholic tradition.[13] He advocates instead a return to the model of monastic and ecclesiastical prisons as "the normative means of punishment" in Catholicism.[14]

This essay explores the contours of the conversation between the bishops and Skotnicki and adds a third Catholic voice to the discussion. After describing the arguments of the USCCB and Skotnicki, as well as the remaining gaps in their discussions, I propose that monastic and ecclesiastical prisons ought not to be the lynchpin of a Catholic theory of criminal justice. Instead Catholics ought to approach issues of criminal justice from a position that emphasizes the centrality of the sacraments to our faith as we engage in work for justice, love, and forgiveness in the world. Placing the sacraments, especially the Eucharist and Penance, at the center of a Catholic response to crime and criminal justice, rather than monastic and ecclesiastical prisons, provides a stronger traditional foundation for the bishops' call for rehabilitation and restorative justice. Furthermore, it provides a stronger traditional foundation for a Catholic pursuit of social justice, a necessary corollary in overcoming the crises within our criminal justice systems.

Two Catholic Voices: The USCCB and Andrew Skotnicki

The USCCB composed "Responsibility, Rehabilitation, and Restoration" in 2000 to build upon Pope John Paul II's message earlier that year, "Jubilee in Prisons."[15] Their statement reflects a tension within all Catholic approaches to dealing with crime, punishment, and justice. On the one hand, Catholic tradition insists that criminal behavior that harms others and violates the rights of human persons cannot be tolerated. On the other hand, the church also upholds the inherent dignity of all children of God, including victims and of-fenders, and maintains that every person bears the potential for redemption and restoration to full relationship with both God and neighbor. These two beliefs lead the bishops to conclude, "The common good is undermined by criminal behavior that threatens the lives and dignity of others and by policies that seem to give up on those who have broken the law."[16] In light of this conclusion, the bishops hope in this statement to find some resolution to this tension and some response rooted in Catholic tradition to crises in US criminal justice systems. "We are convinced that our tradition and our faith offer better alternatives [than more prisons and more executions] that can hold offenders accountable and challenge them to change their lives; reach out to victims *and* reject vengeance; restore a sense of community and resist the violence that has engulfed so much of our culture" (emphasis in original).[17]

After a brief description of current problems with criminal justice systems in the United States, the bishops turn to resources from the "scriptural, theo-logical, and sacramental heritage" of the Catholic Church to build a framework for their response, which they hope allows them to "move away from the so-called 'soft' and 'tough' approaches to crime and punishment offered by those on opposite ends of the political spectrum."[18] The bishops find support for their via media within Old Testament traditions that demonstrate God's justice and mercy in the context of the covenant community and the extension of these traditions in the New Testament with the life, death, and resurrection of Jesus Christ. In the life of Jesus Christ, they find the roots of the tension described earlier as he both battled oppression and called for the transformation of sin-ful lives. The bishops also note that Jesus himself was a prisoner who called his disciples to visit the imprisoned (Matthew 25). In addition to scriptural sources, the bishops draw upon Catholic social teaching to justify their stance. They par-ticularly cite the value of human life, the recognition of human dignity, the im-portance of participation in family and community for human beings, the op-tion for the poor and vulnerable, and the principles of subsidiarity and solidarity as offering direction for Catholic responses to crime, justice, and punishment. Finally, the bishops suggest, "Our sacramental life can help us make sense of our paradoxical approach to crime and punishment."[19] While they mention the Eucharist in passing, they find that the sacrament of Penance provides the fun-damental Catholic model for "taking responsibility, making amends, and rein-tegrating into the community."[20] From these resources of the Catholic heritage, the bishops conclude that although punishment of wrongdoers is justified in Catholic tradition, punishment must always be meted out for the purpose of reincorporating offenders into the body of the community, never for the sake of punishment itself.

The bishops propose several policy directions for a Catholic response to criminal justice crises in the United States. They maintain that, although some people will inevitably need to be removed from society for public safety, punishment from a Christian perspective ought to be directed not toward incapacitation, deterrence, or retribution but always toward rehabilitation and restoration of offenders to community and, when possible, toward restitution for victims. Reforms of criminal justice systems need to be accompanied by work for crime prevention and social justice, especially poverty reduction. The bishops also support efforts to meet the needs of victims of crime and communities, particularly through restorative justice programs. Offenders must have access to spiritual guidance as well as to treatment for mental illness and substance abuse when necessary. Finally, the bishops advocate a variety of community alternatives to incarceration that may reduce incidents of crime, including community policing, neighborhood watch, and "broken windows" policing. They conclude that together these policies navigate the way between the insistence that we cannot ignore criminal behavior and the recognition that all people, including criminal offenders, are children of God created for responsible, rehabilitated, and restored relationship with God and neighbor.

Andrew Skotnicki's criticisms of the bishops' statement are twofold. First, he argues that the bishops "lack analytical depth concerning contemporary criminology," resulting in their advocacy of policies that exacerbate the punitiveness and racial, ethnic, and class bias of criminal justice systems.[21] He writes, "The Catholic bishops of the United States have found themselves in the rather strange position of advocating a number of policies that are hallowed by the very forces to which they have expressed opposition."[22] To a limited degree, Skotnicki's first criticism of the bishops is warranted, although it does not entirely undermine their recommendations for reform of our criminal justice systems.[23] It seems that the bishops could correct their missteps with only a brief addendum that clarifies their recommendations for alternatives to incarceration.

Skotnicki's first criticism, then, does not seem to get at the heart of his problem with the bishops' approach to crime, justice, and punishment. The central issue that Skotnicki raises against the bishops, and his second criticism, is that he finds in their call for rehabilitation and restoration "an insufficient appreciation for the foundational importance of the prison and the essential element of the 'time' sentence as contributing factors in the dynamic of punishment and renewal."[24] He argues that Catholic tradition has long insisted that prisons are necessary to inspire contrition in those offenders who feel no remorse and that, in these cases, some level of retribution is necessary to bring about offenders' cooperation with rehabilitation and restoration. According to Skotnicki, the bishops do not see that a truly Catholic approach to these issues must include prisons as the normative means of punishment.

Skotnicki develops his argument for prisons in a Catholic theory of criminal justice most fully in his book *Criminal Justice and the Catholic Church*. He organizes his presentation of this theory around four questions that he argues any theory of criminal justice must answer; his answers to the first three questions largely agree with what the USCCB might say. Skotnicki's main area of disagreement with them lies in his answer to the final question. Nevertheless, Skotnicki's responses to all four questions depend upon one another, so a full understanding of his argument requires consideration of each question in turn.

Who are the offenders? Skotnicki argues that Catholics must see the criminal offender as Christ himself, "see the prisoner . . . [as] the battered body of Jesus."[25] We will then come to recognize prisoners as human persons, sinful, but still bearing the image of God. Identifying prisoners with Jesus Christ ought to lead all Christians, in Skotnicki's view, to compassionate care, rather than to limitless punishment.

What is the justification for punishing criminal offenders? Skotnicki answers in two parts. First, he draws upon Augustine and Aquinas to show that Catholic tradition has held that the state has a moral obligation to punish people who violate the law because of its duties to maintain order and to establish justice in society. The efforts of the state to realize order and justice, however, will always be limited because the state cannot bring about redemption in its fullest sense. For Skotnicki, the ultimate justification of punishment is neither order nor justice but atonement—an internal journey for offenders toward repentance, which potentially results in God's forgiveness and liberation.[26]

In light of this justification for punishment, Skotnicki asks, *What is the end at which forcible intervention aims?* He proposes two ends for punishment. First, it ought to aim for social reintegration of offenders after a period of enforced exile. Second, it ought to lead to internal reform, resulting in the liberation and reconciliation of offenders with God and neighbor.[27]

Skotnicki's responses to these three questions do not present perspectives significantly different from those of the USCCB; his disagreements with the bishops arise with his fourth question: *By what means will the end of punishment be accomplished?* Through a historical survey of the formation of Western penal systems, Skotnicki argues that Catholic tradition upholds the prison as the normative means of punishment. He finds that penal systems in the West are rooted in the development of, first, monastic prisons and, later, ecclesiastical prisons under the jurisdiction of the church from the late patristic period through the Middle Ages. These prisons were centered upon the monastic ideal that "the cell is a place for people serious about finding their true identity and rooting out the influences and impulses that lead to alienation from self, from others, from nature, and from God."[28] Drawing upon this elevation of isolation as a means for self-reform within monasteries, the church created monastic and ecclesiastical prisons as alternatives to secular punishments, which typically used prisons merely as holding cells in anticipation of "real" punishments (usually corporal or monetary in nature). Prisons became "the basic disciplinary apparatus in the church and, by extension, in Western jurisprudence" with the development of canon law in the twelfth and thirteenth centuries.[29] The Catholic Church continued to use monastic and ecclesiastical prisons throughout the next few centuries in religious criminal justice systems that ran parallel to secular systems. Skotnicki admits that the use of these prisons for punishment throughout the history of the church was "ambiguous" and that "prisoners in Catholic institutions often did not 'live happily.'"[30] Nevertheless, he finds virtue in the Catholic use of prisons where the image of the prisoner as Christ was maintained along with the justification of atonement and the ends of internal reform and social reintegration; he suggests that monastic and ecclesiastical prisons were often recognized, even by offenders, as more merciful and humane than secular punishments.[31] Skotnicki seems to view the pinnacle of Catholic influence upon Western penal systems as the creation of the penitentiary in the early nineteenth century in the United States by Quaker reformers who drew upon monastic and ecclesiastical models to create secular prisons building upon the idea "that the combination of work, silence, prayer, and spiritual counsel could mend what was wrong in the human heart."[32] Skotnicki concludes, "Imprisonment is then not the only means to bring the offender back to personal well-being and normal social interaction but, criticisms and misuse notwithstanding, it is clearly the preferred means to accomplish the ends of criminal justice unique to the Catholic tradition."[33]

Skotnicki's second criticism of the bishops' stance on rehabilitation and restoration is that the bishops have ignored what he views as the primary means of punishment in a Catholic theory of criminal justice: the prison. The only means of tying together the threads of a Catholic understanding of crime, punishment, and justice, in Skotnicki's view, is the use of time sentences in prisons so that prisoners may come to recognize their wrongdoing and seek reconciliation with God and neighbor. Skotnicki fears that the bishops have lost sight of the value of incarceration as punishment, and he seems to stake a lot on this argument. He writes, "The question that undoubtedly arises in the mind of the reader is whether the theory outlined here . . . can work in practice. The material presented . . . suggests that if the idea of confinement cannot work, then the entire monastic system, *as well as Catholic anthropology and spirituality*, is in question, not to mention its penitential ethos."[34] Skotnicki seems to believe that if the prison cannot work as the means of achieving social reintegration and internal reform of prisoners, then it may be that much of Catholic tradition, not just a Catholic theory of criminal justice, is undermined.

The stakes that Skotnicki places in his theory of criminal justice ought to lead to questions not only about whether it can work in practice but also about whether prisons really are the normative means of punishment within Catholic tradition. The former question concerns the effectiveness of prisons in terms of social reintegration and internal reform of prisoners. In failing to answer this question fully, Skotnicki himself is guilty of his first criticism of the bishops, a lack of analytical depth concerning contemporary criminology. He presents no criminological evidence that prisons in the United States (or anywhere else, for that matter) are effective. He does not account for criminological data that suggest that about two-thirds of released prisoners in the United States are re-arrested within three years of reentry into the community, half are reconvicted, and one-quarter are sentenced to prison for a new crime.[35] Nor does he account for data that indicate that recidivism does not seem to correspond to the length of a prisoner's sentence.[36] Modern US prisons clearly do not "work" as far as Skotnicki's stated ends for criminal justice systems are concerned.

With respect to this question, however, Skotnicki might respond that he would not expect to achieve these ends in modern US prisons because they do not practice what he is preaching in terms of Catholic tradition; these prisons are therefore not a true test of his theory. Given the praise he gives to Quaker penitentiaries, a reader might then suppose that those penal institutions would offer a fair test of Skotnicki's theory. While recidivism data are not available for these institutions, Charles Dickens visited the United States in 1842 in order to see their innovations firsthand. Although Skotnicki draws upon Dickens's visit, as well as that of Alexis de Tocqueville, to praise penitentiaries,[37] he fails to mention that Dickens was not pleased with what he found.

> The system here is rigid, strict, and hopeless solitary confinement. I believe it, in its effects, to be cruel and wrong. In its intentions, I am well convinced that it is *kind, humane, and meant for reformation*; but I am persuaded that those who devised this system of Prison Discipline, and those benevolent gentlemen who carry it into execution, *do not know what they are doing*. I believe that few men are capable of estimating the immense amount of torture and agony which this dreadful punishment, prolonged for years, inflicts upon its sufferers.[38]

The historical record thus suggests that even early penitentiaries did not re--alize in practice Skotnicki's theory of criminal justice. To the question of whether a theory of criminal justice that uses prisons as normative means of punishment can work, any level of intellectual honesty requires the answer that it never has before.

With this conclusion, Skotnicki may worry that the failure of his theory on practical grounds destabilizes the whole of Catholic tradition. Such could be the case, however, only if he is correct that incarceration is foundational within a Catholic theory of criminal justice. I contend that few Catholics would view the prison as a redemptive, or even an accurate, representation of the core of their tradition. Rather, the sacraments lie at the center of Catholic faith and practice. In the sacramental life, particularly in the practices of the Eucharist and Penance, we may find a stronger foundation for a Catholic theory of criminal justice, one that supports the call of the bishops of the United States for responsibility, rehabilitation, and restoration.

A Sacramental Response to Criminal (and Social) Justice

On the surface, an appeal to the sacraments as a foundation for a Catholic theory of criminal justice may seem misguided. Several problems—including the privatization and individualization of Christian worship practices, the reduction of the connection between liturgy and ethics to themed worship services, fears of "politicizing" religious rituals, and divisions among Christian denominations about the sacraments—perhaps speak against this endeavor. Despite these difficulties, full consideration of the sacraments of Eucharist and Penance in Catholic tradition may offer a stronger foundation for a Catholic theory of criminal justice that both provides a social critique of those factors that have contributed to our criminal justice crises and fulfills the USCCB's hopes for restorative and rehabilitative alternatives to prison. Furthermore, this consideration may also open space for ecumenical conversations about the relationships between sacramental practices in various traditions and work for justice.

The Catholic Church has not always drawn on the richness of the sacraments, especially the Eucharist, in its reflections upon and work toward justice, whether social justice or criminal justice. In "Responsibility, Rehabilitation, and Restoration," the US bishops mention the Eucharist in passing as a "real encounter with the Saving Lord and central Catholic sign of justice and mercy," but they do not explain in detail the relevance of the Eucharist to crime, punishment, or justice.[39] However, New Testament texts that describe the institution of the Eucharist by Jesus Christ and its celebration in early Christian communities validate the bishops' cursory reference to this sacrament. During the Last Supper, Jesus drew his disciples together and offered to them bread and wine, his body and blood, telling them of his death and resurrection for the forgiveness of sins.[40] His celebration of the Last Supper fulfills the covenant established with Israel for the reconciliation of all creation with God and provides a foretaste of the reign of God in its fullness. It also brings to mind the numerous other meals described in the Gospels in which Jesus ate with people who were excluded from society, but whom he would welcome in God's kingdom. In Luke's account of the Last Supper, Jesus responds to a dispute among the disciples by instructing them that those who would become servants of others and would stand with him in his trials would receive the kingdom of God.[41] Following Jesus' death and resurrection, the early Christian community endeavored to "do this in remembrance" of him through the celebration of the Eucharist as a communal meal. Addressing the Corinthians, Paul explains that by taking the bread and wine, participants in the Eucharist share in the body and blood of Christ and so are made one body with one another.[42] He warns them that those who take the bread and wine unworthily "eat and drink judgment against themselves."[43] The community ought not to eat or drink without "discerning the body," without addressing divisions within the community and ensuring that all brothers and sisters have gathered at the table. The New Testament accounts of the Last Supper and early celebrations of the Eucharist indicate that, through the ongoing practice of this sacrament, Christians remembered Jesus' victory over the principalities and powers of this world not only by sharing the bread and wine but also by coming together as a community and "reaching out to all those who are excluded and sharing with them all that one has,"[44] thus embodying God's justice.

The description of the Eucharist in New Testament texts highlights a tension within its celebration. As we partake in the Eucharist in the present moment (whenever in history that moment may be) we are called to remember Jesus Christ's death and resurrection in the past and to anticipate the coming of the God's reign in its fullness in the future. The Eucharist collapses time so that its participants may experience God's past, present, and future simultaneously. William Cavanaugh describes this experience of the Eucharist as producing a desire for what is "not yet" even amidst what has "already" come with Jesus Christ. "If the Eucharist is indeed a memorial of the whole Christ . . . then it recalls more than the past events of Jesus' life, death, and resurrection, but also expresses an ardent longing for the completion of the Kingdom Christ inaugurated."[45] Through participation in the Eucharist, Christians glimpse God's reign in which life overcomes death, peace conquers violence, sin is forgiven, all of creation is reconciled, the covenant is fulfilled, and God's love and justice reign. We find hope in the body of Christ, experienced in both the elements of the Eucharist and the community gathered at the table. The Eucharist awakens what Andrea Bieler and Luise Schotroff call our "eschatological imagination," which enables us to see our world as it could become fully in the reign of God as well as to recognize the extent to which our world remains fallen. "This is exactly what the eschatological imagination holds: the reality of brokenness and a hope for wholeness."[46] The tension between the "already" and the "not yet" in eschatological imagination awoken in the Eucharist is the source of the ardent longing described by Cavanaugh for God's life, peace, forgiveness, love, and justice.

This longing is not otherworldly; rather, the Eucharist is bodily, communal, and political. Thus, well-considered celebration of the Eucharist ought to draw Christians into "deep confrontation with human alienation."[47] Kevin Seasoltz writes,

> In our contemporary world there are many who are lowered by society; those
> who are thought to be unworthy or inferior are pushed lower and lower in

the community until their own sense of dignity and worth is decimated too. . . . Christian ministry to these people must be ministry and service after the manner of Jesus. That means the very ones who are pushed or kept down by society are the ones to be raised up so they achieve that sense of dignity and worth essential to the redeemed human condition.[48]

As the Eucharist fosters visions of God's justice, which sometimes contrasts sharply with justice interpreted in human terms, Christians ought to become increasingly aware of injustices in our midst that demean and degrade our neighbors. Ruptures within our communities, violations of the bodies of human persons, and exclusions from the political life of our society ought to inspire Christians to work for redemption, healing, and inclusion of all people.

Among the sources of human alienation in our society that we—Catholic, Protestant, Orthodox, and non-Christian—must all confront are both crime and the crises in US criminal justice systems as they are marked by social injustice. For Catholics, this confrontation ought to be founded upon their eschatological imaginations nourished by the Eucharist within the sacramental life. Emphasizing the centrality of the Eucharist in Catholic tradition may help provide stronger support for the US bishops' insistence upon the inherent dignity of all human persons and the enduring potential within all people, including victims and offenders, for redemption and restoration to full relationship with God and neighbor. Jesus Christ's institution of the Eucharist demands that its participants serve those who are "pushed or kept down" and, within our context, that may include serving both victims and offenders of crime through support of and engagement in restitution, rehabilitation, and restorative justice. In working for the inclusion and restoration of victims and offenders of crime in community, the church witnesses to its hope in the establishment of justice under God's reign even as we continue to live in the brokenness of our world.

Catholic responses to crime and to crises in US criminal justice systems marked by social injustice ought to occur on several levels. The US bishops and Skotnicki agree that criminal behavior cannot be tolerated, but they disagree about the means for responding to wrongdoing. While Skotnicki argues that the prison is foundational within a Catholic theory of criminal justice, placing the Eucharist at the center of such a theory would suggest that another sacrament, Penance, has actually been the normative means within Catholic tradition for responding to wrongdoing. The sacraments of Eucharist and Penance have been closely linked throughout the history of the church; Penance arguably cannot be understood fully outside of the context of the Eucharistic community. The Christian community seeks unity by evaluating when members conform to the powers of the world rather than to the ways of discipleship, thereby cutting themselves off from the body of Christ. Ideally, in judging those who violate other individuals or the community, the church extends the opportunity to become reincorporated into the body of Christ through Penance. While modern practices of this sacrament often seem individualistic and privatized, penitential practices in the early church were communal and public. While Penance today is often perceived as metaphorical self-flagellation for the sake of alleviating unhealthy guilt, the purpose of these practices was seen as "medicinal," restoring the wholeness of the wrongdoer for full communion with the body of Christ and resulting in reconciliation. Penance, not prison, has been the normative means in Catholicism for achieving the ends of social reintegration and internal reform of wrongdoers.[49]

Of course, the sacrament of Penance cannot be instituted as the central practice of a modern Western penal system. Nevertheless, some similarities between early Christian penitential practices and modern restorative justice practices may provide a stronger theological framework for the latter within Catholic tradition than that offered by the US bishops in their statement. Restorative justice includes a variety of practices that generally involve bringing together victims, offenders, and often community members to reach consensus about how to "repair the harm" caused by a crime. These practices have an affinity with early Christian penitential practices. Oddly, Skotnicki describes the penitential practices of the early church but does not recognize this affinity.[50] These procedures began when penitents confessed their sins and asked the community for an ascetical regimen that would retrain them in the ways of Christ. Often penitents were "excommunicated," although they continued to participate in worship and other community activities while not partaking of the Eucharist. While penitents were sometimes segregated within the community, they undertook their ascetical regimen in continual relationship with the community, which oversaw and monitored penitents, "making the community an intimate partner in the renewal of the delinquent member."[51] Upon completion of their disciplinary sentences, penitents would be forgiven and restored to full communion. The US bishops also discuss penitential procedures in "Responsibility, Rehabilitation, and Restoration," although they do not discuss the similarities of these practices with restorative justice practices. Elaborating upon these connections may clarify the foundations for restorative justice within Catholic sacramental traditions of Eucharist and Penance.

Among the points of connection between the sacrament of Penance and restorative justice is, first, the emphasis on the communal context of wrongdoing, whether such wrongdoing is viewed as sin or crime. For both Penance and restorative justice, wrongdoing is seen not only as a violation of a rule or law but also as a harm done to other persons and to the communities in which we live. Both practices also aim toward restoration of all members of the community, both wrongdoers and those people who have been harmed, and toward the continuation of relationship in ways that enable all persons to flourish. Neither advocates retribution, but both insist upon wrongdoers taking responsibility for their actions and making things right as much as is humanly possible. In short, practices of Penance and restorative justice, at least in their ideal forms, endeavor to achieve the hopes of the bishops to hold people accountable while challenging them to change their lives, to reject vengeance, to reach out to victims, and to restore a sense of community. Recognizing the connections between Penance and restorative justice may encourage Catholics to support efforts to implement restorative justice in our criminal justice systems and perhaps even to get involved in restorative justice programs in their communities.

Against these arguments for restorative justice, Skotnicki might respond that the expectation that restorative justice practices could foster significant change in the behavior of wrongdoers is unrealistic.[52] In fairness, restorative justice does require offenders to admit their wrongdoing and to choose to repair the harm that they have caused; if someone willfully denies culpability, then other approaches to criminal justice will be necessary. Beyond the issue of recalcitrant offenders, however, is Skotnicki's question about the effectiveness of restorative justice in reducing recidivism. Although much more work still needs to be done to address this question, the best data to date show that while punitive responses to crime such as incarceration increase recidivism, restorative justice interventions on average significantly decrease recidivism, although the effect is small.[53] This evidence suggests that restorative justice practices, not prison, are among the best means available to achieve the end of punishment described by Skotnicki. Whether restorative justice leads to multilayered internal reform or social reintegration is difficult to prove; nevertheless, at least in terms of recidivism, it seems to be significantly better than prison.

The "medicinal" understanding of Penance may also serve as a basis for supporting rehabilitative efforts within criminal justice systems. The acts of satisfaction in Penance, which are "the external sign of one's desire to amend one's life,"[54] are not to be understood as punishments for the sake of punishment, but as regimens for retraining oneself in the ways of Christ. In many ways, penitential regimens may be thought of as analogous to rehabilitative efforts to encourage and facilitate healthful change in the behaviors and attitudes of criminal offenders. Rehabilitative practices that serve these purposes can then be supported within a Catholic sacramental framework.

In contrast to the USCCB, Skotnicki seems skeptical of rehabilitative reforms of our criminal justice systems; his skepticism, however, seems based upon outdated criminological arguments from the 1970s that "nothing works" in the use of rehabilitation.[55] Criminologists have made great strides over the last four decades in describing evidence-based rehabilitative practices that decrease recidivism. They have found that appropriate, well-implemented rehabilitative interventions with high-risk offenders show the highest rate of recidivism reduction when compared with both incarceration and restorative justice.[56] This support among criminologists along with the commensurability of rehabilitation with the purposes and practices of Penance ought to lead Catholics to support efforts to make our criminal justice systems more rehabilitative, less retributive, and less dependent upon the prison.

Both restorative justice and rehabilitation require the active participation of offenders who admit their wrongdoing, take responsibility, and desire change in their lives. Of course, not every person who commits a crime will meet these criteria, so we will continue to need prisons in our society. Catholics must ask, however, whether prisons really are the normative means of punishment in our tradition or whether we ought to admit that our use of prisons throughout our history reflects a tragic failure to achieve the appropriate ends of punishment, that is, social reintegration and internal reform, through other means. The US bishops recognize a role for incarceration in our criminal justice systems, but they remind us that where incarceration is necessary, it is never a sufficient response to criminal offenders. "Not all offenders are open to treatment, but all deserve to be challenged and encouraged to turn their lives around."[57] The normative means of integration into the body of Christ and of ongoing internal reform in Catholicism are the sacraments, not prisons. Our calls of criminal justice reform must then be viewed through a sacramental lens that fosters restoration and rehabilitation while calling for a significantly reduced role for incarceration.

The discussion thus far has focused on how rehabilitative and restorative responses to crime can be related to Catholic interpretations of the sacraments of Eucharist and Penance as well as supported by contemporary criminology. Criminal justice reform in the United States, however, cannot remain so narrowly focused given the broader social context of the crises in these systems. The central problem with these systems is not necessarily a problem with high crime rates.[58] Given the data describing our criminal justice systems, we must admit that this crisis is largely the result of a more significant failure to realize social justice throughout our communities. A sacramental response to criminal justice must entail work for social justice beyond these systems as well. The stark realities of racial, ethnic, and class disparities within criminal justice systems ought to alert us to factors other than crime rates that have contributed to the unprecedented numbers of people in US jails and prisons and the demographic composition of incarcerated populations. The call to reduce crime is insufficient in any proposal to fix our criminal justice systems; any responsible effort to reform criminal justice must also respond to the call to fight injustice in all of its forms.

For Catholics, we ought to hear the call to seek social justice most loudly and clearly in our celebration of the Eucharist. This sacrament offers a foretaste of God's reign in which everyone is welcomed to Christ's table, especially those who are excluded from society. As we celebrate this sacrament, we remember and protest the death of Jesus as a criminal at the hands of the Roman Empire. We are made into one body while we are also confronted with the brokenness of the body of Christ as well as the pervasive dynamics of exclusion and division in our churches, communities, and society. Paul calls us to discern the body, to recognize the sources of brokenness, exclusion, and division amongst us and to work toward healing, inclusion, and unity. When we fail to do so, we eat and drink judgment against ourselves, and we must seek the discipline of Penance so that we may become reconciled with the ways of Christ rather than walk in the ways of the principalities and powers of this world. People who commit crime are not the only people who need social reintegration and internal reform; the Eucharist reminds us that we are all called to these tasks, especially through the endeavor for social justice. Through this effort, Catholics should strive to counter the racial, ethnic, and class disparities that remain significant factors in our criminal justice crises.

The pursuit of social justice, however, ought not to be rooted solely in a sense of conviction for our failures as church, community, and society. For Catholics, we must also base this work in the hope for the in-breaking of God's reign disclosed in the Eucharist. We celebrate Christ's resurrection and anticipate the coming of God's life, peace, forgiveness, love, and justice in fullness. The eschatological imagination nourished by the Eucharist, which makes known both the brokenness and redemption of the world, ought to create a yearning to confront the alienation that degrades and demeans our neighbors on the basis of race, ethnicity, and class. This "tension" within the celebration of the Eucharist ought to impel its participants into the pursuit of social justice in the world as an aspect of living within God's reign already in our midst. Catholics specifically, but also Christians in general, who find hope in the celebration of the Eucharist, may be fed for the work for social justice that can reduce the tragic use of prison as the means for breaking people, dividing and excluding them from our midst.

This Eucharistic vision of social justice ought to encourage Catholics to join the ranks of "those who envision a society that promotes public safety primarily through investments in strengthening families and communities, rather than through the expansion of the criminal justice system."[59] These investments must include commitment to improve public health, educational, economic, infrastructural, and social service access for all members of our communities.[60] Alongside advocacy for restorative justice and rehabilitation programs, Catholic responses to crises in US criminal justice systems ought to support efforts for economic development of impoverished neighborhoods; the reduction of residential instability through reform of housing programs and increased housing subsidies; and improvement of schools, particularly where schools have operated as "pipelines to prison" for children living in poverty or who are members of racial or ethnic minorities.[61] Our communities should provide mentoring programs, supervised recreational programs during after-school hours, and cognitive-behavioral programs that teach children and youth to cope with anger and frustration in socially acceptable, legal, and nonviolent ways. We ought to attend also to pressures on families on the margins of our society. Home visitation, marital and family counseling, and parental training have been shown to reduce stress faced by families, to improve their overall well-being, and to decrease rates of delinquency and criminal behavior among all of their members. We ought to confront more openly the ongoing plagues of racism and ethnocentrism in our communities, particularly as they shape those whom we incarcerate. By working for social justice through these means, Catholics may combat the breakdown of families and communities that contributes in numerous ways to our criminal justice crises. In their statement, the bishops recognize the value of these strategies as they recommend similar measures alongside their call for restorative justice and rehabilitation.

Conclusion

Andrew Skotnicki argues that the prison is the normative means of punishment in Catholic tradition, and he worries that its rejection by the USCCB reflects a lack of appreciation of the penitential ethos of Catholicism as well as its anthropology and spirituality. He criticizes the bishops for rejecting what he sees as the core of a Catholic theory of criminal justice and for lacking analytical depth with respect to contemporary criminology. Skotnicki's critique, however, can be turned back onto his own argument. First, his texts reflect inadequate attention to developments in criminology since the 1970s that indicate that restorative justice and rehabilitation provide the most adequate means for achieving the end of criminal justice interventions delineated within Catholic tradition. Second, his narrow focus on monastic and ecclesiastical prisons obscures the true center of Catholicism: the sacramental life lived in response to Jesus Christ and in anticipation of his return in the fullness of God's reign of life, peace, forgiveness, love, and justice. The sacraments, not the prison, are the core of Catholic anthropology and spirituality. Consideration of the sacramental life, particularly as lived through the Eucharist and Penance, supports the call of the US bishops for restorative and rehabilitative reforms in a Catholic theory of criminal justice. Furthermore, the sacraments, especially the Eucharist, call us to look beyond a Catholic theory of criminal justice to situate our responses to crime within the broader pursuit of social justice. By turning our attention from the prison to the sacraments as the center of a Catholic response to crime and criminal justice, Catholics may come to appreciate and perhaps to act upon the summons of the US bishops: "Working together, we believe our faith calls us to protect public safety, promote the common good, and restore community. We believe a Catholic ethic of responsibility, rehabilitation, and restoration can become the foundation for the necessary reform of our broken criminal justice system."[62] Such an ethic located within a broader sacramental ethic could become the foundation for the necessary reform of our churches, communities, and societies in pursuit of both criminal and social justice.

Notes

1. Heather C. West, "Prison Inmates at Midyear 2009—Statistical Tables," Bureau of Justice Statistics, US Department of Justice, June 2010, http://bjs.ojp.usdoj.gov/content-pub/pdf/pim09st.pdf.

2. Ibid.

3. Ibid.; and Bureau of Justice Statistics, "Key Facts at a Glance: Correctional Populations," US Department of Justice, July 2010, http://bjs.ojp.usdoj.gov/content/glance/tables/corr2tab.cfm. These rates do not include jail inmates, who bring the overall rate of incarceration up to 762 people per 100,000.

4. Adam Liptak, "US Prison Population Dwarfs that of Other Nations," *New York Times*, April 23, 2008.

5. Roy Walmsley, "World Prison Population List," 8th ed., International Centre for Prison Studies, King's College London (January 2009), www.kcl.ac.uk/depsta/law/research/icps/downloads/wppl-8th_41.pdf. The United States incarcerates more than 700,000 more people than the second nation on this list, China, which incarcerates 1.6 million people.

6. West, "Prison Inmates at Midyear 2009."

7. Ibid.

8. Bureau of Justice Statistics, "Defense Counsel in Criminal Cases," US Department of Justice, November 2000, http://bjs.ojp.usdoj.gov/content/pub/pdf/dccc.pdf.

9. Increases in incarceration rates did coincide with drops in crime rates during the 1990s, although, at best, only about 25 percent of decreasing crime rates could be attributed to locking up offenders. Nevertheless, increases in incarceration rates also coincided with increases in crime rates in the 1980s. The relationship between incarceration and crime rates is complex, and often the interpretation of this relationship reflects selective interpretation of the data. See Ryan S. King, Marc Mauer, and Malcolm C. Young, "Incarceration and Crime: A Complex Relationship," The Sentencing Project, January 2005, www.sentencingproject.org/doc/publications/inc_iandc_complex.pdf. For a more detailed discussion, see Marc Mauer, *Race to Incarcerate*, 2nd ed. (New York: New Press, 2006).

10. David C. Garland, *Punishment and Modern Society: A Study in Social Theory* (Chicago: University of Chicago Press, 1990), 6.

11. Lee Griffith, *The Fall of the Prison: Biblical Perspectives on Prison Abolition* (Grand Rapids, MI: Eerdmans, 1993); Christopher D. Marshall, *Beyond Retribution: A New Testament Vision for Justice, Crime, and Punishment* (Grand Rapids, MI: Eerdmans, 2001); Timothy Gorringe, *God's Just Vengeance: Crime, Violence, and the Rhetoric of Salvation* (Cambridge: Cambridge University Press, 1996); T. Richard Snyder, *The Protestant Ethic and the Spirit*

of Punishment (Grand Rapids, MI: Eerdmans, 2001); Mark Lewis Taylor, *The Executed God: The Way of the Cross in Lockdown America* (Minneapolis: Fortress Press, 2001); and James Samuel Logan, *Good Punishment?: Christian Moral Practice and US Imprisonment* (Grand Rapids, MI: Eerdmans, 2008).

12. USCCB, "Responsibility, Rehabilitation, and Restoration: A Catholic Perspective on Crime and Criminal Justice," USCCB website, November, 15, 2000, www.nccbuscc .org/sdwp/criminal.shtml.

13. Andrew Skotnicki, "Foundations Once Destroyed: The Catholic Church and Criminal Justice," *Theological Studies* 65, no. 4 (2004): 812.

14. Andrew Skotnicki, *Criminal Justice and the Catholic Church* (Lanham, MD: Rowman & Littlefield, 2008). See especially chapter 4, "Prison as the Normative Means of Punishment," 73–114.

15. Pope John Paul II, "Jubilee in Prisons," The Vatican, July 9, 2000, www.vatican.va/holy_ father/john_paul_ii/messages/documents/hf_jp-ii_mes_20000630_jubilprisoners_en.html.

16. USCCB, "Responsibility, Rehabilitation, and Restoration."

17. Ibid.

18. Ibid.

19. Ibid.

20. Ibid.

21. Skotnicki, "Foundations Once Destroyed," 812.

22. Ibid. Skotnicki cites movements for "penal harm" and "social control" within contemporary criminology as the forces in opposition with the bishops' position. Penal harm encourages punitive responses to crime, in which punishment in itself is the final end; social control is "a systems management approach that 'aggregates' the individual, understanding him or her solely as a member of a group, uncoupled from social history and subjective interpretations, and defined in terms of risk." Social control emphasizes incapacitation based on one's racial, ethnic, and class background (that is, "risk level"), which results in "the detecting, monitoring, and control of a permanent criminal class" ("Foundations Once Destroyed," 814).

23. The only fair critique of the bishops I could detect based on Skotnicki's argument is that they ought not to have recommended "broken windows" policing, which they mention briefly as an example of an alternative community-based effort at crime control. See James Q. Wilson and George L. Kelling, "Broken Windows: The Police and Neighborhood Safety," *Atlantic Magazine*, March 1982, www.theatlantic.com/magazine/archive-1982/03/broken-windows/4465/. For critiques, see Bernard E. Harcourt, *Illusion of Order: The False Promise of Broken Windows Policing* (Cambridge, MA: Harvard University Press, 2001); and Gary Stewart, "Black Codes and Broken Windows: The Legacy of Racial Hegemony in Anti-Gang Civil Injunction," *Yale Law Journal* 107, no. 7 (1998): 2249–79.

24. Skotnicki, "Foundations Once Destroyed," 810.

25. Skotnicki, *Criminal Justice*, 17–27.

26. Ibid., 37–50.

27. Ibid., 58–65.

28. Ibid., 135.

29. Ibid., 87–88.

30. Ibid., 101. See also 95–97.

31. Ibid., 91–92.

32. Ibid., 122–23.

33. Ibid., 137.

34. Ibid., 137. Emphasis mine.

35. Bureau of Justice Statistics, "Recidivism," US Department of Justice, June 16, 2010, http://bjs.ojp.usdoj.gov/index.cfm?ty=tp&tid=17. These figures do not include released prisoners who returned to prison for parole violations.

36. Marc Mauer, "The Hidden Problem of Time Served in Prison," *Social Research* 74, no. 2 (2007): 701–6. Prisoners serving five years in prison are as likely to reoffend as prisoners serving one year in prison; the decrease in recidivism of those who serve between five and ten years is explained mostly by prisoners "aging out" of criminal behavior.

37. Skotnicki is clearly aware of Dickens's writings on this subject as he cites them in both *Criminal Justice and the Catholic Church* and an earlier book based upon his dissertation, *Religion and the Development of the American Penal System*. See Skotnicki, *Criminal Justice*, 122. Also, *Religion and the Development of the American Penal System* (Lanham, MD: University Press of America, 2000), 142.

38. Charles Dickens, *American Notes*, introduction by Christopher Lasch (1842; repr. Gloucester, MA: Peter Smith, 1968), 120. Emphasis mine.

39. USCCB, "Responsibility, Rehabilitation, and Restoration." Many theologians, both Catholic and non-Catholic, have highlighted the significance of sacraments, particularly the Eucharist, for Christian responses to sin, injustice, and violence. See, for example, Andrea Bieler and Luise Schotroff, *The Eucharist: Bodies, Bread, and Resurrection* (Minneapolis: Fortress Press, 2007); John P. Hogan, "The Eucharist and Social Justice," in *Romero's Legacy: The Call to Peace and Justice*, ed. Pilar Hogan Closkey and John P. Hogan, 25–34 (Lanham, MD: Sheed and Ward, 2007); Judith A. Merkle, "The Eucharist and Justice," *Liturgical Ministry* 17, no. 3 (2008): 133–38; Thomas W. Porter, ed., *Conflict and Communion: Reconciliation and Restorative Justice at Christ's Table* (Nashville: Discipleship Resources, 2006); and Margaret Scott, *The Eucharist and Social Justice* (New York: Paulist Press, 2008). Likewise, Catholic feminists have discussed the relationship between sacraments, especially the Eucharist, and justice, particularly in light of the denial of ordination to women and the cultural, social, and religious subordination of women. See, for example, Susan Ross, "Liturgy and Ethics: Feminist Perspectives," *Annual of the Society of Christian Ethics* 20 (2000): 263–74.

40. See Mk 14:12–26; Mt 26:17–30; and Lk 22:7–38. Also, Jn 6:52–58 and 13.

41. Lk 22:24–30.

42. 1 Cor 10:16–17.

43. 1 Cor 11:29.

44. R. Kevin Seasoltz, "Justice and the Eucharist," *Worship* 58, no. 6 (1984): 507–25, at 513.

45. William Cavanaugh, *Torture and Eucharist* (Malden, MA: Blackwell Publishers, 1998), 226.

46. Bieler and Schotroff, *Eucharist*, 7.

47. Seasoltz, "Justice and the Eucharist," 511.

48. Ibid., 522.

49. For discussions of the development of the sacrament of Penance and its relationship to Eucharist, see Monika K. Hellwig, *Sign of Reconciliation and Conversion: The Sacrament of Penance for Our Times* (Wilmington, DE: Michael Glazier, Inc., 1982); and Bernhard Poschmann, *Penance and the Anointing of the Sick* (New York: Herder and Herder, 1964).

50. Skotnicki's failure to recognize this affinity may be rooted in some misreading of the restorative justice movement shown in his "How Is Justice Restored?" *Studies in Christian*

Ethics 19, no. 2 (2006): 187–204. He criticizes restorative justice on three points: (1) that restorative justice advocates fail to recognize the necessity of punishment for criminal offenses; (2) that they lack a consistent normative foundation for understanding justice, reducing justice to contextual interpretations alone; and (3) that restorative justice cannot bring about substantive change in the character of offenders. For a comprehensive rebuttal, see Kathleen Daly, "The Past, Present, and Future of Restorative Justice: Some Critical Reflections," *Contemporary Justice Review* 1, no. 1 (1998): 21–45.

51. Skotnicki, *Criminal Justice*, 79.

52. Skotnicki, "Foundations Once Destroyed," 805, and "How Is Justice Restored?" 197.

53. James Bonta, Rebecca Jesseman, Tanya Rugge, and Robert Cormier, "Restorative Justice and Recidivism: Promises Made, Promises Kept?" in *Handbook of Restorative Justice: A Global Perspective*, ed. Dennis Sullivan and Larry Tifft, 108–20 (New York: Routledge, 2006).

54. USCCB, "Responsibility."

55. Skotnicki, *Criminal Justice*, 138. The argument that "nothing works" in the use of rehabilitation stems from Robert Martinson's much cited—and much critiqued—article, "What Works: Questions and Answers about Prison Reform," *Public Interest* 35 (Spring 1974): 22–54.

56. Bonta and colleagues define "appropriate rehabilitative interventions" in terms of three factors: risk, need, and responsiveness. When programs address each of these factors, they contribute to a decrease in reoffending of about 26 percent. If treatment is delivered in the community rather than in prison or residential settings, recidivism is reduced even more, by about 35 percent (Bonta et al.,"Restorative Justice and Recidivism").

57. USCCB, "Responsibility."

58. Mauer, *Race to Incarcerate*, 113–29.

59. Ibid., xiv.

60. For whether and how these different types of investments can contribute to lower rates of crime as well as lower rates of incarceration, see, for example, James C. Howell, Barry Krisberg, J. David Hawkins, and John J. Wilson, eds. *A Sourcebook: Serious, Violent, and Chronic Juvenile Offenders* (Thousand Oaks, CA: Sage, 1995); Rolf Loeber and David P. Farrington, eds., *Serious and Violent Juvenile Offenders: Risk Factors and Successful Interventions* (Thousand Oaks, CA: Sage Publications, 1998); Lawrence W. Sherman, David P. Farrington, Brandon C. Welsh, and Doris Layton MacKenzie, eds. *Evidence-based Crime Prevention* (London: Routledge, 2002); Robin Hamilton and Kay McKinney, *Job Training for Juveniles: Project CRAFT* (Washington, DC: Office of Juvenile Justice and Delinquency Prevention, 1999); Elaine Morley, Shelli B. Rossman, Mary Kopczynski, Janeen Buck, and Caterina Gouvis, "Comprehensive Responses to Youth at Risk: Interim Findings from the SafeFutures Initiative," (Washington, DC: Office of Juvenile Justice and Delinquency Prevention, 2000), https://www.ncjrs.gov/pdffiles1/ojjdp/183841.pdf; and Timothy N. Thornton, Carole A. Craft, Linda L. Dahlberg, Barbara S. Lynch, and Katie Baer, *Best Practices of Youth Violence Prevention: A Sourcebook for Community Action* (Atlanta: Centers for Disease Control and Prevention, National Center for Injury Prevention and Control, 2002), available at www.cdc.gov/violenceprevention/pub/YV_bestpractices.html.

61. "America's Cradle to Prison Pipeline," Children's Defense Fund (October 2007), www.childrensdefense.org/child-research-data-publications/data/cradle-prison-pipeline-report-2007-full-highres.pdf.

62. USCCB, "Responsibility, Rehabilitation, and Restoration."

Mass Incarceration and Theological Images of Justice

Kathryn Getek Soltis

THE NUMBINGLY HIGH RATE OF INCARCERATION IN THE UNITED STATES poses a challenge to our images of justice, particularly given the indirect consequences for families and communities. Two key theological sources for justice, the *lex talionis* and the (mis)interpretation of Anselmian satisfaction, offer key insights for adjudicating between restoration and retribution. Yet a Christian ethical response capable of addressing mass incarceration must also examine the collateral consequences of imprisonment. This essay ultimately argues for an image of justice that, while sensitive to restoration and retribution, is also attentive to community membership and the full scope of human relationality.

Nearly 2.3 million people are currently behind bars in the United States.[1] Of these, 760,000 men and women are in local jails while more than 1.5 million are in the custody of federal and state prisons. This latter population has experienced a 700 percent increase since 1970 when the US prison population was only 190,000.[2] Considered cumulatively, 1 in every 37 US adults has served time in a prison at some point.[3] Indeed, the United States imprisons far more people, both in absolute numbers and in rate of incarceration, than any other country in the world.[4]

The entire American correctional population exceeds 7 million people. That is, 1 in every 32 adult residents is currently under correctional supervision, whether through prisons, jails, probation, or parole.[5] Close to two-thirds of the estimated 600,000 individuals admitted into prison over the course of a year are there because they failed to complete probation or parole.[6] Overall, it is estimated that 95 percent of inmates will eventually return home. However, within three years, 67 percent of these former inmates will be rearrested and 52 percent will be reincarcerated.[7] Every year an astonishing 13.5 million adults pass through our nation's prisons and jails.[8]

Rather than a direct response to crime, the astronomical growth of incarceration in the United States over the last several decades is largely due to policy choices. Prominent criminal justice scholar Todd Clear identifies three waves of penal code reform that contributed to this growth.[9] First, many states abolished parole in the 1970s, thereby altering and eliminating rehabilitative programs. The second wave resulted from drug-law reform in the 1980s, influenced in part by growing concerns about crack cocaine. Finally, the third wave was a product of tough-on-crime sentencing for violent offenses and recidivists, those who reenter the system.

We are in the midst of a phenomenon identified as mass incarceration or mass imprisonment. This is more than a problem of mere magnitude. Behind these shocking numbers are insidious patterns of social and racial inequality, devastating damage to communities, and a host of suffering families and children. These are some of the collateral consequences of mass imprisonment and, as I argue in this essay, such consequences must be placed at the center of our pursuit of justice.

Clear concludes that the appropriate response to mass imprisonment must be a combination of sentencing reforms as well as "philosophical realignment."[10] In short, it is not simply a problem of social policy but of our image of justice. Contemporary theological and philosophical discourse on matters of justice and punishment has largely focused on the relationship between retributive and restorative approaches.

On the one hand, some scholars have regarded retribution and restoration as fundamentally opposed to one another. For example, in *Changing Lenses*, a classic text of the restorative justice movement, Howard Zehr contrasts retribution and restoration as two distinct lenses.[11] In the traditional justice paradigm of retribution, the primary concern is to determine what the offender deserves, thereby focusing on guilt with an orientation toward the past. Restorative justice involves the victim, the offender, and the community in a forward-looking process that repairs and, where possible, reconciles these relationships. Elsewhere, Zehr acknowledges that both approaches to justice share an impulse toward righting the balance in a proportionate manner.[12] Still, he maintains that the methods differ in significant ways. Whereas retributive theory suggests that pain will vindicate, restorative justice finds vindication in an acknowledgment of the victim's needs along with efforts to encourage offenders to take responsibility and address the causes of their behavior.[13]

On the other hand, theologian Andrew Skotnicki calls for the embrace of retribution alongside rehabilitation. Seeing important roles for isolation, contrition, and conversion, Skotnicki critiques the strongly restorative approach to criminal justice articulated by the US Catholic Bishops in 2000.[14] Philosopher Antony Duff views punishment as a secular penance and concludes that "restoration is not only compatible with retribution: it *requires* retribution."[15]

Adjudication between restorative and retributive images of justice is indeed necessary. However, added to this must be greater attention to familial and social contexts, the collateral consequences of mass imprisonment. In what follows, my argument proceeds in three sections. First, I examine two key theological sources for criminal justice: the *lex talionis* of "an eye for an eye" and Anselm's theory of satisfaction. I suggest that a proper understanding of these images can mediate to some extent between restoration and retribution. Second, I identify collateral consequences of mass incarceration and argue against an overly individualistic image of justice. In the third section, I argue for a theological image of justice that regards the full scope of personal and social relationality. Such an image, I contend, is a necessary framework for Christian ethical responses that critique mass incarceration and attempt to reform the American prison.

Two Theological Images of Justice

The law of retaliation, the *lex talionis* ("an eye for an eye, a tooth for a tooth"), is a potent and ubiquitous image of justice. Found in multiple ancient Near Eastern sources, including but not exclusive to the Pentateuch, the *lex talionis* appears in both contemporary religious and secular discourse. In general, it appeals to ideas of equilibrium, closure, and victims' rights.

First, the law of retaliation communicates a basic human sense of equivalence and of "evening the score." For some, an injury or an offense swings a cosmic balance to the advantage of the offender; justice remains askew until the balance is righted by an equal injury to that offender. While a powerful image, it relies entirely upon the notion of an immaterial equilibrium. A second aspect of an "eye for an eye" is its apparent ability to bring closure to an offense. The principle maps out a path to settle all violations and quarrels. Victims can look forward to a moment that closes off the period of suffering that commenced with the crime. Finally, the *lex talionis* gives rights to those who have had their rights violated through crime. The law restores power to victims by offering them a claim to the equivalent suffering of the offender. The image of a balance emerges yet again, suggesting a zero-sum game in which the deliverance of victims hinges upon the punishment of offenders. Much of the growth of imprisonment at the end of the twentieth century is in fact linked with the rise of advocacy for victims and victims' rights.

While notions of equilibrium, closure, and victims' rights are not without some legitimacy, the appeal to an "eye for an eye" requires further context. It is widely recognized that this principle, as it appeared in the Old Testament (Ex 21:23–25; Lev 24: 19–20; Deut 19:21), was a restraint on revenge or retaliation.[16] An offender could not be dealt with more harshly than the offense itself; in other words, justice was no more than an eye for an eye. In addition, the principle's strict equivalence ensured that those with more power or wealth had no advantage over the poor and vulnerable of society. The *lex talionis* set standards of fairness and proportionate compensation. Instead of requiring vengeance, it provided a basis for settling disputes in an equitable manner, avoided excessive retaliation, and protected those who were powerless.

The nonliteral character of the *lex talionis* is also instructive. In the case of intentional murder, there is general agreement that "life for life" did indeed apply in ancient Israel. However, several scholars suggest that all other injuries were handled according to moral but not physical equivalence.[17] A comprehensive study of the issue by James Davis surveys sixteen recent interpreters of the *lex talionis*.[18] Davis suggests that a literal application was a viable, though perhaps not majority, view in the first century CE during a time of intense debate on the matter. Still, the *lex talionis* was widely interpreted as allowing if not preferring financial compensation for injury.

Within the biblical text itself, there is already evidence that literal equivalence is not the heart of the law of retaliation. In Exodus 21:26–27, when a master injures his slave, destroying the function of an eye or knocking out a tooth, the master is to release the slave as compensation for the injury. Yet a literal retribution would have required that harm come to the master's own eye or tooth.[19] In this case, precise retaliation is trumped by liberation. In commentary on these verses, Walter Brueggemann notes that the "cost of an eye or a tooth to the master might deter brutality, but emancipation changes fundamental social relations."[20] The *lex talionis* ought not to be understood as establishing an absolute equilibrium or an unqualified right of victims to be vindicated through equivalent injury. Indeed, the majority of evidence suggests that an "eye for an eye" helped define monetary fines for the compensation of victims.

A proper interpretation of the *lex talionis* is further complicated by its apparent rejection in the New Testament in Jesus's Sermon on the Mount (Mt 5:38–42). Some interpreters note that the "eye for an eye" formulation is taken out of its legal context when it appears in the Gospel of Matthew, suggesting that the judicial principle of equivalent compensation is left intact on an institutional level and only rendered illegitimate within the sphere of private action.[21] Another line of interpretation presents the Sermon on the Mount as transcending the *lex talionis*. In this view, Jesus' commands to turn the other cheek and to surrender one's cloak constitute a new standard of righteousness modeled after divine justice and appropriate to the eschatological kingdom.[22] Without attempting to settle this matter here, it is instructive to recognize that the *lex talionis* and the Sermon on the Mount are somewhat compatible. Davis notes that the *lex talionis* "sought to prevent personal acts of revenge by taking matters of justice out of individual hands and placing them in a court context. Jesus sought to prevent such acts by calling for positive actions of excelling love, which would help diffuse situations of conflict."[23] No doubt there is something new in Jesus' preaching; yet it is not at complete cross-purposes with "an eye for an eye," assuming we understand the latter properly.

While the law of retaliation's concern for equivalence may not be sufficient for justice, it underscores a legitimate element of it. Indeed, the identification of harm and the attempt to make due restitution are among the foundational ideas of restorative justice if they are in service of restoring just relationships. Thus, the *lex talionis* can mediate restoration and retribution by recommending due punishment or compensation that is ultimately directed toward repair and restoration.

A second theological image of justice emerges out of a version of atonement. In his book, *God's Just Vengeance*, Timothy Gorringe argues that the satisfaction theory of atonement "provided one of the subtlest and most profound" justifications for retributive justice.[24] This satisfaction theory understands the crucifixion of Christ as a necessary compensation for human sin. Humanity disobeys and incurs an enormous debt to God. Since God's justice requires that this debt be paid, God becomes human and pays on our behalf. Gorringe notes that the theory emerged in the eleventh century at the same time that criminal law took shape. The theological framework reinforced legal retributive thinking by demonstrating that sin and crime must be punished without exception. As the criminal law became identified as an instrument of God's justice, there arose a certain mysticism of pain that offered redemption to those who paid in suffering.[25]

A theology of satisfaction reinforces two significant ideas relevant for punishment and incarceration: the importance of suffering and the obligation to punish. First, satisfaction theory suggests that suffering is the primary, if not exclusive, method to pay the so-called debt of crime. The offender's emotional loss and psychological trauma ought to match if not exceed the original transgression. Second, the satisfaction theory of atonement suggests an absolute obligation to punish, implying a stark opposition between justice and mercy. In this view, the reduction of an offender's deserved punishment is an injustice that cannot be tolerated. This point resonates with the victims' rights usage of the *lex talionis*; however, satisfaction theory tends to shift focus away from individual victims and directs it to the larger sense of order and law. Theologically, this redirection coheres with the notion that every sin is ultimately an offense against God, not merely the individuals who are harmed.

Gorringe and others identify eleventh-century theologian St. Anselm of Canterbury as the major innovator of the satisfaction theory of atonement. Anselm's theological account has long been recognized in the Christian tradition as a vehicle for retributive thinking about punishment and the necessary payment of debt. However, recent scholarship demonstrates that a strong retributive interpretation misreads significant portions of Anselm's theology.

Anselm is clear about the requirement of satisfaction for sins; however, the concept of satisfaction is distinct from that of punishment.

In his explication of satisfaction theory in his treatise, *Cur Deus Homo*, Anselm clearly states that every sin must be followed by either satisfaction or punishment.[26] As Anselm describes it in the life and death of Christ, satisfaction is offered through obedience and maintaining justice.[27] Satisfaction, a restoration of God's ordering of things, comes about through the infinitely just will of Christ. This pathway to atonement is entirely separate from the option of punishment, which denotes a penalty endured against one's will. Since it was the infinitely just will of Christ that carried out the atonement, Anselm claims that God opted for satisfaction rather than punishment. It is our obedience, not our suffering, that satisfies God; we restore God's order for the world when we are just, not when we are in pain.

Anselm suggests that punishment is not an actual option for God because it is God's nature to bring to perfection what God began.[28] The despicable acts of human beings do not hold the power to reverse God's original purpose for the world. The justice of God renders what is due: that God's will for creation be realized.

The infinitely just will of Christ not only makes the restoration of God's purposes possible but also entreats and empowers humanity to pursue the justice that we owe to God.[29] Humans partake in the satisfaction of Christ by becoming just people, by striving for the virtue of justice. It is the possibility of satisfaction that allows Anselm to reconcile mercy and justice by the end of the treatise.[30] Despite the highly retributive manner in which the satisfaction theory of atonement has been passed down through the tradition, Anselm's text supports a more restorative approach by grounding justice in the disposition to realize the will of God.[31] Punishment, as an end in itself, can never accomplish such justice. Indeed, were justice merely concerned with upholding the terms of debt, it would make God's will to restore humanity an abrogation of justice rather than its fulfillment.

Despite Anselm's introduction of satisfaction as an alternative to punishment, it did not take long for the theory to become aligned with the idea of a punitive, vicarious sacrifice made to appease the wrath of God. Mere decades after Anselm, both Hugh and Richard of St. Victor taught that Christ satisfied divine justice through the suffering of a substitutionary punishment.[32] In the thirteenth century, Thomas Aquinas also maintained a close association of satisfaction and punishment.[33]

Anselm's own writing provides nuance to the importance of suffering and the obligation to punish. First, it is instructive to note that, for Anselm, Christ does not pay humanity's debt by enduring humanity's punishment. Rather, Christ satisfies the debt by offering God what is owed and then beyond what is owed. The payment is not one of suffering but of overflowing love and obedience. Second, Anselm also destabilizes the absolute obligation to punish. In addition to Anselm's concern for the payment of debt, there is also a need to fulfill God's original purposes. It is this latter imperative that eliminates the punishment of humanity as a possibility for repayment. While Anselm expresses the necessity of realizing God's intentions for creation in a framework that resonates with a retributive penal theory (i.e., with obligatory compensation for offense), the restorative purposes of God are paramount. In this way, mercy need not be regarded as a violation of justice.

In review, I suggest that the *lex talionis* may be exploited to construct an image of justice that demands equilibrium, promises closure, and bestows on victims the right to an offender's punishment. Similarly, the theory of satisfaction may be exploited to claim that punishment is obligatory and suffering is necessary. These, in fact, are all versions of arguments that have been used to justify the US penal system, especially the shift toward tough-on-crime sentencing policy. However, a closer examination of these theological sources suggests a different image of justice. Although suffering may be involved when confronting one's own wrongdoing, for Anselm's theory of satisfaction, it is not the suffering itself that compensates but the will to restore right order. Both Anselm and the *lex talionis* can mediate between restoration and retribution, which suggests that punishment and compensation are legitimate so long as they are directed toward the retrieval of relationships and the realization of original purposes.

Both theological images of justice can reject the notion of punishment for its own sake. Justice ought never to be reduced to the calculation of the damage of a crime and the proper distribution of proportionate pain or suffering. The intrinsic value is not found in punishment, equivalence, compensation, or suffering but in the rectification of relationships accomplished through them.

This rectification is a critical claim about justice, one that leans in the direction of restoration but maintains a valid space for retribution as an instrument in the service of restorative ends. Even so, the adjudication between restoration and retribution is not wholly sufficient because it continues to regard the offender as individually responsible and individually held accountable. Empirically, there is a very different narrative that accompanies the phenomenon of mass incarceration, and it is to such collateral consequences that I now turn.

Collateral Consequences of Mass Incarceration

In the last decade a growing number of scholars have attended to the collateral consequences of incarceration, particularly in light of the phenomenon of mass imprisonment.[34] However, as a matter of policy, these realities are almost entirely neglected. Sociologists John Hagan and Ronit Dinovitzer believe that Americans would be far less inclined to accept the high rates of incarceration if we were more aware of the collateral consequences, especially for children and parents. In the meantime, they contend, we are making penal policy without adequate information.[35] In this section I identify selected collateral consequences as they impact the individual offender, families and children, and the community.

For an individual offender after release, numerous invisible punishments diminish the basic rights and privileges of citizenship.[36] These include possible exclusion from public housing, suspension or revocation of the license to drive, and denial of the right to vote. Of all the negative effects of incarceration, however, one of the most obvious is the effect on future employment. Individual offenders face the prospect of long-term reduced earnings and unstable employment.[37] Various material disadvantages and the general stigma associated with incarceration also extend beyond the individual offender to impact families and communities.

There is a clear link between incarceration and increased burden on the offender's family, especially with regard to children of the imprisoned. According to a 2008 report from the Bureau of Justice Statistics, more than half of incarcerated men and women are parents of children under the age of eighteen.[38] The report estimates that 1.7 million children have an incarcerated parent, representing 2.3 percent of minors in the United States. Slightly more than half of incarcerated parents were the primary financial support for their children and slightly fewer than half lived with their children before arrest. Based on an extensive consideration of criminological and sociological literature, Hagan and Dinovitzer identify three prominent effects of parental imprisonment on children. "These involve the strains of economic deprivation, the loss of parental socialization through role modeling, support, and supervision, and the stigma and shame of societal labeling."[39]

A parent's imprisonment will often result in deprivation, whether directly through lost income or indirectly through the loss of other positive contributions to the family. A remaining parent or the extended family members often have less time and money to offer; older children may be required to take on greater responsibilities in terms of child care and labor. Evidence suggests that even the incarceration of a nonresident parent may have a significant negative effect upon children since such parents often contribute income as well as child care and support to the resident parent. At the same time, it must be noted that the incarceration of some parents may relieve burdens from the family. Without denying such cases, Hagan and Dinovitzer suggest that overall "it is more likely imprisonment is harmful to children even in dysfunctional families, because imprisonment will more often compound than mitigate preexisting family problems."[40]

The negative impact on the socialization of children can be significant because even parents oriented toward crime can help to guide younger members of the family in positive directions.[41] Moreover, the imprisonment of a parent can lead to anxiety, shame, sadness, and isolation. While young children may tend to withdraw and regress developmentally, adolescents may act out and be at risk for delinquency, drug addiction, and gang involvement.[42] The stigmatization experienced as a result of a parent's imprisonment can lead to similar problems for children, sometimes setting in motion a chain reaction of antisocial behavior.[43]

These challenges often increase for children with incarcerated mothers. Because there are fewer women's facilities, mothers are at higher risk for being located at greater distances from their children than are fathers. One study of federal prisons concluded that an average female inmate is more than 160 miles farther from her family than the average male inmate is.[44] Other studies suggest that at least half of children with imprisoned mothers have not seen or visited their mothers since their time of incarceration.[45]

The damaging impact of incarceration extends not only to offenders, families, and children but to their communities as well. Indeed, the pattern of incarceration within groups, geographically and socially, leads to extensive marginalization. Bruce Western and Becky Pettit speak of a new group of "social outcasts who are joined by the shared experience of incarceration, crime, poverty, racial minority, and low education." They suggest that this "social and economic disadvantage, crystallizing in penal confinement, is sustained over the life course and transmitted from one generation to the next."[46] Imprisonment has become a typical life event for young minority men, particularly African Americans. In 2008, a widely publicized study by the Pew Center on the States noted that white men over eighteen are in prison at a rate of 1 in 106 while the rate for black men is 1 in 15. Black men between the ages of twenty and thirty-four are imprisoned at a rate of 1 in 9.[47] Moreover, in 1980, 10 percent of young African American men who dropped out of high school were in prison or jail; in 2008 this rate had climbed to 37 percent.[48]

Hagan and Dinovitzer note that the damaging concentration of effects is brought into relief by comparing the communities from which prisoners typically come and the location of the new prison settings to which they are sent. Prisons bring new jobs to a community, creating economic and social capital, while the prisoners themselves are disproportionately removed from minority communities. The loss of working men from a neighborhood produces community instability such that many minority communities do not have a sufficient workforce to sustain viable labor market activity.[49] One study asserts that children in ghetto communities are more likely to know someone who has been involved in the criminal justice system than to know someone who is employed in a profession such as law or medicine.[50]

Western and Pettit suggest that the social inequality produced by mass incarceration is significant because it is invisible, cumulative, and intergenerational. The inequality is invisible since incarcerated populations are commonly excluded from official counts of economic well-being such as unemployment rates.[51] The cumulative influence refers to the fact that incarceration increases the disadvantage of those who are already most marginalized in society. I have already discussed intergenerational effects, the enduring negative effects on families and children. However, it is important to note that these intergenerational effects also interact with inequality among social groups. Among white children, 1.75 percent had an incarcerated parent in 2008. The rate for Latino children was 3.5 percent, roughly double. African American children have been most significantly affected with 1.2 million or about 11 percent with an incarcerated parent in 2008.[52]

The work of sociologists and criminologists in bringing these collateral consequences to light has been an enormous contribution. However, most only leverage these data in order to argue that mass imprisonment is ultimately ineffective—perhaps more accurately, counterproductive—as a tool for public safety. Thus, they suggest, in the name of public safety we ought to reduce imprisonment and invest in education and employment. This reinvestment is a critical move, but it stops short of challenging us to reexamine our images of justice. It opts out of deeper theological and philosophical questions by turning to utilitarian concerns for greatest social benefit. However, I argue that we must attend to collateral consequences because of justice, not in spite of justice. This claim requires that we significantly revise our moral imagination.

A Revised Image of Justice

The realities of human interdependence and communal belonging suggest that punishment can never be merely confined to the guilty. The idea of retribution as self-contained and providing closure is a myth. How then do we account for the fact that the means to restore violated relationships may cause significant harm to collateral relations of family and community? One of the greatest challenges for our image of justice is to extricate it from a narrow, individualistic view of offenders and instead place full relationality and moral agency at the center of our pursuit of justice.

Evidence of a highly individualized context for justice can be found in the way we regard the punitive significance of incarceration. The primary feature of imprisonment is often identified as the deprivation of personal liberty.[53] From this view, the offender's loss of freedom is deemed to be the most appropriate response to the violation of the freedoms and rights of others. Yet, while the forfeited liberties are real and do result in suffering, I contend that the most devastating loss experienced in prison is separation from one's community.[54] By "community," I have in mind those relationships that contribute to human flourishing and participate in the common good. The burden placed on an offender's communal connectedness ought to be the primary lens for understanding incarceration rather than the loss of an offender's capacity for self-determination or autonomy. Indeed, a person's social membership is the very condition of possibility for the exercise of freedom.[55] Thus, the ultimate burden of confinement can be described as the deprivation of the full range of participation in social life and the loss of connectedness. The most fitting description for incarceration, then, is a practice of "social exclusion."[56]

This hermeneutic of social exclusion is relevant for considering the total and coercive nature of imprisonment. When society finds cause to impose social exclusion on one of its members, there are consequent obligations due not only to the inmate but also to the inmate's family, particularly dependents, and other members of the community who will experience significant loss and hardship. As a total institution, the prison cannot adequately function by mere avoidance of basic human rights violations of prisoners. Since it exercises expansive control over the lives of inmates, the prison is obliged to offer positive accounts of the good, which bear in mind also the full range of relationships at stake.[57] This obligation is true not only with regard to the inmates themselves but also in relation to the community at large. For the sake of justice, the prison's basic structure and function must take account of and mitigate the profound relational interruptions that it imposes.

To account for the collateral consequences of mass incarceration, the full scope of an offender's relationality must be at the center of justice, not only those relationships harmed by crime. As noted earlier, the collateral consequences of incarceration bring an offender's connectedness to families and communities into focus. Thus, justice must not only be concerned with redress and repair but also maintaining and nourishing the right relationships that already exist. If citizens and policymakers plainly accept the social exclusion of offenders and wait until the conclusion of a sentence to consider reintegration, justice is already long overdue. Reintegration is the starting point of punishment rather than a question after its completion. The alienation experienced by an offender ought not to be the response to crime; this alienation is the experience of crime itself. It is by violating the community that one is alienated and set at a distance. In these terms, we can see that the social alienation and marginalization that contribute to the commission of crime are also violations and crimes themselves. We and our communities are implicated in creating, sustaining, and failing to address patterns of damaging social and economic inequality. In many cases, mass incarceration only reinforces the exclusion that had been in place long before a crime had been committed. Thus, whether the burden of guilt falls to the offender, to his society, or is shared between the two, the object of justice is not only to restore injured relationships but also to re-store belonging. Justice demands that membership is maintained and nourished to the fullest extent possible, and it demands that the imposition of any exclu-sion is always in the service of such membership.

Punishment, as a due burden or harm, importantly communicates and rep-resents the violation of the community.[58] However, the mode of punishment must simultaneously communicate and facilitate the continued membership of the offender in that community. Here the mediation of retribution and restora-tion can intersect with the common good of society. The restoration of rela-tionships and membership must give purpose to punishment. At the same time, the retributive determination of what is due prevents excessive punishment that would seek reform without paying heed to desert. The exile and return of an entire people may be an apt theological image to represent a justice that both is restorative and accounts for the full scope of relationality and moral agency. The prophets speak of a whole people who are sent into exile, not only of ban-ished individuals. It is the justice of God that is called upon to restore them to the land and restore them as a whole people. A critical juncture in the edito-rial framework of Isaiah is the opening of chapter 56: "Thus says the Lord: Ob-serve judgment, do justice, for my salvation is about to come, my justice, about to be revealed" (Isa 56:1).[59] The verse is a synthesis of two distinctive word pairs employed in First and Second Isaiah, respectively. The pair "judgment and jus-tice" (or "justice and righteousness") is employed in First Isaiah to signify so-cial justice to the poor and weak. In Second Isaiah, the "salvation and justice" word pair arises, expressing God's action that is saving and righteous. In this combination of both word pairs in the opening verse of Third Isaiah (56:1), Old Testament scholar Richard Clifford identifies a careful editor who asserts that the initial indictment of Israel can be overcome in a renewal of Zion.[60] Bringing a people out of exile, God enacts justice through a divine act of sal-vation and that same justice is demanded of the people. Thus, having received God's justice, the people themselves are to become agents of justice.[61] Justice does not merely repair situations but brings about a just people. Indeed, what is primarily restored is the possibility for justice to be enacted in and by the community. In this way, the primary test of justice is whether it results in per-sons and communities becoming more just. This result in turn relies on a con-cern for the full scope of relationality and moral agency of all the members of the community.

Clear's model of "community justice" resonates with the theological image of justice described above.[62] He proposes that a central criterion for the jus-tice system ought to be its contribution to the quality of life in communities. Essentially, Clear's "community justice" could be described as a paradigm in which the common good is the primary goal of the justice system. Similar to my proposal, Clear emphasizes that criminals must be treated as part of their communities. As a result, he recommends minimal use of imprisonment and the positive communication of behavioral norms through the meaningful networks of family and community. In addition to community-centered efforts to prevent incarceration, Clear advocates initiatives to serve the needs of recently released prisoners and those serving probation and parole. However, Clear remains largely silent on the implications of a "community justice" paradigm for the prison itself. Yet, as I have tried to suggest here, an image of justice that attends to the full relationality and social context of offenders can have a significant impact on the way we envision the function of incarceration.

When our image of justice takes into account this relationality, the prison must be structured around the development of inmates as just moral agents. This relationality manifests itself in a variety of ways. Interactions with fellow inmates such as peer counseling and tutoring ought to be encouraged and formally structured into the correctional environment. The expectations for correctional staff must be reformulated so that all staff members are responsible for cultivating and modeling just relationships. These expectations must replace the current divide between the primary staff members who are responsible for security and custody and the secondary staff of teachers, social workers, and chaplains who may attempt more positive interventions. In addition, family contact must be regarded as integral to the enterprise of justice, for example, emphasizing visitation and parenting programs that mentor and facilitate positive relationships with children.[63] Finally, inmates must be provided significant opportunities to contribute to the good of the wider community during the time of incarceration. Such possibilities include, for example, agricultural work to support local food banks, mentorship of at-risk youth, and restorative projects with community members to produce mural art.[64] In short, the prison must be reimagined as a place of enacting justice, both for the inmates within its walls and for the families and communities beyond them.

Conclusion

Mass incarceration has and continues to have a devastating impact on the United States, particularly on some of its most vulnerable members. The collateral consequences of this phenomenon underscore the need for appropriate images of justice with which we can proceed and reform. As we have seen from the *lex talionis* and Anselmian satisfaction, the priority of restoration does not eliminate punishment and compensation but constrains our use of them. Ironically, mass incarceration has created conditions that even the *lex talionis* and Anselmian satisfaction try to avoid. An "eye for an eye" was intended to promote fairness and apply to rich and poor equally. Yet our criminal justice system exacerbates class divisions, placing additional burdens on those already marginalized. As a limiting principle, the *lex talionis* placed constraints on the effects of punishment. Yet today we observe enduring, lifelong penalties for offenders, and we witness how families and communities are ravaged, especially by the loss of young minority men. One scholar of the *lex talionis* has even argued that the ancient Israelites would not have imposed strict, literal retribution since they would have been aware that such retribution can itself be an injustice.[65] Some form of monetary or labor-based compensation would be preferable to a literal retribution for two reasons. First, such compensation would have been able to give real benefit to the victim and the victim's family. Second, a literal application would have created injustice for the offender's own family. This interpretation suggests that justice must take into account the connectedness of the offender and his or her continuing role in the community. It supports my contention that justice applied regardless of social context cannot be true justice.

In addition, while Anselm suggests that satisfaction is accomplished by maintaining a just will rather than through suffering, the emphasis of mass incarceration points in the opposite direction. Years of imprisonment, characterized by idleness and incapacitation, prevent development of a just will. While some programs for education, behavior, and wellness are available within correctional facilities, they are typically funded through the small discretionary portion of the corrections budget. They are viewed as extrinsic to the project of justice that requires little more than effective custody for the duration of the sentence. Oddly, we tend to determine whether an offender receives so-called justice at the courthouse when the length and type of correctional custody is assigned. The nature of the subsequent years in custody is usually irrelevant. Whether an inmate completes treatment programs or receives education or job training is not relevant to "justice being served." It is irrelevant whether an inmate is able to maintain positive relations with family, even despite the fact that such familial connections are critical for the success of an inmate's return to society.[66] Instead, programs, visits, and phone calls are merely viewed as elective opportunities and privileges. Indeed, many times family contact is used primarily as an incentive mechanism to help maintain control in a given facility.[67]

Ultimately, while the *lex talionis* and satisfaction theory begin to point us in the proper direction, we require a theological image of justice that challenges an excessively individualized sense of responsibility and punishment. Justice is not only about restoring and repairing but also about maintaining and nourishing the full scope of relationality. Simply put, the goal of justice is to make individuals and communities more just. Even those whose participation in society is diminished through incarceration continue to be members of the community. In the context of mass incarceration, we are exiled as a people. To move forward, we must find a way to return as a people and become a community of true justice.

Notes

1. Lauren E. Glaze, "Correctional Populations in the United States, 2009," NCJ 231681 *Bureau of Justice Statistics Bulletin*, December 2010, US Department of Justice, Bureau of Justice Statistics, http://bjs.ojp.usdoj.gov/content/pub/pdf/cpus09.pdf.

2. Pew Charitable Trusts, Public Safety Performance Project, "Public Safety, Public Spending: Forecasting America's Prison Population 2007–2011," February 14, 2007, ii, 1, www.pewcenteronthestates.org/uploadedFiles/Public%20Safety%20Public%20 Spending.pdf.

3. Thomas P. Bonczar, "Prevalence of Imprisonment in the US Population, 1974–2001," NCJ 197976 *Bureau of Justice Statistics Special Report*, August 2003, US Department of Justice, Bureau of Justice Statistics, 1, http://bjs.ojp.usdoj.gov/content/pub/pdf/piusp01.pdf.

4. International Centre for Prison Studies, "Highest to Lowest," World Prison Brief, http://www.prisonstudies.org/info/worldbrief/wpb_stats.php?area=all&category=wb _poptotal. (December 31, 2009, latest date determined by figures for the United States, http://www.prisonstudies.org/info/worldbrief/wpb_country.php?country=190.)

5. Pew, "Public Safety, Public Spending," 3; also see table 1, p. 2.

6. Ibid., 6.

7. John J. Gibbons and Nicholas de B. Katzenbach, "Confronting Confinement: A Report of the Commission on Safety and Abuse in America's Prisons," Vera Institute of Justice, 11, 106, www.prisoncommission.org/pdfs/Confronting_Confinement.pdf.

8. Ibid., 11.

9. Todd Clear, *Imprisoning Communities: How Mass Incarceration Makes Disadvantaged Neighborhoods Worse* (New York: Oxford University Press, 2007), 53.

10. Ibid., 6.

11. Howard Zehr, *Changing Lenses: A New Focus for Crime and Justice* (Scottdale, PA: Herald Press, 2005).

12. Howard Zehr, *The Little Book of Restorative Justice* (Intercourse, PA: Good Books, 2002), 58–59.

13. Ibid., 59.

14. See Andrew Skotnicki, *Criminal Justice and the Catholic Church* (Lanham, MD: Rowman and Littlefield, 2008); and Skotnicki, "Foundations Once Destroyed: The Catholic Church and Criminal Justice," *Theological Studies* 65, no. 4 (2004): 792–816.

15. Antony Duff, "Restoration and Retribution," in *Restorative Justice and Criminal Justice: Competing or Reconcilable Paradigms?* ed. Andrew von Hirsch, Julian Roberts, Anthony E. Bottoms, Kent Roach, and Mara Schiff (Oxford: Hart Publishing, 2003), 43. See also Gerry Johnstone, *Restorative Justice: Ideas, Values, Debates* (Portland, OR: Willan Publishing, 2002), 106–7. Emphasis in original.

16. See, for example, Christopher Marshall, *Beyond Retribution: A New Testament Vision for Justice, Crime, and Punishment* (Grand Rapids, MI: Eerdmans, 2001), 79ff.

17. See, for example, ibid., 80–84; and J. K. Mikliszanski, "The Law of Retaliation and the Pentateuch" *Journal of Biblical Literature* 66, no. 3 (1947): 295–303.

18. James F. Davis, *Lex Talionis in Early Judaism and the Exhortation of Jesus in Matthew 5:38–42* (London: T & T Clark, 2005).

19. Marshall makes a similar point about the master and slave in his argument against the literal application of the *lex talionis*. In addition, he notes that medical costs are to be paid for the one who is incapacitated in a fight (Ex 21:18–19). Marshall, *Beyond Retribution*, 82.

20. Walter Brueggemann, "Exodus," *New Interpreter's Bible: Genesis to Leviticus*, vol. 1 (Nashville: Abingdon Press, 1994), 864.

21. See, for example, John Barton and John Muddiman, eds. *The Oxford Bible Commentary* (New York: Oxford University Press, 2001), 140, 855.

22. See Marshall, *Beyond Retribution*, 85; and Davis, *Lex Talionis in Early Judaism*, 149.

23. Davis, *Lex Talionis in Early Judaism*, 168.

24. Timothy Gorringe, *God's Just Vengeance: Crime, Violence and the Rhetoric of Salvation* (Cambridge: Cambridge University Press, 1996), 12.

25. Ibid., 102.

26. Anselm, *Cur Deus Homo (Why God Became Man)*, 100–83, in *A Scholastic Miscellany: Anselm to Ockham*, ed. and trans. Eugene Fairweather (Philadelphia: Westminster Press, 1956), bk. 1, ch. 15 (124). Hereafter, *CDH*.

27. See *CDH*, bk. 1, ch. 9 (112–13).

28. R. W. Southern, *Saint Anselm: A Portrait in a Landscape* (Cambridge: Cambridge University Press, 1990), 207.

29. *CDH*, bk. 2, ch. 18 (177).

30. "[God's mercy] is in such harmony with his justice that it cannot be conceived to be greater or more just." *CDH*, bk. 2, ch. 20 (181).

31. See Peter Schmiechen, *Saving Power: Theories of Atonement and Forms of the Church* (Grand Rapids, MI: Eerdmans, 2005). Schmiechen's chapter on Anselm is titled, "The Restoration of Creation."

32. Gorringe, *God's Just Vengeance*, 115–16.

33. Thomas Aquinas, *Summa theologica*, trans. Fathers of the English Dominican Province. (Allen, TX: Christian Classics, 1948), I–II.87.6. Aquinas does make a distinction between satisfactory punishment and punishment simply. Satisfactory punishment is that which is voluntarily accepted (although it is still punishment and, absolutely speaking, it is against the person's will). Satisfaction, for Aquinas, designates punishment that is endured with consent (since the person wills to be reunited with God); the term also applies to those who willingly endure punishment on behalf of another (e.g., Christ who bore a satisfactory punishment for our sins). See I–II.87.7 for additional explanation of this distinction.

34. For example, see Dina R. Rose and Todd Clear, "Incarceration, Social Capital, and Crime: Implications for Social Disorganization Theory," *Criminology* 36, no. 3 (1998): 441–80; John Hagan and Ronit Dinovitzer, "Collateral Consequences of Imprisonment for Children, Communities, and Prisoners," *Prisons (Crime and Justice: A Review of Research 26)*, ed. Michael Tonry and Joan Petersilia, 121–62 (Chicago: University of Chicago Press, 1999); Marc Mauer and Meda Chesney-Lind, eds., *Invisible Punishment: The Collateral Consequences of Mass Imprisonment* (New York: New Press, 2002); Mary Pattillo, David Newman, and Bruce Western, eds., *Imprisoning America: The Social Effects of Mass Incarceration* (New York: Russell Sage Foundation, 2004); and Clear, *Imprisoning Communities*.

35. Hagan and Dinovitzer, "Collateral Consequences," 152.

36. Jeremy Travis, "Invisible Punishment: An Instrument of Social Exclusion," in *Invisible Punishment: The Collateral Consequences of Mass Imprisonment*, ed. Marc Mauer and Meda Chesney-Lind, 15–36 (New York: New Press, 2002).

37. Hagan and Dinovitzer, "Collateral Consequences," 134. See also Harry J. Holzer, "Collateral Costs: Effects of Incarceration on Employment and Earnings among Young Workers," in *Do Prisons Make Us Safer?* ed. Steven Raphael and Michael A. Stoll (New York: Russell Sage Foundation, 2009).

38. Lauren E. Glaze and Laura M. Maruschak, "Parents in Prison and Their Minor Children," NCJ 222984, *Bureau of Justice Statistics Special Report*, August 2008, http://bjs.ojp.usdoj.gov/content/pub/pdf/pptmc.pdf.

39. Hagan and Dinovitzer, "Collateral Consequences," 123.

40. Ibid., 125.

41. Ibid. See also Travis Hirschi, *Causes of Delinquency* (Berkeley: University of California Press, 1969).

42. Bruce Western and Becky Pettit, "Incarceration and Social Inequality," *Daedalus* (Summer 2010): 17n8. Western and Pettit reference new research demonstrating that children of incarcerated parents, especially boys, are at greater risk for developmental delays and behavioral problems. See Christopher Wildeman, "Paternal Incarceration and Children's Physically Aggressive Behaviors: Evidence from the Fragile Families and Child Wellbeing Study," working paper 2008-02-FF (Fragile Families and Child Wellbeing Study, 2008). See also Hagan and Dinovitzer, "Collateral Consequences," 145. Hagan and Dinovitzer (147) note a study that suggests children of incarcerated parents may be six times more likely to end up incarcerated themselves.

43. Hagan and Dinovitzer, "Collateral Consequences," 127.

44. John Coughenour, "Separate and Unequal: Women in the Federal Criminal Justice System," *Federal Sentencing Reporter* 8 (1995): 142–44.

45. Tracy L. Snell and Danielle C. Morton, "Women in Prison," Survey of State Prison Inmates, 1991, US Department of Justice, Bureau of Justice Statistics, March 1994, www.iiav.nl/epublications/1994/women_in_prison.pdf.

46. Western and Pettit, "Incarceration and Social Inequality," 8.

47. Pew Center on the States, "One in 100: Behind Bars in America 2008," The Pew Charitable Trusts, 2008, www.pewcenteronthestates.org/uploadedFiles/One%20in%20100.pdf.

48. Western and Pettit, "Incarceration and Social Inequality," 10.

49. Hagan and Dinovitzer, "Collateral Consequences," 135.

50. See A. C. Case and L. F. Katz, *The Company You Keep: The Effects of Family and Neighborhood on Disadvantaged Youths* (Cambridge, MA: National Bureau of Economic Research, 1991).

51. Western and Pettit, "Incarceration and Social Inequality," 12.

52. Ibid., 16–17.

53. The most influential voice on behalf of this perspective is Gesham M. Sykes who published *The Society of Captives: A Study of a Maximum Security Prison* in 1958 (Princeton University Press). See Yvonne Jewkes and Helen Johnston, eds. *Prison Readings: A Critical Introduction to Prisons and Imprisonment* (Portland, OR: Willan Publishing, 2006), 159.

54. In his studies of long-term imprisonment, Timothy Flanagan suggests that the loss of outside relationships is the most painful aspect of confinement. Flanagan, "The Pains of Long-Term Imprisonment: A Comparison of British and American Perspectives," *British Journal of Criminology* 20, no. 2 (1980): 148–56.

55. I appeal here to a common good tradition that understands the good of the individual as inseparable from the good of the community. For example, David Hollenbach suggests that self-determination "is not a solo activity but has social preconditions. Moreover, these

social preconditions are not external to the person who makes the free choices; they are internally constitutive of the capacity for freedom itself." Hollenbach, *The Common Good and Christian Ethics* (New York: Cambridge University Press, 2002), 75.

56. By "social exclusion," I do not claim that inmates are deprived of all social interactions (unless they are in solitary confinement). During incarceration, there are possibilities for relationships and community, both negative and positive. However, even inmates who find positive relationships in prison are still separated from important and nourishing relationships with the wider community. The prison structures and controls this latter separation, and so it is this "social exclusion" to which I refer.

57. Although a full account of human flourishing may exceed the capacity of a prison operating within a pluralist society, the growing data regarding collateral consequences of imprisonment demonstrate how a public consensus might be formed around key concerns of the common good.

58. Oliver O'Donovan helpfully articulates this communicative role for justice-as-judgment in *The Ways of Judgment: The Bampton Lectures, 2003* (Grand Rapids, MI: Eerdmans, 2005), 31–51.

59. Richard Clifford, "The Major Prophets, Baruch, and Lamentations," in *The Catholic Study Bible: The New American Bible*, 2nd ed., ed. Donald Senior and John J. Collins (New York: Oxford University Press, 2006), 293–94.

60. Ibid., 294.

61. See Stephen Charles Mott, *Biblical Ethics and Social Change* (New York: Oxford University Press, 1982), 60; and Thomas L. Leclerc, *Yahweh Is Exalted in Justice: Solidarity and Conflict in Isaiah* (Minneapolis: Fortress Press, 2001), 89–90.

62. Clear, *Imprisoning Communities*, 190–208.

63. See Randall Turner and Jeff Peck, "Long-Distance Dads: Restoring Incarcerated Fathers to Their Children," *Corrections Today* 64, no. 2 (April 2002): 72–75; and Marilyn Moses, "Keeping Incarcerated Mothers and Their Daughters Together: Girl Scouts beyond Bars," Program Focus, National Institute of Justice, US Department of Justice, 1995, https://www.ncjrs.gov/pdffiles/girlsct.pdf.

64. See Matthew Katz, "'Productivity' in the Community," *Corrections Today* 64, no. 3 (June 2002): 65; Cheryl Wittenauer, "Justice in Bloom: Gardens Offer Inmates a Way to Give Back," *Boston Globe* (A17), October 21, 2007; Esteban Parra, "Help from behind the Wall," *News Journal/DelawareOnline*, November 18, 2008, http://doc.delaware.gov/news/08press11.pdf; and Charles Lawson, "Art and Its Transformative Power," *Community Arts Network*, December 2007, http://wayback.archive-it.org/2077/20100903214505/http://www.communityarts.net/readingroom/archivefiles/2007/12/art_and_its_tra.php.

65. Yung Suk Kim, "*Lex Talionis* in Exod 21:22–25: Its Origin and Context," *Journal of Hebrew Scriptures* 6 (2006): 1–11.

66. For example, see Gibbons and Katzenbach, "Confronting Confinement"; and Elizabeth Craig, "Building Bonds from the Inside Out," *Corrections Today* 68, no. 7 (December 2006): 42–45.

67. David M. Rosen, "Mass Imprisonment and the Family: A Legal Perspective," *Marriage & Family Review* 32, no. 3–4 (2001): 63–82.

The Place of Desert in Theological Conceptions of Distributive Justice: Insights from Calvin and Rawls

Michael R. Turner

DOES A STANDARD OF DESERT BELONG IN CHRISTIAN CONCEPTIONS OF distributive justice? This essay places John Calvin and John Rawls, two of desert's most incisive critics, in conversation to examine the theological and philosophical issues raised by this question. Calvin and Rawls make similar arguments against deservingness as a moral principle, but Calvin emerges as the more adamant detractor, noting that God's grace and humanity's corrupt nature make the validity of positive human desert claims virtually unthinkable. Still, the moral force of desert invites a reevaluation of both Calvin's and Rawls's objections and the fittingness of this principle to theological conceptions of distributive justice.

Introduction

When Christian thinkers discuss economic justice in the context of a market system, they often introduce notions of grace as a way of critiquing the dominant mechanism of modern economic exchange.[1] Such a strategy is understandable given the disparate values and objectives that capitalism and grace tend to uphold. Since capitalism operates largely on principles of scarcity, self-interest, and merit, one might argue that the influence of more grace-imbued principles such as abundance, the common good, and beneficence will lead to a more just market or perhaps even to a better economic system altogether. Yet despite calls for a more grace-centered economy, the ideas of earning one's way and of deserving the fruits of one's labor retain considerable moral force. Few would deny the relevance of deservingness in arenas such as criminal justice, but as a principle for the distribution of society's goods, it can become deeply problematic, especially for Christians. As part of a larger project that assesses the appropriate role of desert in a Christian conception of distributive justice, this essay examines a longstanding, fundamental objection to desert in an effort to reconsider the principle's theological warrant.

John Calvin and John Rawls serve as central figures in this discussion. Their respective contributions to the theological and philosophical discourse on desert and the enduring influence of their work make them essential, if unlikely, interlocutors. Calvin's well-known exaltation of divine grace over human desert has had a decisive impact on countless Christian thinkers. Indeed, the legacy of his work arguably constitutes a major reason for the notable disinterest that many theologians exhibit for deservingness today. Rawls's regard for this principle bears striking similarity to Calvin's despite obvious differences in the contexts and aims of their work. Each thinker views desert as a direct challenge to the sovereign authority that establishes and maintains society's moral structure. For Calvin, that sovereign is, of course, God; for Rawls it is the set of principles to which society's members must hypothetically agree, as presented in his theory of justice. Putting their distinct concerns in conversation not only highlights one of the most trenchant criticisms of desert from both theological and philosophical points of view but also situates the religious tension between grace and desert in the political context of a modern pluralistic democratic society. Thus, substantial groundwork can be laid for assessing the suitability of desert in a contemporary Christian conception of distributive justice.

I begin the discussion with a brief overview of desert, followed by a sketch of society's moral structure as seen by Calvin and Rawls, respectively. I then demonstrate how desert challenges the grounds of these structures in similar ways before offering critiques of Calvin and Rawls with an eye toward future work in justifying the inclusion of desert in a theological conception of distributive justice.

The Concept of Desert

Because the idea of deserving appears in a befuddling array of contexts, settling on a precise definition of the concept can pose a problem. Works of art, for example, are said to deserve praise; major issues can deserve our attention, and proposed legislation might deserve popular support. But, as Joel Feinberg points out, these notions of desert typically do not pertain to matters of justice in the same way personal desert does: Desert claims about people are more directly and perhaps even necessarily tied to justice.[2] One may add, however, that not all personal desert claims carry the same moral import. Advertisers make this clear when they invoke personal desert as a way of enticing people to affirm, reward, or indulge themselves with the consumption of certain goods and services. The claim that a hard-working individual deserves a particular brand of ice cream simply does not function on the same moral plane as the claim that such a person deserves a raise. Regardless of context, though, Feinberg notes that desert claims follow the basic form "X deserves Y in virtue of Z," where X is some person or group, Y is a mode of treatment, and Z is some fact about the person or group (such as a trait or an action) that warrants the mode of treatment.[3] Institutions may establish policies or laws that ground desert claims, but deservingness can also be seen as a preinstitutional moral concept.[4] One might say, therefore, that Team A is entitled to a victory because it scored more points but that Team B deserved to win because it played a better game; league rules may declare the winner, but common, preexisting beliefs insist either way that games go best when the better-performing team wins.

Calvin and Rawls use the concept of desert in substantially the same way, albeit in different contexts. Calvin's discourse on human deservingness, ranging from the quotidian to the soteriological, argues that Thomas Aquinas and other medieval thinkers gravely err in believing that people can merit their temporal goods or salvation in any way. The reformer insists that humans cannot legitimately take credit for their productive labor or their morally good works for the same basic reason: Every laudable inclination, effort, and skill that allows people to perform these tasks comes from God, and the condition of sin makes humans too indebted to God to make any positive personal desert claim valid. Rawls, working in the context of modern democratic societies, discusses desert primarily in terms of distributive justice. He is keen to avoid using desert as a first principle of justice since desert claims for him ultimately rely on factors that lie outside an individual's control yet can deeply affect the share of society's goods that each person receives. Both Calvin and Rawls are thus concerned essentially with personal desert, and given Feinberg's formal definition, there does not appear to be a significant difference in what these thinkers mean when they invoke the concept; both seek to delineate the proper treatment people should receive given the possession of certain traits or the performance of certain actions.

The Moral Structure of Society: Calvin and Rawls

Calvin's theology is shaped by a deep awareness of both divine sovereignty and human infirmity. These two realities point to humanity's utter dependence on God for not only physical sustenance but spiritual nourishment as well. The initial design of creation offered humanity everything it needed to flourish,[5] but disobedience led to humanity's banishment from the full abundance of God's creation as well as to the corruption of the will.[6] Calvin sees further consequences of sin in the dramatic vicissitudes of nature, the demands of hard labor for sustenance, and the fractured bonds of humanity.[7] Still, God maintains dominion over every aspect of creation and thereby offers hope for a full and upright life for each Christian.[8] God's sovereign grace provides the redemption that makes good works possible, the law that inclines people to do them, and the institutions of family, church, and polity that comprise the necessary support to carry out these works.

Original sin caused God's natural gifts to humanity, soundness of mind and uprightness of heart, to be damaged such that people no longer distinguish good from evil. Likewise, the supernatural gifts of faith—love of God, charity toward neighbor, and zeal for righteousness—were withdrawn such that humans no longer seek God or even the good on their own.[9] Unable to discern righteous living, much less achieve or even desire it, humanity is saddled with an existence characterized by moral confusion and misdirection; the will labors in bondage, inclined to the passions rather than to God, and enslaves the person to sin. Yet the sacrifice of Christ redeems the fallen "by arousing love and desire and zeal for righteousness in our hearts; or, to speak more correctly, by bending, forming, directing, our hearts to righteousness. [God] completes his work, moreover, by confirming us to perseverance."[10] The will, aided by God's grace, is thus enabled to pursue good works with both courageous persistence and the humble gratitude that is due God for making it possible.[11]

Even with a rightly oriented will, though, Calvin believes that people still need a spur to act. Fortunately, God provides this spur in the third use of the law. Luther famously identifies two functions of God's law: illuminating divine righteousness, which convicts human beings of their own wickedness, and eliciting the fear of punishment, which restrains evildoers.[12] Calvin identifies a third use for Christians, which he claims is the law's primary function: "to learn more thoroughly each day the nature of the Lord's will to which they aspire, and . . . by frequent meditation upon it to be aroused to obedience, be strengthened in it, and be drawn back from the slippery path of transgression."[13] Because even the most faithful are encumbered by "the weight of the flesh," which leads them astray or lulls them into idleness, the law rouses people from their moral stupor and prods them to righteous behavior.[14] The law for Calvin, though, is not merely a divine whip; it also testifies to the promise of God's grace, a sure sign of God's sovereign love for humanity.[15]

Study and application of the law is a lifetime endeavor, requiring commitment, discipline, insight, and deep reflection on the part of the believer.[16] Because these traits and activities often present distinct challenges, God graciously offers guidance and support in the institutions of family, polity, and church.[17] Among their many functions, these institutions create and maintain the social bonds Christians need to grow physically and spiritually in their pursuits of faithful lives in service to God. In families, husbands and wives work for the benefit of one another, and each plays a vital role in developing the other's relationship with God.[18] As parents, married couples have a duty to nurture their children and to serve as a primary means of their spiritual development. In fact, Calvin thinks of pious families as "so many little Churches" that are responsible for the instruction of their members.[19] Parents should correct and punish children when necessary, careful to avoid the extremes of severity and indulgence; with proper rearing, children will be in the best position to devote their own lives to God when they come of age.[20]

Polity and church are also part of God's design, organizing, regulating, and instructing people in their pursuits of safe, peaceful, and pious existences. Calvin conceives these institutions as a twofold government consisting of the political kingdom, which addresses the outward person and the responsibilities of citizenship, and the spiritual kingdom, which ministers to the soul and instructs the faithful in personal devotion to God.[21] Both civil and church leaders are called by God to their offices to act as collaborators in the protection and edification of the populace.[22] In different ways, these leaders serve as God's representatives on Earth. Defying the magistrate amounts to rebelling against God, and everyone (including the magistrate) is to listen to the minister as if God's own voice were speaking.[23] Unlike secular leaders, though, pastors are servants to their congregations, too, since God possesses sole dominion over spiritual matters.[24] Even as teachers, members of the clergy may be seen as students and their preaching remains subject to the scrutiny of congregants to ensure the Word of God is rightly conveyed. As Calvin insists, God, not the minister, is to be heard during the sermon.[25]

In sum, the moral structure of society according to Calvin is a product of God's sovereignty, manifest especially in humanity's redemption, divine law, and society's institutions. In the face of humanity's corruption, God offers the means, inclination, and support for righteous living. Perhaps few will ultimately lead a pious life, but those who do owe all their gratitude and honor to God. Primarily for this reason, Calvin objects vehemently to the recognition of positive personal desert claims. Affirming human deservingness necessarily detracts from the recognition that is due God alone. Before examining Calvin's arguments in detail, though, it will be helpful to present Rawls's view of society's moral structure in order to highlight the similarities apparent in his rejection of desert as well.

Rawls's theory of justice is deeply informed by the contingencies of human existence. People are born with various talents and propensities, and they grow up in vastly different environments. Such distinctions help determine personal identities, but they also can create unfair conditions through which people exploit one another. Rawls's methodology attempts to eliminate the arbitrary elements of life that offer advantages to some but not to everyone. He believes the random nature of certain privileges justifies his insistence that desert should not figure among the first principles of justice. The overall objective of Rawls's work is to posit what he calls a "realistic utopia"; he wants to examine the extent to which a just, sustainable, and worthwhile collective existence in a democratic system is possible.[26] While his methods entail ideal theory, thought experiments, a hypothetical point of view, and assumed behaviors, his ambition is decidedly real-world and pragmatic. The point of articulating a "realistic utopia" is not simply to explore the practical limits of concepts such as democracy, society, and justice but also to establish a theoretically sound ideal of justice to which contemporary democratic societies might aspire.[27] The following sketch of Rawls's thought centers on two concepts that are particularly relevant to his assessment of desert as a principle of justice: the basic structure of society and the original position.

For Rawls, the primary subject of political justice is the basic structure of society, a term that refers to "the way in which the main political and social institutions of society fit together into one system of social cooperation, and the way they assign basic rights and duties and regulate the division of advantages that arises from social cooperation over time."[28] Society's basic structure includes its political and legal frameworks, its economic system, and even the family unit. Such institutions comprise the overall social organization in which groups and individuals conduct their activities. How well people in a society ultimately flourish often depends largely on the operation of society's basic structure.[29] If the basic structure's institutions are trustworthy, competent, effective, and above all just, individuals stand a much better chance of thriving than if these institutions are, say, corrupt or prejudiced. Rawls therefore concentrates on developing the principles that underlie the basic structure itself; for if everyone considers the principles to be just and if everyone further agrees that the basic structure faithfully upholds these principles, Rawls believes society has the best chance of achieving the ideal of self-sustaining justice.[30]

A key problem, of course, is deriving these principles in a way that ensures people will both agree to and abide by them. Rawls's approach entails the original position, a strictly hypothetical stance designed to establish principles of justice that would hold under a "veil of ignorance." Persons in the original position do not know beforehand their places in society, class positions, or social standings; they do not know what natural assets and abilities they possess, their psychological propensities, or even their conceptions of the good.[31] The original position is designed to ensure that "no one is advantaged or disadvantaged in the choice of principles by the outcome of natural chance or the contingency of social circumstances. Since all are similarly situated and no one is able to design principles to favor his particular condition, the principles of justice are the result of a fair agreement or bargain."[32] Rawls maintains that, after due consideration, people in the original position will affirm two fundamental principles: basic rights and duties are to be equally assigned, and social and economic inequalities are to be allowed so long as they benefit everyone, especially the least-advantaged members of society.[33] The first principle underscores everyone's desire for equal access to the same system of basic liberties; the second, known as the difference principle, recognizes that people are more inclined to ensure the well-being of the least fortunate when their own standings in society are undetermined.

While establishing the principles of justice is critical, the enterprise would amount to nothing if they proved unstable over time. Gauging the stability of these principles entails determining whether people who grow up under the institutions specified by the agreed-upon principles develop a firm enough sense of justice to incline widespread allegiance to the institutions.[34] In other words, the institutions grounded by these principles need to be able to resist tendencies toward injustice, and the institutions do this in part by educating the populace in the very principles of justice that established them. Rawls is careful to point out that a political conception of justice means that the institutions are not instructing the populace in a comprehensive moral doctrine; instead, members of society accept the political conception as either part of or an adjunct to their own comprehensive moral doctrines.[35] For Rawls, personal moral development takes place in a sequence of stages, each consisting of the various institutions in which people participate as they mature.[36] Families, civic groups, religious organizations, and employers contribute to the moral development of the individual by stipulating various sets of precepts and standards that help the person to understand and fulfill her appropriate roles within these associations. One learns how to be a good child, friend, student, and employee according to distinct guidelines. In time, the individual also learns how to be a just person, which entails understanding the morality of principles in a political context. As long as people believe that their institutions adequately support the accepted principles of justice, the stability of these institutions and of a just society is relatively ensured. The moral structure of society for Rawls is thus ultimately determined by the principles of justice that establish the institutions, which in turn educate the populace in the norm of fairness.

Why Desert Is Problematic

As indicated earlier, desert is problematic for both Calvin and Rawls because it undermines the sovereign authority of society's moral structure. For Calvin, the problem arises when people make positive desert claims for themselves or for one another, because such claims necessarily detract from God's sovereignty and the recognition that God is due. Good works deserve praise, but Calvin believes works are good only because God accepts them as good, not because the person performing them is good or because the nature of the actions themselves is good.[37] The corrupt will, although autonomous and able to choose among various options, cannot choose between good and evil because this capacity was lost to original sin. So humans must now suffer the reality of a bound will, which, because of its corruptness, is held captive to wicked desires and can choose only evil.[38] This condition makes positive personal desert claims ultimately vain. "Scripture shows what all our works deserve when it states that they cannot bear God's gaze because they are full of uncleanness. . . . There is no doubt that whatever is praiseworthy in works is God's grace; there is not a drop that we ought by rights to ascribe to ourselves."[39]

Some might object that humans must contribute something good to their works, inasmuch as an individual's effort and actions are necessary to their performance. Calvin grants that both human and divine inputs are involved, but he insists that the ultimate source of personal ability, effort, and action is not found in the individual. As with other gifts, these things come from God alone. "It is not that we ourselves do nothing or that we without any movement of our will are driven to act by pressure from him, but that we act while being acted upon by him. We will as he guides our heart, we endeavor as he rouses us, we succeed in our endeavor as he gives us strength, so that we are animate and living tools, while he is the leader and the finisher of the work."[40] The implication for human deservingness is that no one can take credit for good works, even in part, because no one can take credit for all the elements that ultimately contribute to the works actually being performed. Individuals may participate in this activity, but God initiates, guides, and sustains their efforts in every case and therefore deserves all the praise. By this argument, Calvin effectively insists that, to truly deserve, one must deserve all the way down: no positive desert is due unless credit can be claimed for every aspect of the work's performance.[41]

The notion of desert is problematic for Rawls, too, because it fundamentally undermines the authority of his first principles of justice. These principles derive their moral force primarily from their method of establishment, which entails the elimination of what Rawls considers to be the morally arbitrary aspects of the social world that lead to certain advantages for some but not for others.[42] He claims that because "it is one of the fixed points of our moral judgments that no one deserves his place in the distribution of natural assets any more than he deserves his initial starting place in society," the principles that ground the basic structure of society must discount these undeserved elements of our existence in order to be just.[43] Consent to the principles of justice must take place from a position of fairness, which means forgoing not only advantages over others prior to the agreement but also the prospect of gaining advantages over others as a result of the agreement. A condition of fairness is precisely what the idea of the original position is designed to establish, and introducing deservingness into the deliberation of first principles of justice necessarily prioritizes some members of society over others.

In presenting his theory, Rawls appears to make a claim about the nature of desert that resonates with Calvin's argument. The passage that best exemplifies this point (and has garnered much attention from critics) states: "We do not deserve our place in the distribution of native endowments, any more than we deserve our initial starting place in society. That we deserve the superior character that enables us to make the effort to cultivate our abilities is also problematic; for such character depends in good part upon fortunate family and social circumstances in early life for which we can claim no credit."[44]

That people do not deserve their natural endowments or starting places in society seems largely accepted; people enter the world by actions wholly outside themselves, and, according to most Western traditions at least, individuals cannot be held responsible for either the natural attributes with which they arrive or the environmental conditions into which they are born.[45] More contentious, however, is the idea that people do not deserve the character traits that allow them to advance socially or economically because these traits depend on factors for which they can claim no credit. The upshot of this argument appears to be that in order to deserve, one must deserve the very bases for one's desert claims. If a person could take credit for the character traits that allow her to improve her social or economic status, one might infer from Rawls's statement that she would be entitled to the additional fruits of her efforts, perhaps even benefits to the disadvantaged notwithstanding. Rawls never explicitly states that deservingness requires one to deserve all the way down, but he never explicitly refutes this idea, either. The argument with which he rejects desert as a first principle of justice recalls Calvin's point that humans simply cannot take ultimate credit for their positive actions.

Unlike Calvin, though, Rawls affirms desert as a moral standard in certain contexts. In brief, his theory recognizes three ideas of moral desert: that which concerns the moral worth of a person's actions or character as indicated by a comprehensive moral doctrine; that which is specified by a set of public rules designed for a specific purpose; and that which he refers to as legitimate expectations.[46] Only the first of these cannot be included in a political conception of justice because it draws from comprehensive moral doctrines for its content. This notion of desert might be used to justify why a person ought to go to heaven, or to make the claim that good people ought to flourish in life. The second idea specifies deservingness according to a particular set of public rules, such as those in games. Systems of cooperation that satisfy the difference principle are another example because "they serve to encourage individuals to educate their endowments and to use them for the general good."[47] In the case of education, there is no guarantee that getting a degree will lead to a successful career, just as in games there is no guarantee that the better competitor will win, but in both cases, one's deserving status depends on adherence to the public rules established for that particular purpose; no moral assessment is made of a person's character or her particular actions in order to confer the reward. Rawls's final idea of desert, that of legitimate expectations, highlights the difficulties that are introduced with considerations of effort and productivity.

The Problem of Effort and Productivity

Do people who demonstrate greater effort or generate more production in their work deserve greater rewards? Both Calvin and Rawls effectively say yes, but their rejection of desert raises some difficulties in defending their positions. Calvin in particular runs into problems when he discusses the distribution of material goods. He acknowledges that, even in the abundance of divine benevolence, God does not distribute sustenance equally or with complete regularity to human beings. Individuals receive their blessings of shelter, food, and wealth in varying degrees, just as entire societies face intermittent periods of want and plenty. Because earthly goods are intended to nourish both the physical and spiritual well-being of humanity, Calvin sees the different levels of divine distribution as fitting responses to the diverse physical and spiritual needs people have: "God will bless us on the earth, but it will be . . . according to the measure of our infirmity."[48] Calvin nevertheless sees grace as the principle governing divine distributions. God grants humanity not only love and mercy but also life and sustenance without consideration for personal merit. Grace, therefore, ought to serve as the primary standard for distributions among humans, too. "As our heavenly Father freely bestows upon us all things, so we ought to be imitators of his unmerited kindness in doing good . . . because, in laying out our resources, we are simply the dispensers of his favor."[49] If humans are to be like God, then it seems that desert has no role in the just distribution of material goods.

Yet Calvin makes a clear distinction between the material distributions that come from God and those that occur among people. The latter kind may rightfully take into account effort, talent, and other measures of distinction, as his exegesis of the manna narrative in Exodus 16 illustrates.

> The case of ordinary food is different; for it is necessary for the preservation of human society that each should possess what is his own; that some should acquire property by purchase, that to others it should come by hereditary right, to others by the title of presentation, that each should increase his means in proportion to his diligence, or bodily strength, or other qualifications. In fine, political government requires, that each should enjoy what belongs to him; and hence it would be absurd to prescribe, as to our common food, the law which is here laid down as to the manna.[50]

God's distribution of manna took place during the Israelites' flight from Egypt, when sustenance was especially scarce and survival a daily concern. Moses instructed the people to gather only what they needed, and all were satisfied. Yet Calvin does not regard this narrative as a mandate for all economic distributions for all times. He realizes that peaceful economic relations in his own time depend at least in part on such normative standards as respect for property rights, widespread generosity, and rewards that reflect individual contribution.

Not surprisingly, he refuses to couch the last of these in terms of desert, but the implication seems clear. In economic relationships, people have a fundamental and firm belief that rendering one's due entails, among other things, considerations of desert.

Still, Calvin appears to equivocate, if not directly contradict himself, at times on this very point. In certain discussions of labor and wages, he recognizes that distinctions in effort and skill warrant differences in compensation, yet on other occasions he insists that no one truly deserves the earnings one receives. Defending the first claim, he observes that God grants us distinctive talents that are to be fully employed using our concomitant gifts of motivation and diligence.[51] Whatever the gains, people are called to use their God-given talents productively; failure to do so results in well-deserved deprivation.[52] As the indolent rightly suffer want, the diligent should benefit from the fruits of their labor —especially the poor, who rely on timely compensation for their very survival.[53] Civil law often mandates prompt remuneration, but Calvin believes this law would pertain whether codified or not, given its spiritual nature.[54] In these observations, Calvin appears to affirm a robust and theologically grounded standard of desert for the laborer.

Elsewhere, however, he insists just as adamantly that people cannot take credit for their output or their earnings, even if these derive directly from the workers' diligent efforts and personal labor, for all things ultimately come from God alone.[55] The farmer may seem to deserve the fruits of his labor by virtue of his tilling the soil, planting the seeds, tending the fields, and harvesting the crops, but Calvin points out that it is God who gives the farmer not only the earth, seed, and vegetation but also the will, knowledge, and strength to produce the harvest in the first place, so the farmer has no basis for claiming desert of anything. While this logic may seem severe, Calvin insists the farmer and those like him are not denied their due: "Who gives human beings forethought, physical ability, the strength for work, resources and skills? Is it not God who puts everything into their hands?"[56] Considering the breadth and depth of God's contribution to human endeavors, people simply lack any basis for making desert claims for their labor. Calvin sees God's hand in every aspect of human existence, and this understanding of God's sovereignty grounds his negative assessment of personal desert. At the root of every human achievement lie God's blessings; any claim to deserve the fruits of one's labor necessarily discredits God.

Rawls also wants to avoid recognizing desert claims when assessing the impact of production and effort on wages. The virtues of hard work, dedication, and efficiency may be seen as various expressions of moral desert, so these cannot be used as bases of distribution because of their ties to comprehensive moral doctrines. Rawls therefore introduces the ideas of legitimate expectations and entitlements instead. These operate fittingly in a political conception of justice because they do not issue from any comprehensive moral doctrine. Institutions,

for example, set up schemes of compensation that produce legitimate expectations for the payments to which an employee may be entitled; determining the
nature or amount of compensation in no way involves a moral worth assessment
of the person's character or actions. When people receive higher wages for superior contributions under Rawls's framework, they are due their compensation
not because the virtue of hard work or raw talent deserves to be rewarded;
rather, the principles of a market economy simply dictate that greater contributors receive more pay.[57] In the economic institution of a market system, highly
productive employees generally enjoy greater demand, and employers are willing to offer more pay in order to attract them. A similar principle applies to
those with unique or exceptional abilities. "The premiums earned by scarce natural talents . . . are to cover the costs of training and to encourage the efforts of
learning, as well as to direct ability to where it best furthers the common interest. The distributive shares that result do not correlate with moral worth, since
the initial endowment of natural assets and the contingencies of their growth
and nurture in life are arbitrary from a moral point of view."[58] Again, it is not
that great athletes deserve high earnings because of their moral worth; they simply are entitled to extra compensation by virtue of their advanced training and
the substantial market demand for their talents.

Rawls has a more difficult time, however, accounting for the inclination to
reward outstanding effort, as he acknowledges, "The precept which seems intuitively to come closest to rewarding moral desert is that of distribution according to effort, or perhaps better, conscientious effort."[59] Here, appeals to
the market do not seem to fare as well. While it is rather unlikely that many
people have been hired, promoted, or paid large bonuses simply for making a
good effort, demonstrations of conscientious effort remain highly regarded, and
people often want to see such exhibitions aptly rewarded. Rawls cautions again,
though, that "the effort a person is willing to make is influenced by his natural abilities and skills and the alternatives open to him. The better endowed
are more likely, other things equal, to strive conscientiously, and there seems
to be no way to discount for their greater good fortune."[60] Thus, outside an
institutional formula for rewarding effort, it would be unfair to distribute social goods according to this standard. The conscientious and diligent worker
may be said to deserve some reward for her effort, but she is not entitled to
such unless an institution established by the principles of justice so stipulates.

Critique of the Principal Arguments Regarding Desert

Putting Calvin and Rawls in conversation on the moral status of desert underscores a major argument against this standard in both Christian and philosophical discourse. A brief critique of each thinker provides some points of refer-

ence that may prove useful in delineating an appropriate role for desert in a Christian conception of distributive justice. Looking at Calvin's work, the major question seems to be whether affirming desert claims necessarily entails a subversion of God's moral sovereignty. Many Christians may agree with Calvin that God is ultimately responsible for all that humans are and thus in the end deserves all the credit for their achievements, but it seems this observation could also lead to a conception of desert that actually presumes grace from the start rather than apparently denying or ignoring it. If one's God-given talents and the family and social situation into which one is born cannot be deserved, then humans enter the world already subject to God's grace, and that grace is already implied in every desert claim. Since no one can deserve all the way down, grace provides the starting point for desert claims even to make sense. This observation requires a fundamental shift in the way many typically conceive desert. Returning to Feinberg's scheme, desert claims that recognize grace from the beginning might take the form of "X deserves Y in virtue of Z, given A," where A represents the relevant preexisting factors that make possible the claimant's relationship to the desert basis. Granted, accounting for all the factors that A may represent and working out a systematic way of compensating for these factors pose what may be an insurmountable problem. And it may not be the case that all desert claims require this depth of analysis to attain just resolutions. Still, conceiving desert claims in ways that explicitly consider not only the bases of the claims but also the givens that help establish the bases themselves may prove decisive in the pursuit of justice. Additional work is needed, therefore, to determine the kinds of circumstances that warrant this level of analysis.

Rawls stands apart from Calvin in his willingness to acknowledge the validity of desert in certain contexts. As observed, however, he affirms only institutional desert (entitlements) as part of his political conception of justice since desert claims that rely on moral worth draw from comprehensive moral doctrines for their content. One may question Rawls on whether such a stark line ought to or even can be drawn between individual moral worth and the just distribution of, say, employment opportunities and compensation. Background checks, for example, are commonly used by companies and firms for conditions of employment, and people who work in medical, legal, religious, political, and teaching professions are routinely held to higher standards of morality than those who work in many other careers. The recent public outcry over bonus payments made to American International Group (AIG) and other Wall Street executives who were responsible for one of the largest financial market failures in history also points to the deep connection many people make between personal earnings and moral integrity.[61] While some argue that these executives are entitled to their bonuses because the institutions of contract law, compensation agreements, or the market warrant them being paid, others insist that these executives simply do not deserve the bonuses and therefore should not be paid, entitlements notwithstanding.[62] The separation of entitlement and moral desert seems a necessary aspect of Rawls's work, given the distinct aims and parameters of his project, but such elements are not essential to a Christian conception of distributive justice. The challenge, then, lies in clarifying from a theological perspective the circumstances that pertain to make moral desert claims a valid consideration in the distribution of society's goods.

Conclusion

This essay has brought together Calvin and Rawls in an attempt to highlight some of the problems and possibilities that emerge when desert is considered as a standard of justice from a Christian perspective. Many theologians hold deep reservations about desert because of its inherent tensions with grace, but the moral force of human deservingness seems undeniable, as the work of even two of its most ardent detractors indicates. Both Calvin and Rawls struggle to account for the apparent propriety of rewarding the more diligent and productive with more pay despite their shared fundamental reservations about desert's capacity to reflect adequately the countless predetermined elements that contribute to the laborer's work. Some theological groundwork is therefore necessary to identify the proper bearing desert should bring to matters of distributive justice.

This essay suggests two areas that warrant further development. First, desert may be reconceived to presume the impact of grace on the deserving. No one can deserve the circumstances into which one is born, yet personal achievement is often directly tied to the specific capacities, inclinations, and socioeconomic background one receives upon entering the world. Ideally, these factors should be taken into account when resolving desert claims. For example, many people agree that job opportunities ought to be filled by the most qualified applicants; hiring a less-qualified candidate over one who brings the best set of knowledge, skills, and upward potential to a position seems intuitively wrong. Opponents of affirmative action, in fact, have long used this argument to support their stance, saying employment should be earned but affirmative action inevitably awards jobs to the less deserving.[63] This claim, however, seems to rely on a rather rudimentary notion of desert. A more robust conception would consider the impact of inherited factors on the development of one's marketable qualifications. The disadvantaged often have to work longer and harder to develop their knowledge and skills and may thus deserve as much (if not more) consideration as the more privileged who possess greater skills and expertise but face fewer challenges in attaining them. Recognizing diverse starting positions in the concept of desert affirms that many disadvantaged people may be equally deserving of consideration for job positions even if their qualifications do not measure up absolutely.[64] As a practical matter, instituting this kind of accommodation raises numerous difficulties, such as identifying which inherited factors contribute to or collectively constitute meaningful disadvantages and deciding whether standards should be established in terms of groups or individuals. Some obstacles may in fact prove intractable. Still, reconceiving desert as described would underscore the reality that everyone enters life subject to distinctive manifestations of grace as well as various social and economic constructs. Given their significance in human flourishing, these factors should be accorded due consideration in the just distribution of social and economic goods.

Also in need of theological attention are the substantive and functional distinctions between moral worth and entitlement. Prevailing practices indicate that people do not separate considerations of moral worth and the just distributions of employment and compensation absolutely. The outrage over AIG executive bonus payments suggests that desert claims may actually have greater moral force than entitlement claims. Indeed, in response to the recent financial crisis, regulatory changes now grant stock owners an official voice for making their desert claims and other demands heard. In January 2011 the Securities and Exchange Commission adopted "say on pay" rules that allow shareholders of publicly traded companies to vote on the compensation and separation packages executives receive.[65] While these votes are nonbinding, "no" votes constitute a significant source of embarrassment for companies and garner unwanted attention from the press. Early results show that executive deservingness is a key determinant in shareholder voting. A study of the first one hundred proxy filings of Fortune 500 companies in 2011, for example, confirms that companies who link performance and pay are more likely to approve executive compensation with "yes" votes.[66] Another analysis shows that, of the four companies receiving "no" votes in the first quarter of 2011, three appear to be related to executive performance.[67] The long-term impact of "say on pay" voting remains to be seen, but returns so far evince not only substantial changes in the size and structure of executive pay but also a keen interest on the part of shareholders to remain vigilant.[68] Rules focusing on executive deservingness may be welcome, but they leave open the question of how performance itself ought to be measured. The standards of short-term profits and stock price need improving because, while they may boost immediate shareholder returns, they are too narrow and misguided to address a company's long-term sustainability. Better standards of executive desert might be drawn from a much broader set of criteria that more accurately reflects the various beneficiaries of sound management, both within the company and without. Owners and boards of directors should reward executives for not only increasing shareholder wealth for investors and employees but also maintaining the company as a going concern for the benefit of the greater community.

As these brief examples indicate, desert enjoys wide affirmation as a principle of distributive justice in a variety of applications. Christian thinkers therefore need to consider more thoroughly the relationship between grace and desert and the theological warrant each principle holds for the just distribution of society's goods. The analysis presented here constitutes only a small, initial step in this larger task, but the project must be pursued at length if the moral relevance of desert is to receive its due.

Notes

1. See, for example, John Milbank, "Politics: Socialism by Grace," in *Being Reconciled: Ontology and Pardon* (London: Routledge, 2003); Milbank, "Can Morality Be Christian?" in *The Word Made Strange: Theology, Language, Culture* (Oxford: Blackwell Publishers, 1997); Milbank, "The Transcendality of the Gift: A Summary," in *The Future of Love: Essays in Political Theology* (Eugene, OR: Cascade Books, 2009); Kathryn Tanner, *Economy of Grace* (Minneapolis: Fortress Press, 2005); and Timothy J. Gorringe, *Capital and the Kingdom: Theological Ethics and Economic Order* (New York: Orbis Books, 1994).

2. Joel Feinberg, "Justice and Personal Desert," in *Doing and Deserving: Essays in the Theory of Responsibility* (Princeton, NJ: Princeton University Press, 1970), 55.

3. Ibid., 61. I have changed the variables slightly for clarity.

4. Whether desert is fundamentally an institutional or preinstitutional moral concept has been subject to debate. For a discussion of the debates and an attempt at a third position, see Owen McLeod, "Desert and Institutions," in *What Do We Deserve? A Reader on Justice and Desert*, (Oxford: Oxford University Press, 1999), 186–95.

5. John Calvin, *Commentaries on the First Book of Moses Called Genesis*, vol. 1 of *Calvin's Commentaries*, complete from the Calvin Translation Society (Grand Rapids, MI: Christian Classics Ethereal Library, CCEL), www.ccel.org/ccel/calvin/commentaries.html, Gn 2:9. All references to Calvin's commentaries are from CCEL.

6. John Calvin, *Institutes of the Christian Religion*, ed. John T. McNeill, trans. Ford Lewis Battles (Philadelphia: Westminster Press, 1960), 1.15.8.

7. Calvin, *Commentaries on Genesis*, Gn 3:17, 2:18.

8. For Calvin, God is "everlasting Governor and Preserver . . . not only [because] he drives the celestial frame as well as its several parts by a universal motion, but also [because] he sustains, nourishes, and cares for, everything he has made, even to the least sparrow." Calvin, *Institutes of the Christian Religion*, 1.16.1.

9. Ibid., 2.2.12.

10. Ibid., 2.3.6.

11. Ibid., 3.15.3.

12. See Martin Luther, "Secular Authority: To What Extent It Should Be Obeyed," in *Martin Luther: Selections from His Writings*, ed. John Dillenberger (New York: Doubleday, 1962), 369–70.

13. Calvin, *Institutes of the Christian Religion*, 2.7.12.

14. Ibid.

15. Ibid., 2.5.7.

16. Calvin, *Commentaries on the Four Last Books of Moses Arranged in the Form of a Harmony*, vol. 1, Dt 6:6–9.

17. "Laws, for Calvin . . . give access to the *principles* of social control. But the good order of society also depends on *institutions*. Calvin's social and political universe was ordered by three major institutions, related more or less hierarchically, which, he believed, had been essentially unchanged since the world began. First came the family, above that the polity, and over all the church. All three had been established by God to enforce in human society the principles of order visible in the cosmos." William J. Bouwsma, *John Calvin: A Sixteenth Century Portrait* (Oxford: Oxford University Press, 1988), 76.

18. This is not to say that Calvin sees the husband and wife as equals. The man, as superior, is to marry a woman who will help him lead a life of faith; the woman, as wife, cannot obey Christ without obeying her husband. The marriage itself nevertheless centers on a bond of mutual love and devotion. See Herman J. Selderhuis, *John Calvin: A Pilgrim's Life* (Downers Grove, IL: InterVarsity Press, 2009), 178; and John Calvin, *Commentaries on the Epistle of Paul to the Galatians and Ephesians*, Eph 5:22–25.

19. John Calvin, *Commentaries on the Epistles of Paul the Apostle to the Corinthians*, vol. 1, 1 Cor 16:19.

20. Ibid., 1 Cor 7:37.

21. Calvin, *Institutes of the Christian Religion*, 3.19.15.

22. Ibid., 4.11.3.

23. Ibid., 4.20.4 and 4.20.23; 4.11.4 and 4.1.5.

24. John Calvin, *Commentaries on the Epistles of Paul the Apostle to the Corinthians*, vol. 2, 2 Cor 1:24, 4:5.

25. John Calvin, *Commentary on the Book of the Prophet Isaiah*, vol. 1, Is 2:3; Calvin, *Commentaries on Corinthians*, vol. 1, 1 Cor 3:22.

26. John Rawls, *Justice as Fairness: A Restatement* (Cambridge, MA: Belknap/Harvard University Press, 2001), 4.

27. Ibid., 13.

28. Ibid., 10.

29. This constitutes, in part, one of the reasons the basic structure is the primary subject of Rawls's political conception of justice: "Even in a well-ordered society. . . . our prospects over life are deeply affected by social, natural, and fortuitous contingencies, and by the way the basic structure, by setting up inequalities, uses those contingencies to meet certain social purposes." See §16 in ibid., 55–57.

30. When these conditions prevail and when citizens possess "a normally effective sense of justice," Rawls calls this a well-ordered society. See ibid., 8–9.

31. John Rawls, *A Theory of Justice*, rev. ed. (Cambridge, MA: Belknap/Harvard University Press, 1999), 11.

32. Ibid., 11.

33. Rawls provides a more detailed final version of these principles, along with rules of their priority, in §46 of ibid.

34. Rawls, *Justice as Fairness*, 184.

35. Ibid., 187.

36. For a detailed description of these stages, see Rawls, *Theory of Justice*, §§70–72.

37. Calvin, *Institutes of the Christian Religion*, 3.15.3.

38. Ibid., 2.2.12.

39. Ibid., 3.15.3.

40. John Calvin, *The Bondage and Liberation of the Will: A Defense of the Orthodox Doctrine of Human Choice against Phighius*, ed. A. N. S. Lane, trans. G. I. Davies (Grand Rapids, MI: Baker Books, 1996), 152.

41. The phrase "all the way down" is from Robert Nozick's critique of Rawls on the subject of desert in his *Anarchy, State, and Utopia* (New York: Basic Books, 1974), 225.

42. Rawls, *Theory of Justice*, 13–14.

43. Ibid., 274.

44. Ibid., 89. For some of his critics, see Nozick, *Anarchy, State, and Utopia*; Michael Sandel, *Liberalism and the Limits of Justice* (Cambridge: Cambridge University Press, 1982); George Sher, *Desert* (Princeton, NJ: Princeton University Press, 1987); David Miller, *Principles of Social Justice* (Cambridge, MA: Harvard University Press, 1999); and Samuel Scheffler, *Boundaries and Allegiances: Problems of Justice and Responsibility in Liberal Thought* (Oxford: Oxford University Press, 2001).

45. Hindu and other perspectives that affirm reincarnation and the influence of previous existences on a person's new life obviously complicate this claim.

46. Rawls, *Justice as Fairness*, 73.

47. Ibid., 74.

48. Calvin, *Commentaries on the Twelve Minor Prophets*, vol. 2, Jl 3:18.

49. Calvin, *Commentaries on Corinthians*, vol. 2, 2 Cor 8:4.

50. Calvin, *Commentaries on the Four Last Books of Moses*, vol. 1, Ex 16:17.

51. "But whatever gifts the Lord has bestowed upon us, let us know that it is committed to us as so much money, that it may yield some gain; for nothing could be more unreasonable than that we should allow to remain buried, or should apply to no use, God's favors, the value of which consists in yielding fruit." John Calvin, *Commentary on a Harmony of the Evangelists, Matthew, Mark, and Luke*, vol. 2, Lk 19:13.

52. "From its being written in Psalm 128:2, 'Thou art blessed, eating of the labor of thy hands,' also in Proverbs 10:4, the blessing of the Lord is upon the hands of him that laboreth, it is certain that indolence and idleness are accursed of God. Besides, we know that man was created with this view, that he might do something. Not only does Scripture testify this to us, but nature itself taught it to the heathen. Hence it is reasonable, that those, who wish to exempt themselves from the common law, should also be deprived of food, the reward of labor." Calvin, *Commentaries on the Epistle of Paul to the Philippians, Colossians, and Thessalonians*, 2 Thes 3:10.

53. Calvin, *Commentaries on the Book of the Prophet of Jeremiah and the Lamentations*, vol. 3, Jer 22:13.

54. Calvin, *Commentaries on the Four Last Books of Moses*, vol. 3, Dt 24:14.

55. Calvin, *Commentary on a Harmony of the Evangelists, Matthew, Mark, and Luke*, vol. 1, Mt 6:11.

56. The full quote emphasizes the point: "In considering people at work, we estimate whether they are industrious, apt and dexterous. We examine that. Thus at least it seems that when a person has worked with his mind to it, skillfully, being attentive, using the right means, avoiding harm—it looks as if we do him wrong to say he has done nothing and that it was a free gift from God, for experience goes against this. But Moses replies to all this by saying that although men work, they strive with a view to being provident in their own interest, but that they would be well advised and prudent in ensuring that God not be deprived of his honor. Why? Who gives human beings forethought, physical ability, the

strength for work, resources and skills? Is it not God who puts everything into their hands?" Calvin, Sermon LXI on Deuteronomy 8:14–20, quoted in Andre Bieler, *Calvin's Economic and Social Thought*, ed. Edward Dommen and trans. James Greig (Geneva: World Alliance of Reformed Churches, 2005), 352–53.

57. Rawls, *Theory of Justice*, 273–74.

58. Ibid., 274.

59. Ibid.

60. Ibid.

61. In 2009 AIG paid $168 million in bonuses to employees in its Financial Products unit, whose derivatives deals nearly brought down the company in 2008 and led to a $180 billion loan package from the federal government to keep AIG afloat. In 2010 the company paid $100 million in bonuses to the same employees.

62. See, for example, "The Case for Paying out Bonuses at AIG," *New York Times*, March 17, 2009, www.nytimes.com/2009/03/17/business/17sorkin.html; and "Obama Will Move to Block AIG Bonus Payments. Said It Is 'Hard to Understand' Why AIG Traders Deserve Money," *Chicago Sun-Times*, March 16, 2009, http://blogs.suntimes.com/sweet/2009/03/obama_hard_to_understand_why_a.html.

63. The scholarly literature on affirmative action is vast. For a survey of discussions on the topic, including the central role of desert, see Robert Fullinwider, "Affirmative Action," *The Stanford Encyclopedia of Philosophy* (Winter 2010), ed. Edward N. Zalta, http://plato.stanford.edu/archives/win2010/entries/affirmative-action/.

64. The point here is not to suggest that every job opportunity ought to be awarded to the disadvantaged but rather that the designation "best qualified" does not automatically translate to that of "most deserving" in terms of a person's candidacy for employment.

65. U. S. Securities and Exchange Commission, "SEC Adopts Rules for Say-on-Pay and Golden Parachute Compensation as Required under Dodd-Frank Act," January 25, 2011, www.sec.gov/news/press/2011/2011-25.htm.

66. Yonat Assayag and Russell Miller, "The Focus Is on Performance," NACD Directorship, April 20, 2011, www.directorship.com/say-on-pay-the-focus-is-on-performance/2/.

67. Robin Ferracone, "Early Takeaways from 'No' Votes on Say on Pay," April 6, 2011, http://blogs.forbes.com/robinferracone/2011/04/06/early-takeaways-from-no-votes-on-say-on-pay/.

68. Among the changes in compensation that Assayag and Miller note in their study, nearly forty companies eliminated excise tax gross-ups (whereby companies cover excise taxes for certain executives) from either existing or future arrangements; three companies reduced severance multiples for CEOs from three times cash compensation to two times cash compensation; and thirty-four companies adopted or enhanced clawback provisions, whereby firms can force executives to pay back some of their compensation because of wrongdoing. Shareholders also vote on the frequency of "say on pay" voting, from annually to every three years, and most companies' shareholders appear to prefer annual votes. See Assayag and Miller, "Focus Is on Performance."

Children's Situated Right to Work

Cristina L. H. Traina

ALTHOUGH "CHILD LABOR" IS UNIVERSALLY CONDEMNED, CHILD WORK
will be a feature of global life for the foreseeable future because many children
without adequate access to the requisites of human dignity must work to gain
them. With help from the recent work of John Wall, Mary M. Doyle Roche, Bonnie J. Miller-McLemore, and others, the author claims children's right to work
in Ethna Regan's sense, as an expression of a "situated universal." Rights on
this view are real but contingent. They are means to protect universal human
goods and vulnerabilities under attack in particular situations. In this case, a
situated right to work protects children's flourishing in a global culture still
shaped by liberal and capitalist institutions, even as it criticizes that culture's
injustices and exclusions.

Contemporary American theologians tend to discuss child work in one
of two modes.[1] We condemn "the worst forms of child labor"—forms
presumably found only across oceans—and demand that university
bookstores cease selling products made in sweatshops. We also decry the
leisure culture of American childrearing, debate whether education can stand
in for "work," and recommend that children be required to wash dishes, mow
the lawn, and take out the trash. Both modes of thinking have merit, but neither mode advances our awareness of or thinking about a global phenomenon that will be with us for the foreseeable future: children who work out of
economic necessity. We may prophetically decry their need to work, but the
long-term, happy goal of eliminating that need must not eclipse our more immediate, gritty responsibility to children now and in the near term. We need
to develop a robust ethical description of children as intentional social and
economic agents—as workers—and to articulate both their right to work and
their rights as workers in a way that protects their flourishing rather than invites their exploitation.[2]

The present essay does not accomplish all of these goals. Rather, it is a pre-
liminary experiment in articulating the ground of children's right to work with

the help of authors whose work on children has led them to criticize and re-formulate liberal visions of rights. I argue that as full persons participating in interdependent human society, children have a situated right to appropriate, meaningful work that precedes and grounds their right to protection from harmful work and to protection from exploitation. This right follows from the human right to work, which is itself a means to the universal ends of individ-ual and communal flourishing rather than an end in itself. In addition, I argue that contemporary Christian moral reflection contains ingredients that we need to articulate this argument sturdily, in particular to elaborate the place of rights in theological ethics. I do not—although we must—articulate political strate-gies or legislative language for enacting and protecting these rights. And I do not—although we must—apply this discussion to the burgeoning child labor movement, which both stakes out children's political and social agency and risks creating problematic expectations that vulnerable people can free themselves from exploitation.[3]

I begin by describing the problem. Then I note changes in the conversation about ethics and childhood in recent decades. Finally, I discuss contemporary authors who embrace these shifts and whose recent work on children, rights, or both converges in an extraordinary way. I highlight the recent work of John Wall, Ethna Regan, and Mary Margaret Doyle Roche, with support from David Jensen, Pamela Couture, Bonnie Miller-McLemore, and a child-focused strand of social science literature. These authors fill out the anthropological vision that helps us to describe the robust grounds and the limits of human rights that in-clude children, and they also help us to articulate the human vulnerabilities that are of particular concern for working children.

Working Children

Children have always worked, and children still work.[4] According to Human Rights Watch, at least seven hundred thousand children under age eighteen cur-rently work on American farms—either for hire or for their own families.[5] As recently as 2002, 90 percent of the world's domestic workers were girls between the ages of twelve and seventeen.[6] UNICEF data show that about 30 percent of African children, 12 percent of Asian children, and 10 percent of Latin American and Caribbean children aged five to fourteen engage in work de-manding enough to be considered harmful to them.[7] Keeping in mind that UNICEF considers household work harmful to children ages five to fourteen only when it reaches the threshold of twenty-eight hours per week, and ac-knowledging significant unpaid domestic labor below the "harm" threshold, un-der-the-radar odd jobs, and informal assistance to adults in their paid work, it quickly becomes clear that working children are more the rule than the exception in the contemporary world.

How should we think about the meaning of these statistics for children's concrete lives? Most children who work do so out of personal or family need. Like adults, children genuinely resent work that is dangerous, harmful, difficult, exceptionally tiring, coerced, or overly time-consuming.[8] Not surprisingly, high levels of child economic activity correlate with reduced levels of school attendance and with later illiteracy, a problem that also distresses many children.[9] Still, based on their ethnographic studies of working children, a growing number of researchers argue that many want to work despite these frankly acknowledged problems. Manfred Liebel and others show that beyond supplying necessities, work provides children a sense of pride, social identity, and accomplishment. Poor children are keenly aware of the substantial contributions they make to their families' support, or even simply to their own.[10] Better-off children like the independence that their supplemental incomes provide.[11]

These researchers do not accept children's enthusiasm for work uncritically. Nor do I. The backdrop for this essay is a conviction that sinfulness and injustice endure on the grand scale, limiting children's meaningful choices and wounding them spiritually as well as materially. I ask, what must we insist that children, as human beings and moral agents, be free to do even within this situation of exploitation and need? What rights do they have, especially within this enduring situation? Prophetic denunciation and political caution are appropriate and necessary, but I am holding them aside in order to hone the tools we employ for them.[12]

The Situation

For several important reasons, historical Christian ethics provides few direct resources for evaluating child work. First and most obviously, it was simply assumed that most children worked, in households or alongside parents if not directly for pay; this was not a question for great moral debate.[13] Second, the way in which adults in positions of social power see children and their work has changed. A century ago, Christian opponents of the Child Labor Amendment argued that it would erode parental—in fact, paternal—authority in the household, limiting fathers' God-given power to determine both their children's upbringing and the disposal of their children's labor. They assumed that children were weak, vulnerable nonagents whose labor was an asset their fathers employed in the course of fulfilling their paternal responsibility to provide for their families.[14] That vision rested on the authority of the father and a defensive stance toward the presumed evil moral influences of society and the state; society interacted with children through their parents, not directly.[15]

Now, children are considered full persons who should own their own bodies and their labor and who, despite their need for intimate care in families, have participation rights and make direct claims on society for education and protection. Politically, the jury is out on children's present agency and subjectivity, but at least all agree that society must invest in their future productivity, citizenship, and wisdom and must sometimes limit parental authority in order to accomplish these social objectives.[16]

Third, if children are full persons, not persons-in-the-making, then adult advocacy for them must arise from solidarity with them. This solidarity implies not just active dedication to their flourishing as adults see it but also collaboration with them in their ends and acknowledgment of their opinions and assessments. However, solidarity does not imply that adults should treat children exactly as they treat "everyone else." No one is "just like everyone else." Like everyone, children bear the vulnerabilities of their particular stages of life. They are physically and relationally vulnerable, and they have short histories and long futures. Consequently, as I argue further in the following, this solidarity cannot be uncritical. Critical solidarity privileges children's accounts without taking them at face value, and it is attentive to power dynamics of which children may be only vaguely aware, especially to forms of exploitation that prey on their particular vulnerabilities.[17] Of course, both of these points apply to adults too. We must be aware of the particular vulnerabilities of adults' situations, and they too deserve our critical solidarity. The point is that launching the moral argument from childhood rather than from classic, independent, adult male citizenship makes us more aware that vulnerability is not an exceptional situation that requires an exceptional response. It is a universal human characteristic that calls up a universal political and moral obligation.

Rights and Their Basis

Importantly, Ethna Regan, Mary Roche, and John Wall all begin methodologically with engagement and solidarity with children, and all end up transforming our anthropological and social vision by their radical inclusion of children.[18] All of these authors reject a "thin," formal, threshold definition of rights, in which rights simply name the minimal levels of protection, provision, and participation society owes all persons. In this thin vision, rights attach to individuals. Often presented without systematic connections, rights are individually debatable, appearing as lists of discrete elements that can be negotiated separately (think of the phrasing of the recent debates over the right of gays and lesbians to serve openly in the military).[19] Politically, this approach can make rights appear to be ends or goods in themselves and the declaration and protection of rights seem to be society's highest end. In addition, although exceptions extend rights to cover people deemed "irrational"—children, the elderly, the mentally incompetent—rights usually attach to rational pursuit of self-chosen goods. Reason—whether actual, potential, former, or waylaid—is the justification for the right.

The authors discussed in the following worry that liberal accounts of rights depend on an impoverished anthropology.[20] In place of a thin, rational, individualist vision of humanity, they install a holistic, interdependent anthropology. Human dignity includes rationality, certainly, but dignified people are also essentially social, embodied, and finite, living in a particular historical, physical location and in the continuum of their personal histories as well. Never actually autonomous, isolated agents, they depend for their well-being on ever-widening circles of other people working in concert to create the social, economic, political, and emotional systems of support that ground their freedom and flourishing. That is, everyone is embedded in and dependent on the common good.[21] Everyone is supremely, essentially vulnerable. As Roche reiterates, "vulnerability . . . and finitude are not contrary to dignity but are constitutive features of it."[22] Should human community exclude particular people, they will suffer in ways that contradict dignity. And they will suffer not just in an immediate sense, although hunger, lack of education, inadequate medical care, or lack of proper employment is certainly significant in the present. They will suffer as well in the long term because the stress of inadequate support will prevent them from developing their constructive, creative potential.[23] In addition, because they lack the protective cover of communal institutions and relationships, the "destructiveness of the world" will wreak havoc on them spiritually, stunting virtue.[24]

Their insistence on our essential vulnerability and interdependence distinguishes these authors in at least four further important ways. First, individual flourishing is not just about individual good, and individual harm is not just about individual suffering. The flip side of individual vulnerability is common vulnerability. The more individuals are stunted and diverted, the less they tend to contribute to the common good, and the more all suffer as a result of their absence; early damage in this respect magnifies the loss. Conversely, the more individuals are included in the common good, the more resources they can martial to overcome internal and external challenges, the more they tend to develop their gifts and contribute to the whole, the more the community benefits as a result.[25] The fortunes of all are linked; our concern for the goods of individuals has consequences for the good of all.

Second, true personal flourishing, as both Wall and Regan insist, is more than cultivating skills and living well in a material sense, undisturbed by others. It certainly includes these, as well as physical health, fulfillment, warm relationships, and a certain sense of security. Yet flourishing also involves a grateful awareness of interdependence, an outward focus, a "generosity of existence" that collaborates self-consciously with others for the common good.[26] True flourishing includes achieving "the more—virtue, self-transcendence, the good life, personal and communal well-being—to which human beings are called," individually and communally.[27]

This holistic, interdependent anthropology, with its transcendent ends and its taste for the details of real, historical situations, grounds a vision of rights that, while just as flexible as the "thin," liberal version caricatured earlier, is more coherent. Wall overcomes the individualist tone of liberal rights: individuals' claims on society are better thought of as society's obligations to individuals. "Human rights are social responsibilities in that they create the conditions necessary for responding through society to each other"; they are "social responsibilities to the human diversity of otherness."[28] Thus, rights imply a sharing of social power: everyone has "the right to be included in the creation of social relations."[29] Rights discourse ought to be about how to accomplish this inclusion.

Regan agrees that rights discourse seeks "the most effective means of protecting human dignity, challenging poverty and injustice, and ensuring that everyone is included within the potentiality of human flourishing."[30] But she adds that human rights discourse always emerges from real "conflict within a particular historical and geographical context"; in order to accomplish its ends, it "has found expression at different times" in different terms: for example, as "liberties, natural rights, and human rights."[31] Unlike the human goods it seeks to protect, then, rights discourse is pragmatic, provisional, and self-critical, not absolute. Rights discourse is most powerful when we recognize that rights, though real, are constructed in specific situations to accomplish universally applicable goods. They are not goals in themselves; rather they are ways to advance integral human ends.[32] As long as we accept that rights are robust means, then discourses of flourishing, rights, and beatitude are interdependent, not opposed.[33] As Regan argues,

> When children are denied food, shelter, safety, or education, it is not only a violation of human rights. The far deeper violation is that their capacity to flourish as human beings is impaired. When accompanied by the kinds of exploitation that the most vulnerable children experience, their ability to trust and give of themselves in relationships is profoundly, often irreparably, damaged. . . .
>
> The response to children in need is not primarily a response to them as "rights-bearers" but comes from the recognition of their inherent human dignity on which those rights are based. From a Christian perspective, it is a re-

sponse to the disfigurement of *Imago Dei* in the lives of children whose potential is damaged by poverty, exploitation, and violence.[34]

Third, Regan's refusal to absolutize rights discourse implies "situated universalism," which retains the critical power of universal transcendent dignity without imposing a single, universal formulation of human rights. Situated universalism respects the "idea of concrete subjectivity, that is, being a subject whose human nature is concretized in terms of particularities of race, gender, class, and culture, without allowing any dimension of that concreteness to undermine the inalienable dignity of the human person or limit that person's rights."[35] To accomplish their goals, in fact, rights will need to be expressed in different languages with varied emphases in different times and places. In this sense, we can also speak of situated rights. Shifting the focus from rights as absolute, universal ends to rights as situated means thus qualifies human rights discourse's univocal authority in political debate: the goal is to accomplish not the right but the good that the right protects. Precisely for this reason, situated rights should not displace or trump existing complementary discourses of provision, protection, or participation that may already be contributing to flourishing.[36] That is, the signal to develop or revisit rights discourse to cover children's work is that existing moral or political discourses do not seem to be doing the job of protecting the good of children.

Finally, perhaps the most important theological qualification is that although rights discourse is not merely a response to sin (its purpose is to protect the flourishing of embodied, social, developing human beings in all settings), it is especially necessary in the period between the already announcement of the reign of God and the not-yet of its fulfillment, the uneasy coexistence of the earthy and the heavenly city. It is precisely within this overlap of cities that theological engagement with human rights—with its positive discourse and alertness to the reality of violations—takes place. Human rights is a discourse for the provisional time, in the overlapping space of the intermediate realm; it is an effort to make the best city now possible, knowing that it is not a lasting city. Human rights, in this context, could be interpreted as a boundary discourse of *vera iustitia*.[37]

In sum, Wall and Regan think of rights as a necessary, self-critical, prophetic discourse for the in-between time that protects transcendent and concrete, individual and communal holistic flourishing from attack in particular historical circumstances. The flourishing that rights discourse advances includes the common good on a grand scale and the virtues of generosity and expansiveness at the personal level; the discourse depends also on the cultivation of well-being in the most holistic possible sense. Rights are not ends in themselves, but rights do protect and promote universal, interdependent human ends, both historically situated and transcendent. For these reasons theologians must engage rights discourse.

Child Work as a Situated Right

Regan's and Wall's visions of rights imply that articulating a right to work makes sense if work is a path to goods that human dignity and the common good demand, a path to the "more" to which we are called in a particular time and place in which sin somehow threatens and in which other discourses are not "doing the job." We are in such a moment of impoverished discourse, especially with respect to child work: grudging acceptance of the "nonworst forms" of child work as a "lesser evil" hardly provides consistent criteria for judging it. The distance between American arguments that children must be held to account at home and developing-world arguments against the worst forms of labor is profound and incoherent. And United Nations thresholds for unacceptable labor are arbitrary, insensitive to cultural location, and distressingly high.

To articulate situated rights, we must begin with dignity and the goods that acknowledge it. The situated universal goods that work might protect head off in several directions. First, in the contemporary world sustenance demands either productive or wage labor. For most adults, the basic requisites of human dignity—food, shelter, clothing—come through work.[38] The same dignity justifies claims for compensation when people cannot find work. But, second, work is not just a means of provision; an income is also a path to social and political participation and provides resources that can be used for protection.[39] The money workers earn is the entry fee for engaging contemporary capitalist society, including some resilience, if consumers are lucky, against injustices other people commit against them. It is possible to derive other rights from the vulnerabilities that beset everyone: for instance, the right to adequate wages; sick and personal leaves; injury compensation; medical and dental insurance; strikes; and transparent hiring, evaluation, and firing practices. Still other "situated" rights arise from vulnerabilities that are most likely to afflict adults, such as pensions, parental leaves, child care, and elder care. Without backup protections for these goods, workers are vulnerable to exploitation: workers do, because they must, take the available job at the offered wage, even if the job is demeaning or the wage is inadequate. This is why workers' intentional, purposeful acceptance of labor contracts is so often neither free nor just.

The situated rights I have outlined flow from the fact that in the world we inhabit we cannot exist at all without adequate wages from work, nor can the others who depend on our incomes. Ideally, work also provides a third sort of benefit without which dignified people cannot "be becomingly": opportunities to cultivate their skills, establish social and political identities, advance their virtue, and contribute to the household and the common good.[40] Work does not always accomplish all of these transcendent and relational goods (all people can think of jobs they have held that did not, or at least seemed not to at the time), but dignity implies that all have a right to do work that does not undermine them. At this level, adult vulnerabilities come in more inchoate forms. For example, typical adult anxieties about future security that play into employers' hands by discouraging the search for more humane, better paid, or more rewarding work might need to be answered by educational opportunities and universal portable pension plans.

Thus, subordinating worker rights to dignity provides not only strong arguments for a "situated" universal right to work but also some familiar criteria for that right: Work must not erode dignity or any of its own purposes. Exploitive contracts; slavery; violence; inadequate wages; dangerous, meaningless, demeaning, or destructive tasks; a demand for dishonesty or cruelty—each of these circumstances vitiates work. Given work's additional orientation to the good of households and the world, it also should not be a person's sole means of social identity and engagement. For instance, political and charitable activity are essential for social identity but are not normally part of "work," nor are time for intimate relationships, prayer and reflection, recreation, or rest—all constitutive parts of identity and vocation. Recognition of this fact is one reason why, for example, "workaholism" is actually unethical.

This triple portfolio of goods serving dignity—basic maintenance, interpersonal and communal relations, and transcendent ends—has long been applied to adults and used to claim that parents, usually fathers, have the natural right to meaningful work that sustains their families. Living wage movements right up to the present, the failed Child Labor Amendment, and other efforts have relied on these goods.[41] How can these goods be used to make a case for children's work?

If children are full persons and participants in society, then their goods are simply human goods, and work is one means of achieving them. The cases for relational and transcendent goods from work are easiest. As Bonnie Miller-McLemore and Roche argue, work must never be thought of as a way to earn a dignified place in society or family; a dignified life is a right.[42] Yet overemphasis on children's vulnerability and innate dignity and desert can lead us to underestimate their potential to contribute to the common good.[43] Citing the unjust, indirect dependence of developed-world children on children who labor elsewhere, both authors counter that even children are obliged to recognize, and to respond with creativity and dignity to, the common projects of family and communal life.[44] Miller-McLemore also points out the unjust dependence of well-off children on parental, especially maternal, labor.[45] As members of the human community, children are called to active solidarity with others through work, if on a smaller scale than adults.

In addition, work can provide opportunities for self-expression, perfection of skills, generosity, social identity, participation, and, if paid, some independence even for children. Children cite meaning, pride, autonomy, and accomplishment as benefits of work. Social science researchers increasingly recognize children's decisions about work, even in highly constrained situations, as moments of real, carefully considered self-definition and self-disposal.[46]

The question of basic, physical maintenance is more sensitive because arguing that children have a right to wages that will sustain them runs a political risk: it seems to relieve society of its obligations to children. Yet if children truly are full, vulnerable, interdependent, dignified persons, then their needs for sustenance are just as pressing as adults' needs. If they lack familial and social supports, their right to wage or productive work is just as strong.[47] But children's right to provide for themselves (should others not be doing so) does not reduce society's or parents' obligations toward them. Regan's subordination of rights to dignity ensures that this right, though real, is "situated," not abstract. That is, children's right to work for self-support is not a primary right; it is a contingent right, based in their right to a dignified life. When adults and society fail to provide the goods that universal dignity requires, children have a right to work for them, and, for the reason of situated dignity alone, no one has the right to exploit children's work.

Working Children's Special Vulnerabilities

Scholars writing in support of children's full social participation, including work, are not laissez-faire industrialists. Rather, they recognize that a robust, situated account of children's rights, qualified by dignity, logically entails systematic consideration of the vulnerabilities that can vitiate the goods that any activity is supposed to support. As Wall writes, that we should each be treated "as a full member of the human circle" does not mean "that everyone's rights should be exactly the same."[48] Working children need protection from the vulnerabilities peculiar to them as children so that their work will continue to advance the deeper ends their dignity requires.

A huge proportion of children's particular vulnerabilities are tied to the fact that they have short histories and long futures. On account of their short histories, they have little experience of social relationships and little exposure to the ways institutions function on the large scale. Presented with potential work and wage information, they encounter the person who may hire them; however, they have no idea of the systems and institutions operating unseen or of real alternatives to the tasks and wages offered. They are easily manipulated.[49] In addition, although certainly all people's futures are vulnerable to their presents, children's futures are especially so: their presents need extra protection.[50] Not only do their futures comprise most of their lives, but to a greater degree than for adults, trauma, deficits, and harms suffered in childhood can be impossible to overcome in children's later, longer futures. When children's work endangers health, prevents education, erodes play, or isolates, their futures are disrespected. Thus children are endangered—by employers, by families, and even by themselves—more than adults are when they "spend" their futures for short-term gain.[51] Human interdependency multiplies the losses to children's futures, which reverberate throughout families and societies across the globe.

Contemporary theologies of childhood also note children's ability to focus on the present. For example, Jensen celebrates, a bit wistfully, children's virtuous "present-orientation," their ability to become completely absorbed in what is occurring at the moment.[52] This focus suggests not only that children's futures are more vulnerable proportionately than adults', but children's particular virtue of attentiveness, with its necessarily short-term interests, distracts them from cultivating and protecting their futures wisely. The same goes for children's admirable capacity for fantasy and imagination, which exposes them to adult deception.[53] Both leave children open to harm now, and their futures and ours open to harm later.

Pamela Couture notes two further, related vulnerabilities: economic poverty and the poverty of "tenuous connections."[54] The first makes children vulnerable to exploitation in the same way as adults. If they are desperate, children must accept the wages or in-kind payments supplied, whether or not these are adequate. But their small size, political marginality, and lack of experience give them fewer resources to combat this injustice. The second exacerbates the first. Children need stable, reliable relationships with others, especially adults. Without them, they lack the assets they need to navigate even a relatively privileged life, let alone a challenging one. For this reason Kenyan theologian John Manzi and Ugandan theologian Deusdedit Nkurunziza argue that if children work, they must work alongside caring adults who will initiate them into social customs, help them to recognize justice, demonstrate how to respond to injustice, and model free decisions.[55] Without such support, children will be drawn into work that not only is harmful in the near term but also deprives them of the knowledge they need to function constructively in society.

Finally, children are legally and socially vulnerable. Although children's labor movements are one hopeful sign of change, in general children are without leverage unless adults choose to defend their rights or, even better, to establish these rights systematically. As Liebel points out, the evils of direct harm to children and criminality on the parts of employers, both of which deserve condemnation in their own right, must be distinguished from exploitive power relations that, in themselves, equally deny children's dignity. In many cases working children are suffering no real harm, and supervising adults are not guilty of gross immorality or criminality, and yet there is "an unequal social relationship . . . in which one side obtains economic [and qualitative] advantages at the expense of the other side by means of its greater power, and perhaps also by the use of violence. The essence of this situation is that one side becomes the object of the other side."[56] Consequently, exploitation and harm begin to be described as a problem of the object, in other words, child workers, rather than as a problem of the political and economic system.[57] The real difficulty, as Liebel and all the other authors I have cited argue, is that "the system" is designed for protection of the liberties of supposedly autonomous, savvy, independent adults rather than for radical inclusion of universally but differently vulnerable, interdependent persons of all ages.

Here is the final politically uncomfortable implication of children's situated, universal right to work that preserves their current and future dignity. This right includes more than fair wages and access to health care, education, and other requisites of a good life. It also includes the right to freedom from systematic exploitation. Thus, to honor children's dignity as full persons and as workers, society must systematically accommodate children's political and social vulnerabilities, not just their economic vulnerabilities. For Roche and for Liebel and his colleagues, this right includes paths for children to participate in decisions about their own welfare, including work.[58] Child labor organizations are working to establish these rights de facto in many parts of the world, but de jure changes such as lowering the voting age are also worth consideration.

Rights as Means

Paradoxically, this approach seems to apply liberal remedies to a situation in which I have just argued they do not apply, or at least not very well. This discomfort returns us to the pragmatic role of rights discourse. Children's rights discourse serves human dignity and holiness in a situation of mutual interdependence and vulnerability, but it does so by building a fence around human dignity at a concrete historical moment, against the pests that most threaten to despoil dignity at that place and time. In one case, it may do so by establishing children's voting rights; in another, by setting minimum wages and maximum hours; in a third, by paying children to attend school.

This piecemeal approach is dissatisfying, but it is meant to be. Ethna Regan's work implies that, as a strategic discourse, the language of children's work rights should not encompass every human good that theology or even solid political philosophy embraces.[59] Enumerations of rights are temporal, provisional, and partial, rather than absolute. Thus, like all rights discourses, children's rights discourse assumes and must be accompanied by comprehensive companion discourses of dignity and flourishing, such as theology, that articulate the goods that rights are meant to protect.

To argue for rights effectively, then, companion discourses must maintain a critical distance from them. Theologians cannot rest on their laurels when new labor laws are passed or international charters such as the United Nations Convention on the Rights of the Child are formulated. Nor, however, should they be dismayed by these documents. For even successful children's rights discourses will be either regrettably minimalistic and universal or dissatisfyingly local and provisional; they will be interpreted or applied inconsistently; and they will go out of date. These characteristics of rights language explain most of the difficulties of formulating, ratifying, and applying international documents like the United Nations Convention on the Rights of the Child. Theology and other comprehensive discourses of human flourishing can supply critical leverage to update rights discourse when circumstances require elaboration or transformed situations demand changes. This critical distance permits theology to embrace rights pragmatically without fear of the reductionism that is implied when rights are portrayed as comprehensive, absolute descriptions of persons. For instance, the uninterpreted claim that children have a right to work is an invitation to exploitation in a world that apparently needs no inducement to take advantage of their labor. Theology articulates this right conditionally, insisting that children's situated, conditional right to employment is grounded in and must honor children's vulnerabilities and interdependence. The right is derivative, not absolute, and it exists for the good of children, not their employers.

Situated rights are especially helpful for capturing the tension between long-term justice and children's pressing near-term need. In the case of child work, a robust situated rights discourse prophetically condemns social and economic conditions that force children to work to support themselves, but it also reveres working children as they make their way in these hostile circumstances. It condemns a world in which labor is the primary path to virtue, social participation, friendship, and fulfillment for persons of any age, yet it honors children's pleasure in their meaningful work. It announces a future reign of justice, but it protects the current dignity of those in exile.

Notes

1. I have chosen the term "work" to include paid work, materially productive unpaid work, and domestic labor that contributes to the well-being of a household.

2. This call for a bridge discourse echoes Mary M. Doyle Roche, *Children, Consumerism, and the Common Good* (Lanham, MD: Lexington Books, 2009), 20.

3. John Wall worries that applying straight liberationist models of solidarity to childhood will backfire because children's inherent, particular vulnerabilities make it difficult for them to gain power without assistance; Wall, *Ethics in Light of Childhood* (Washington, DC: Georgetown University Press, 2010),120. But this is true for any genuinely marginalized group.

4. As numerous recent histories testify, different societies and periods have conceived of the period we now call "childhood" variously, and critical analysis of the relationships between

these conceptions and the realities of young people is a crucial element in the history of work. In this essay, by children, I mean very simply the chronologically young; I articulate only a partial, critical anthropology of childhood.

5. Human Rights Watch, *Fields of Peril: Child Agricultural Labor in the United States* (New York: Human Rights Watch, 2010), 16–17, www.hrw.org/node/90126. The report makes clear that this is a conservative estimate.

6. UNICEF, "The State of the World's Children, 2002: Leadership" (New York: UNICEF, 2002), 52, www.unicef.org/sowc02/pdf/sowc2002-eng-full.pdf. The 2011 report acknowledges the decline of the worst forms of child labor but retains this statistic. See "The State of the World's Children 2011: Adolescence; An Age of Opportunity" (New York: UNICEF, 2011), 33, www.unicef.org/publications/files/SOWC_2011_Main_Report_EN _02242011.pdf.

7. Nigeria and China are excepted from the statistics. UNICEF has a graded definition for unacceptable levels of labor: ages five to eleven, one hour economic or twenty-eight hours domestic labor; ages twelve to fourteen, fourteen hours economic or twenty-eight hours domestic labor; ages fifteen to seventeen, forty-three hours of either. See UNICEF Childinfo pages, www.childinfo.org/labour_challenge.html.

8. See, for example, the interviews in Human Rights Watch, *Fields of Peril*, 1–4; and UNICEF, "The State of the World's Children, 2002," 72.

9. Federico Blanco Allais and Fred Hagemann, "Child Labour and Education: Evidence from SIMPOC Surveys" (Geneva: International Labour Organization, 2008), working paper, www.ilo.org/ipecinfo/product/download.do?type=document&id=8390.

10. Children's domestic and subsistence labor contributes significantly to family welfare by providing services that might otherwise need to be purchased or in some cases done without (e.g., child care, fuel and water gathering, sewing) or by freeing parents from these tasks to take on productive or economic labor. See Sarah Rollings-Magnusson, *Heavy Burdens on Small Shoulders: The Labour of Pioneer Children on the Canadian Prairies* (Edmonton: University of Alberta Press, 2009), especially 1–17.

11. See, for example, Thomas A. Offit, *Conquistadores de la Calle: Child Street Laborers in Guatemala City* (Austin: University of Texas, 2008); Manfred Liebel, *A Will of Their Own: Cross-Cultural Perspectives on Working Children* (London: Zed Books, 2004); and Beatrice Hungerland, Manfried Liebel, Brian Milne, and Anne Wihstutz, eds., *Working to Be Someone: Child Focused Research and Practice with Working Children* (London: Jessica Kingsley, 2007). These works are representative of a larger social science literature that takes children seriously as social subjects and actors.

12. For detailed treatment of sin's effect on children, see, for example, David Jensen, *Graced Vulnerability: A Theology of Childhood*, foreword by Bonnie Miller-McLemore (Cleveland: Pilgrim Press, 2005).

13. Demonstrating this point would require another essay or even a book. But moral literature, orphanage histories, histories of childhood, apprenticeship law, and other sources collude to suggest that the debates largely concerned the amount and type of work and the beneficiaries of children's earnings. That children should work and needed to do so were not in question.

14. Catholic critics feared that the Child Labor Amendment would set a precedent of government control of children under eighteen, supplying a foundation for state control of education that could eliminate parochial schools and curtail religious freedom. See Vincent A. McQuade, OSA, "The American Catholic Attitude on Child Labor since 1891: A Study of the Formation and Development of a Catholic Attitude on a Specific Social Question" (dissertation, Catholic University of America, 1938), especially 80–88. See also

William Cardinal O'Connell, "Pastoral Letter on the Laborer's Rights" (November 23, 1912), in *The Church and Labor*, ed. John A. Ryan and Joseph Husslein, SJ, 177–86 (New York: Macmillan, 1920), 178. "Progressive" living wage arguments were likewise based on the father's right and responsibility to provide for his family.

15. Orphaned and lower-class children have often been exceptions, expected to care and fend for themselves to a degree.

16. The burden of this essay is that children are not simply "future persons." But the "future persons" argument gives children more status than some alternatives. Respect for children as full persons is not a new idea, but its appearance in American social policy and in globally influential documents like the United Nations Convention on the Rights of the Child is recent (see Preamble, page 1, http://www2.ohchr.org/english/law/pdf/crc.pdf). It has been a subtheme for centuries in the West, helping to govern, for instance, child custody and apprenticeship in the Eastern colonies. See Mary Anne Mason, *From Fathers' Property to Children's Rights: The History of Child Custody in the United States* (New York: Columbia University Press, 1994), 1–47. See Wall, *Ethics in Light of Childhood*, for a succinct discussion of the implications of historical and current Western notions of rights for children's agency (114–20).

17. See Liebel, *Will of Their Own*, 8–12. Solidarity with children must ground critical inquiry—for example, into children's possible objections to the limitations placed on them by their own societies.

18. Regan's book is inspired by the need to take adequate account of the experiences of the street children of Port of Spain, Trinidad. Ethna Regan, *Theology and the Boundary Discourse of Human Rights* (Washington, DC: Georgetown University Press. 2010), 1.

19. Manfred Liebel makes this complaint in *Will of Their Own*, 195–96.

20. See for instance Roche, *Children, Consumerism, and the Common Good*, 83–84.

21. See Roche's succinct definition of the common good: "the sum total of the conditions of social living whereby individuals and communities achieve their perfection, their flourishing, more easily" (ibid., 89). This is a central concept for Regan as well. John Wall, David Jensen, and Bonnie J. Miller-McLemore use the language of common good rarely or not at all, but their elaborate attention to interdependent human community yields similar content; see Bonnie J. Miller-McLemore, "Children, Chores, and Vocation: A Social and Theological Lesson," in *The Vocation of the Child*, Religion, Marriage, and Family Series, ed. Patrick McKinley Brennan, 295–323, (Grand Rapids: Eerdmans, 2008); Wall, *Ethics in Light of Childhood*; and Jensen, *Graced Vulnerability*, especially ch. 2.

22. Roche, *Children, Consumerism, and the Common Good*, 88; see also 9, 129–30.

23. Wall, *Ethics in Light of Childhood*, ch. 4; Regan, *Theology*, 69. Note that Wall's theoretical discussions focus more on ethical anthropology and meaning-making than on the implications of deprivation for individual and communal flourishing.

24. Wall, *Ethics in Light of Childhood*, 24.

25. Ibid., 133. A person who, despite access to the common good, chooses not to contribute will also harm the common good.

26. Regan, *Theology*, 15; and Wall, *Ethics in Light of Childhood*, 92–110.

27. Regan, *Theology*, 217–18.

28. Wall, *Ethics in Light of Childhood*, 131, 138.

29. Ibid., 135.

30. Regan, *Theology*, 16.

31. Ibid., 8.

32. Ibid., 47.

33. Ibid., 215–16.

34. Ibid., 216; see also Jensen, *Graced Vulnerability*, 96–97.

35. Ibid., 11.

36. Ibid., 12. "Participation" is my addition.

37. Ibid., 5.

38. As Thomas Aquinas says, "whatever is a means of preserving human life, and of warding off its obstacles, belongs to the natural law." Thomas Aquinas, *Summa theologica*, tr. Fathers of the English Dominican Province (1948; repr. Westminster, MD: Library of Christian Classics, 1981), I-II, Q. 94 a. 2).

39. See Roche, *Children, Consumerism, and the Common Good*, 105–31, for critical discussions of children's participation in consumer society.

40. Aquinas, *Summa theologica*, II-II q. 141.6. Thanks to Jean Porter for this reference.

41. See John A. Ryan, "Introduction," in *The Church and Labor*, ed. John A. Ryan and Joseph Husslein, SJ, v–xvii (New York: Macmillan, 1920); and O'Connell, "Pastoral Letter."

42. Miller-McLemore, "Children, Chores, and Vocation," 323; and Roche, *Children, Consumerism, and the Common Good*, 92–93.

43. Miller-McLemore, "Children, Chores, and Vocation," 312–14; Roche, *Children, Consumerism, and the Common Good*, 82–83.

44. Miller-McLemore, "Children, Chores, and Vocation," 302–3, 322–23; and Roche, *Children, Consumerism, and the Common Good*, 120, 129–30.

45. Miller-McLemore, "Children, Chores, and Vocation," 300–301.

46. See for instance Antonella Invernizzi, "Children's Work as 'Participation': Thoughts on Ethnographic Data in Lima and the Algarve," in *Working to Be Someone: Child Focused Research and Practice with Working Children*, ed. Beatrice Hungerland, Manfried Liebel, Brian Milne, and Anne Wihstutz, 135–44 (London: Jessica Kingsley, 2007), especially 137.

47. Here I assume that also that children's moral agency and accountability does not reduce others' concurrent accountability for the situations children are in and the choices they must make. See Cristina Traina, "Children and Moral Agency," *JSCE* 29, no. 2 (2009): 19–37.

48. Wall, *Ethics in Light of Childhood*, 132.

49. This is not to say they do not learn quickly. In situations where survival requires hustle, even fairly young children become savvy.

50. This does not mean that children are not yet full persons; it means that children are full persons whose long futures deserve respect, just as the elderly are full persons whose long pasts deserve respect. See Jensen, *Graced Vulnerability*, 43.

51. *Fields of Peril* reports one mother saying, "I tell my daughter, 'I'm so sorry I stole your childhood from you'" (Human Rights Watch, *Fields of Peril*, 23).

52. Jensen, *Graced Vulnerability*, 53, 36–37.

53. Ibid., 36–37, 59.

54. Pamela Couture, *Seeing Children, Seeing God: A Practical Theology of Children and Poverty* (Nashville: Abingdon Press, 2000).

55. John Kizito Manzi, "Theology of Human Work in Reference to Child Labour in Africa," *African Ecclesiastical Review* 46, no. 2 (2004): 102–20, especially 106–9, 115; and Deusdedit

R. K. Nkurunziza, "African Theology of Childhood in Relation to Child Labour," *African Ecclesiastical Review* 46 no. 2 (2004): 121–38, especially 133.

56. Liebel, *Will of Their Own*, 199.

57. Ibid., 198. Liebel in particular is frustrated by the International Labour Organization's (ILO) simultaneous acceptance of unpaid child labor within family businesses and homes and rejection of paid child work. This is a double standard. The ILO unjustly devalues and overlooks some children's work, allowing their families to benefit from free labor, but forbids other children to assist themselves or their families through paid work, perhaps at their own initiative. See 196–97, for example.

58. Roche, *Children, Consumerism, and the Common Good*, 105–7; Liebel, *Will of Their Own*, ch. 8; and nearly all the essays in Hungerland, et al., eds., *Working to Be Someone*.

59. Regan, *Theology*, 7–14.

Book Reviews

Review of
Peace to War: Shifting Allegiances in the Assemblies of God
PAUL ALEXANDER
Scottdale, Pa.: Herald Press, 2009. 432 pp. $24.54.

Who Would Jesus Kill? War, Peace, and the Christian Tradition
MARK J. ALLMAN
Winona, Minn.: St. Mary's Press, 2008. 325 pp. $27.95.

The morality of war is high on the agenda of various traditions of Christian moral reflection, as the two books under discussion demonstrate. In *Peace to War* Paul Alexander provides a well-documented account of that Pentecostal community's shift from pacifism to an uncritical endorsement of American militarism. In *Who Would Jesus Kill?* Mark J. Allman presents a synthetic analysis of dominant strands of Christian moral discourse on war.

Alexander's work contributes to the study of moral reflection within the Assemblies of God and the larger Pentecostal movement. He writes that he was shocked when, as a seminary-educated adult, he learned that his denomination had declared itself officially pacifist in 1917. It was only in 1967 that the Assemblies of God affirmed the authority of individual conscience on participation in warfare, thus repudiating the earlier pacifist stance. Nonetheless, the fifty years of official pacifism has been largely forgotten among American Pentecostals and is surely unknown in other circles.

Alexander shows that, from its origins in early twentieth-century America, Pentecostalism was a movement that largely eschewed violence, being "crucifist" in the sense of stressing the necessity of taking up one's cross and dying to self and the world in obedience to Jesus Christ (3). During World War I, the Assemblies of God supported conscientious objectors and were in solidarity with other pacifists. There are several points of similarity between the Pentecostal and Quaker objections to war, and Alexander demonstrates the direct influence of the American holiness movement (with its Wesleyan roots) on the pacifism of the Assemblies of God.

The author describes Pentecostalism as a movement originally of people of low socioeconomic standing with little desire for harmony with the larger culture. Over time, however, the movement became embarrassed by the social alienation resulting from its pacifist stance. During World War II, the Church emphasized evangelizing soldiers and gave less attention to its official repudiation of participation in combat. Alexander identifies this development as a "shift from a disenfranchised and marginalized social position to mainstream civil religion" (201). There were few Assemblies of God conscientious objectors in World War II, but up to sixty-five thousand "members served in the military either as combatants or noncombatants" (201).

By 1967, in the midst of Vietnam and the social upheaval of the period, the Assemblies of God adopted an official statement that stressed loyalty to the government and "the right of each member" to become a "combatant, a noncombatant, or a conscientious objector" (237). Alexander sees no serious theological or moral argumentation behind this shift away from pacifism; it was a reflection of the denomination's desire to identify with American evangelism and secular culture. In recent decades, Assemblies of God publications and statements have been very promilitary, often portraying military service as a virtuous, desirable occupation for Christians. Support for pacifism is now apparently quite rare in the denomination, as is opposition to the wars in Iraq and Afghanistan.

Alexander concludes that the ethic of the Assemblies of God "has shifted from appeals to Jesus to a norm in line with politically conservative or fundamentalist teachings that support a nationalistic American agenda" (336). In contrast, he calls for the Church to return to a genuinely "crucifistic" praxis that restores the nonviolent peace witness of the New Testament church (338). He argues convincingly that such a standard fits more coherently with the spiritual heritage of Pentecostalism than does the uncritical affirmation of nationalism and militarism. This volume is an excellent piece of scholarship that sheds light on a largely unexplored topic and provides substantial bibliographical resources that will be of great help to other scholars of the history and thought of American Pentecostalism.

Allman's *Who Would Jesus Kill?* is a clearly presented textbook, ideal for use in college or seminary classes. After providing a helpful overview of major methods and issues in Christian ethics, he devotes chapters to pacifism, holy war, just war theory, and contemporary challenges to the just war tradition. He concludes with a brief articulation of his own stance followed by an appendix on Jewish and Muslim teaching on warfare. Chapters include discussion questions, illustrations, outlines, summaries, and sources for further study. The author is obviously an experienced teacher who understands students' habits of thought, reading, and discussion. Quotations from primary texts are short, definitions are clear, and there are many prompts for readers to engage the material critically and personally.

For an introductory text of such broad scope, Allman is impressively precise and thorough in his analysis of salient issues and methods. For example, the chapter on pacifism is informed by accurate descriptions of figures and themes ranging from Justin Martyr to contemporary Catholic social teaching and the "Responsibility to Protect" vulnerable populations, as recently advocated by the United Nations. The chapter on holy war addresses not only the Crusades but also the Thirty Years' War, the French Revolution, and post-9/11 America. Likewise, the author traces the development of just war theory from its classical origins through its various contemporary interpretations. Of particular interest is his lucid analysis of the US Council of Catholic Bishops' apparent affirmation of both the just war standards and pacifism in *The Challenge of Peace*, as well as the virtual pacifism of those who define the criteria of just war so strictly that they are practically impossible to meet.

Allman examines the challenges for just war theory raised by the advocates of preemptive war, especially in the "War on Terror." He describes the moral complexities involved in resisting terrorists and possessing weapons of mass destruction in ways that demonstrate the practical, contemporary relevance of moral discourse about war in an ever-changing world. Likewise, the author's treatment of just peacemaking and postwar justice encourages readers to discern the moral significance of actions before and after a conflict, not simply during the war itself. In this way, he challenges readers to adopt a dynamic perspective on the causes, conduct, and consequences of armed conflict.

Allman concludes that he is "a contemporary just war theorist with a strong affinity for just peacemaking" (265). He resonates with Augustine and Reinhold Niebuhr on the moral brokenness of political institutions and, like them, will not abandon the victims of injustice to their attackers. At the same time, Allman recognizes the tension between that conclusion and the peaceable witness of Jesus Christ. Although one could ask for fuller elaboration of what that conclusion means, the book succeeds admirably as a clear, accessible, and thorough textbook.

The works of Alexander and Allman are both excellent contributions to scholarship on the morality of Christian participation in warfare. *Peace to War* documents a radical change of direction in Pentecostal thinking on pacifism. It is an impressive piece that presents the unknown history of a socially marginalized Christian group as they accommodated to mainstream culture and adjusted their ethical stance accordingly. *Who Would Jesus Kill?* introduces a broad readership to moral discourse on war and peace and challenges them to work through the complexities of the issues at stake fairly and in an informed way. Taken together, they witness to the liveliness and diversity of Christian thinking about the morality of war.

Philip LeMasters
McMurry University

Review of

Rediscovering the Natural Law in Reformed Theological Ethics

STEPHEN J. GRABILL
Grand Rapids, Mich.: Eerdmans, 2006. 310 pp. $38.00.

God's Joust, God's Justice: Law and Religion in the Western Tradition

JOHN WITTE JR.
Grand Rapids, Mich.: Eerdmans, 2006. 498 pp. $32.00.

Intractable Disputes about the Natural Law: Alasdair MacIntyre and Critics

EDITED BY LAWRENCE CUNNINGHAM
South Bend, Ind.: University of Notre Dame Press, 2009. 392 pp. $50.00 cloth, $30.00 paper.

Published in the last five years by Christian scholars of different confessional backgrounds, these three worthwhile books deal with the topics of law (in particular, natural law) and religion. They illustrate a new range of questions occupying Catholic and Protestant thinkers that were not on their radar screens a generation ago.

The first, by Calvin scholar Stephen J. Grabill, aims to contribute to a rediscovery and rehabilitation of natural law reasoning within Reformation scholarship. The author lays responsibility for the widespread antipathy to natural law reasoning in twentieth-century Protestant theology at the feet of Karl Barth, whose radical epistemological skepticism with respect to the human capacity for natural knowledge exercised enormous influence over more than a half century of Reformed scholarship. Barth's rendering of the doctrine of total depravity leaves human nature incapable of being addressed by God through the natural world. Natural lawyers, Barth thought, ignore the radical darkening effects of sin on human reason and rely on an unbiblical account of the operations of nature unaided by grace. Barth attributes this dim view of reasoning to Calvin who, he argues, is singularly committed to an all-inclusive divine command account of the origins of ethical norms.

Grabill persuasively argues that that when Calvin is read in conjunction with other significant Protestant thinkers of the sixteenth and seventeenth centuries, not only is Barth's apodictic pessimism found wanting, but distinct—albeit modest—theoretical rudiments can be found upon which to build an account of natural law consistent with Reformed theology. Grabill also confronts the common claim that the Reformer's divine command morality was hostile to all appeals to concepts such as nature, self-evident first principles, and right reason, and that it was a thoroughgoing voluntarism, painting God as an all-powerful but ultimately arbitrary legislator. This view's origins are located in late medieval nominalism (especially Scotus and Occam), which was undeniably influential in the development of Reformation ethics. Grabill argues, *pace* Barth, that neither Protestant divine command thinking nor late medieval nominalism was strictly voluntaristic. A distinction lost on many contemporary commentators between God's absolute power (*potentia absoluta*) and his ordained power (*potentia ordinata*) allowed nominalist theorists to ground moral normativity remotely in God's will (something Aquinas also did) and to affirm its proximate ground in a moral order, naturally knowable and universally binding.

The book supports its thesis with three chapter-length considerations of influential authors, several of whom, the author complains, have been largely ignored in modern Reformation scholarship. He divides his consideration into three periods within the development of Reformed theology: (1) the "Reformation period" (Peter Martyr Vermigli, 1499–1562; John Calvin, 1509 64); (2) "early orthodoxy" (Jerome Zanchi, 1516–90; Johannes Althusius, 1557–1638); and (3) "high orthodoxy" (Francis Turretin, 1623–87). The writings examined in these chapters illustrate that natural law tradition was received by Reformed scholars of the sixteenth and seventeenth centuries as a "noncontroversial legacy of late medieval scholasticism" (175). These and other dominant voices in the early Reformed tradition believed and argued that human reason, albeit weakened by sin, was still capable of apprehending general principles of the natural law.

Academic texts, analogous to the academics who write them, are marked by virtues and vices. Most texts express a multitude of facts; few are truly erudite, and even fewer reflect the virtue of wisdom. Professor Witte's *God's Joust, God's Justice* is one of those rare texts marked by all three. The book's unifying theme is the relationship between the developing religious tradition in the West and its corresponding legal tradition. It walks the reader briskly from ancient Rome to modern America, tarrying at the Gregorian reforms of law and culture in the late eleventh century, the Reformation dissolution of a unified Christendom (and unified legal landscape) in the sixteenth century, and the religious ideas influencing the political accomplishments of America's founding fathers in the eighteenth century.

The author provides an excellent treatment of the tortured term "rights"—from its classical antecedents in the Roman law concept of *ius* to the birth and proliferation of subjective rights in the modern period. Six of the book's fifteen chapters are dedicated to an extended conversation on the goods and goals of marriage, beginning with Augustine's notion that marriage is a complex social, contractual, and religious association characterized by three fundamental *boni* (the goods of procreation, *bonum proles*; spousal fidelity, *bonum fidei*; and indissoluble bond, *bonum sacramenti*) and ending with the peculiarly modern conception of marriage as an arrangement among consenting adults. The Western tradition, Witte cautions, shows us that because marriage is more than an arrangement between individuals, a scion of the institutional church, or a social unit of civil society but rather a combination of all three, it must be conceived and addressed from these multiple perspectives if all the competing goods upon which it bears are to be adequately respected.

The book's highlight is its discussion of the competing conceptions of religious liberty of Thomas Jefferson ("wall of separation between church and State") and John Adams ("mild and equitable establishment of religion") and its nuanced argument that a balance between the two is needed for a healthy democracy.

Intractable Disputes about the Natural Law, edited by Lawrence S. Cunningham, professor of theology at the University of Notre Dame, is a response to a request made to the president of Notre Dame in 2004 by Joseph Cardinal Ratzinger, then prefect of the Congregation for the Doctrine of the Faith, asking the university to address the problem of contemporary moral disagreement in regard to the question of the existence and content of foundational moral principles. Alasdair MacIntyre was charged with providing a lead essay to which eight academics (six from Notre Dame) offer replies. MacIntyre then concludes the book with a response to the replies.

The lengthy lead essay addresses philosophical problems underlying moral disagreements between people who are presumed to be equally "intelligent, perceptive, and insightful." Natural law theory traditionally proposes that foundational ethical principles are rationally accessible and that once apprehended they are or should be assented to by all rational agents. And yet what we find today is wide-scale disagreement not only at the level of practical norms but also over the question of the plausibility of the concept of natural law itself. MacIntyre sets for himself the ambitious aim of explaining how the precepts of the natural law—closely following Aquinas's account of practical rationality—can be at once accessible to all rational agents and yet unpersuasive to many of those same agents.

Accessible, of course, does not mean rationally compelling, and MacIntyre flatly denies that Thomists can draw upon resources internal to their account to refute the conclusions of their opponents in such a way as to ensure rational assent from those who are being rational. And yet MacIntyre unapologetically defends the thesis that we (humans) can "recognize the authority of the precepts of the natural law" by the use of our rational powers alone, without appeal to divine revelation.

What then is the source of the failure to secure agreement on common moral principles? It stems, he says, from "a variety of failures in practical rationality" on the part of those who reject the basic precepts of the natural law. He provides a sketch of what one of those failures looks like by criticizing the concept of happiness employed by utilitarians. He argues that the concept itself is unintelligible detached from some determinate notion of an end being achieved, happiness being the state of achieving that end. In jettisoning a substantive account of natures and ends, utilitarians are left with a concept of happiness as no more than a psychological state—the feeling of pleasure. But this is too indeterminate to do the work that utilitarians need it to do in their moral theory. Their failure to recognize this deficiency is a failure in practical rationality.

MacIntyre's lead essay is persuasive both in its assessment of the problem of moral disagreement and in its tentative construction of a way forward. I highly recommend it to readers who are interested either in the problems it addresses or simply in MacIntyre's moral philosophy. With notable exceptions, I cannot say the same of the response essays. One exception is Gerald McKenny's interesting examination of Joseph Ratzinger's belief that the natural law, while in principle universal, may no longer be capable of persuading as it once did because of the loss in the West of a unified Christian worldview. Another exception is Kevin Flannery's essay, which shows how Aristotle—the intrepid defender of a determinate concept of the "good life"—clearly thinks that securing practical assent to a rightful account of the *summum bonum* from those who believe it resides in a life of pleasure, riches, or honor is no easy task; deficient conceptions of the good life are not immediately refutable, even when juxtaposed to a cogent rendering of the best way of life. Finally, Thomas Hibbs's examination of Aristotle's moral virtues as appropriated in the moral theory of Aquinas will repay a careful reading.

E. Christian Brugger
Saint John Vianney Theological
Seminary

Review of
Ethics: A Complete Method for Moral Choice

DANIEL C. MAGUIRE
Minneapolis: Fortress, 2010. 320 pp. $35.00.

Daniel Maguire describes *Ethics: A Complete Method for Moral Choice* as an amplification of his earlier textbook *The Moral Choice* (1978). Full of new material, it articulates the method Maguire has developed over a long, illustrious career. Maguire defines ethics initially as "the study of what is good or bad for people and for the rest of nature" (4). But his aim is less to define flourishing than to describe the critical, self-critical process of comprehensive ethical reflection, "the art/science that seeks to bring sensitivity and method to the discernment of moral values" (67, 322).

To this end, four convictions guide Maguire's writing. First, moral reasoning is not dryly analytical but engaged and practical, rooted in the "foundational moral experience" (30), an affective mode of knowing. Second, "whatsoever is true" is fair game for moral reflection. Maguire cites wisdom from all corners of the globe. He also presents—and draws upon the central insights of—classical moral theories like consequentialism, utilitarianism, deontology, relativism, virtue theory, and objectivism, as well as classical theories of justice. The third is "question the question." He demands that we uncover the preconceptions that have determined terms, questions, questioners, and conditions, invisibly shaping moral solutions, and he refuses to accept the authority of any single moral theory. Fourth, humility, integrity, and comprehensiveness, not definitive agreement, characterize good ethical reflection. Honest minds must expect to reach different conclusions on some questions. Throughout, his own trademark opinions are clear, but so is his conviction that his own method provides ample tools for contrary arguments.

Maguire arranges the book inductively. Parts 1 and 2 wrestle with the character of moral truth, emerging with both methodological baselines (ethics as a marriage of affective art and rational science) and practical measures (varieties of justice). Parts 3 and 4 comprise the core of the book. Part 3 introduces the "wheel" of moral discernment, Maguire's model for the process of ethical reflection. Definitional questions occupy the hub: What? Why? How? Who? When? Where? Foreseeable effects? Viable alternatives? Maguire provides tools for deconstructing the obvious answers to these questions, including (among others) means–ends relations, the distinction between volition and velleity, double effect, and the search for creative alternatives. Apparently archaic distinctions acquire freshness and relevance in Maguire's lively, accessible treatment. Part 4 describes the interactions of the spokes, the complementary modes of thought good moral reflection employs. Framed by conscience, they include affectivity, principles, reason and analysis, creative imagination, tragedy (suffering), comedy (humor), authority, and individual and group experience. Natural and social scientific measures of what is good for humans and the earth receive no separate treatment but could easily become a tenth spoke or be incorporated in the existing nine.

Part 5 describes the epistemological dangers of ideologies, reigning myths, abstraction, false analogies, and reductionism. Religious traditions' susceptibilities to these faults are acknowledged, but Maguire emphasizes their history of and potential for creative, subversive, and liberating contributions.

Other important features of the book include varied, provocative suggestions for further reading at the end of each chapter; thoughtful questions for discussion; and highlighted quotations by moral writers of diverse periods and traditions. Plentiful footnotes are rich resources for student papers. A glossary defines some of the terms highlighted in the text. The Fortress Press website provides sample short cases, a guide to teaching, and brief videos.

Ethics is an excellent text for undergraduate ethics courses in both religious and secular institutions. It begs to be paired with a good casebook or with current news items of the instructor's choosing. It also provides a robust critical framework for graduate ethics courses.

Cristina L. H. Traina
Northwestern University

Review of
Moral Dilemmas: An Introduction to
Christian Ethics

J. PHILIP WOGAMAN
Louisville, Ky.: Westminster John Knox Press, 2009. 176 pp. $19.95.

Aristotle warned that lack of experience can impede the study of ethics. Philip Wogaman's *Moral Dilemmas* demonstrates, conversely, that experience and wisdom can contribute enormously to its teaching. Drawing on many years as a professor, pastor, and scholar, Wogaman has written a book wonderfully suitable for multiple audiences.

Not all moral decisions are problematic, but some surely are, and it is the genuine dilemmas that are Wogaman's focus. To address them requires treatment of "the deep basis of the moral life" (the title of chapter 2). This leads to discussions of the religious basis for ethics, acceptable and unacceptable forms of revelation, the authority of the Bible, the importance of virtue and character, and, drawing heavily on H. Richard Niebuhr, "the absolute and relative in moral life" (chapter 3).

Such topics deserve readers' close attention. Here I will focus on the controlling ideas for *Moral Dilemmas*. These emerge when Wogaman turns to the analogy of law and develops the related notions of "presumption" and "burden of proof." So central to the book is this twofold idea that *Moral Dilemmas* could easily have been titled "Moral Presumptions." For Wogaman, the Christian moral vision bears its own presumptions: *for* such things as grace, equality, and the goodness of creation; *against* self-interest and claims to moral perfection. The Christian vision also requires a balance of presumption when it comes to sin vs. human goodness, free will versus determinism, and optimism versus pessimism.

Presumption and burden of proof provide a heuristic framework for addressing ethical dilemmas ranging from sexual intimacy to affirmative action to global warming—and much in between, including war. Wogaman expertly takes up issue after issue, many of which he has addressed elsewhere, and indicates where the presumptions lie, who is faced with the burden of proof to overturn those presumptions, and—sometimes in great detail (for example, in the case of divorce)—what that burden might entail.

Wogaman does not claim definitive solutions to the dilemmas, and the book invites further ecumenical and interreligious discussion. Let me suggest three of several possible discussion points. First, while this book may resonate more with a Protestant audience than a Catholic audience, it will surely benefit the latter. But more sustained attention to the casuistry that has marked (and at times plagued) Catholic moral theology would be fruitful. Old debates about probabilism, for instance, clearly pertain to Wogaman's central concerns. Second, and related to this, should the language of presumptions ever give way, if only rarely, to the language of absolute moral norms? Wogaman's framework will indeed help good-willed people negotiate moral dilemmas. But recalling Blaise Pascal's critique of casuistry in the *Provincial Letters*, might facility with the language of presumptions sometimes also facilitate rationalization in moral decision making? Third, perhaps the language of presumption, if more widely shared, could counter the ultrapartisan, concede-nothing political discourse that often reigns today. But if we are to make progress here, it will be helpful to explore further both the origins of moral presumptions and the dynamics of shifting presumptions. For example, should an increasingly robust presumption in favor of future generations, advocated by Wogaman, shift the moral presumption for life in the case of abortion? More generally, when it comes to reordering individual and societal presumptions, what exactly is the role of moral and religious conversion, and how does this conversion occur?

Good ethics is a matter of questioning our assumptions. In convincing, clear, and remarkably detailed fashion, Wogaman shows readers—which I hope are many—why and how good ethics is most certainly a matter of questioning our presumptions as well.

William P. George
Dominican University

Review of

An Ethics of Biodiversity: Christianity, Ecology, and the Variety of Life

KEVIN J. O'BRIEN
Washington, D.C.: Georgetown University Press, 2010. 240 pp. $26.95.

The achievement of *An Ethics of Biodiversity* lies in its thoughtful engagement with ecological sciences to inform a Christian ethic of biodiversity. Of course, Christian ecological ethicists always use scientific data to describe ecological challenges and prepare theological responses to them. Less often have they first backed up a step, appreciating the choices scientific ecologists make in framing their own analysis of biodiversity as well as the benefits and costs of these choices. Kevin O'Brien considers different scalar perspectives in which ecologists define and analyze biodiversity. Decisions about scalar perspective determine how much of the "variety of life" is viewed and in what level of detail. These choices in turn condition what O'Brien calls our "moral attention" to biodiversity. Drawing on the resources of Catholic sacramental theology and social teaching, O'Brien develops a Christian ethic of biodiversity capable of multiscalar moral attention to the variety of life. *An Ethics of Biodiversity* is therefore an excellent model of moral reasoning and theological reflection in interdisciplinary space. O'Brien's facility with a number of disciplinary languages makes the book an important resource for a wide-ranging audience. That the book is clear and accessible makes it especially appropriate for the uninformed and the newly initiated in the field of Christian ecological ethics.

The five parts of the book address five corresponding questions: What is biodiversity, why does it matter, and how should we pay attention to it? What roles do political policy and moral formation play in responding to biodiversity? And what is the relationship between biodiversity, human diversity, and social justice? In the book's first three parts, O'Brien's strategy is twofold. First, he shows that perspective matters in the way ecologists answer these questions: framings are purposefully chosen, and different framings produce analytical variety. Thus, we learn that the "broad" and "precise" ways in which ecologists define biodiversity reflect different analytical priorities; that the different values scientists, politicians, and economists assign to the variety of life often compete with one another; and that the decisions ecologists and conservationists must make about the scale of their research (on the genetic, species, or ecosystemic levels) and conservation efforts (on the local, community-oriented, or global levels) unavoidably limit their moral attention. Second, O'Brien offers a theological response to these questions, which he takes to both complement and critically engage the analyses of ecological science. For O'Brien, the variety of life has a sacramental quality that points to the irreducible goodness of God's creation, the glory of God, and the mystery of God's work in creation that always transcends human knowing. The sacramentality of creation therefore underwrites an ethic of conservation that requires multiscalar moral attention to biodiversity as the best way to respond to God's creative activity.

Part four argues that both political policy and moral formation are mutually necessary for the protection of biodiversity. In part five O'Brien complicates his case for biodiversity. In conversation with James Cone, Leonardo Boff, and Ivone Gebara, he explores the variety of life as it pertains to marginalized human populations who bear asymmetrically the burdens of ecological degradation and global responses to it.

The scope of this book is comprehensive, and the double edge of this ambitious approach is that some parts of the argument are underdeveloped. For example, O'Brien's sacramental ethics nicely captures the moral value of biodiversity. But when it comes to the inherent violence, "consumption," and "predation" of nature, O'Brien hastens to the mystery of God. The trouble with mystery is that it makes it difficult to know what we ought to be conserving exactly. Of course, a comprehensive ethic of conservation is not possible. But other ethicists have accounted for natural processes by offering finer distinctions between the moral obligations we owe to natural and human communities. This kind of move might have been useful given O'Brien's scalar concern, and particularly helpful in his discussion of social justice in part five of the book. But on the whole, this book has much to teach, and it will be instructive for conservationists, scientific ecologists, policy advocates, clergy, laypersons, theologians, and philosophers alike.

John E. Senior
Wake Forest University School of
Divinity

Review of
Boundaries: A Casebook in Environmental Ethics, 2nd ed.

CHRISTINE E. GUDORF AND JAMES E. HUCHINGSON
Washington, D.C.: Georgetown University Press, 2010. 328 pp. $29.95.

Environmental ethics is a relatively new specialty in ethics that involves determining the duties and responsibilities humans have to animals and the broader ecosystem that sustains life on this planet. Interest in environmental ethics is clearly on the rise. One need only consider the growing concern about environmental degradation and the increasing debate over humanity's use of animals to recognize the need for a deeper and sustained conversation about these (and other) important environmental topics.

Christine Gudorf and James Huchingson's *Boundaries* facilitates that deeper conversation through the use of case studies designed to force readers to consider the principles used to guide environmental decisions as well as the costs of those decisions. The authors masterfully combine clear and thorough writing with heuristic methods to engage readers and facilitate comprehension of the material.

The book's fifteen chapters are organized into four parts. Part 1, containing only two chapters, provides readers with a superb introduction to the variety of theories as well as the challenge of individual rights and public consequences that lie at the heart of many environmental debates. I suggest that the survey of ideas contained in chapter 1 is worth the price of the book on its own. The remaining three parts organize each of the chapters under one of the three key challenges in environmental ethics: (1) how to protect the environment; (2) how to restore a broken environment; and (3) how to manipulate the environment to resolve pressing problems.

Each chapter contains a case study on a thorny environmental issue followed by commentary, discussion questions, and suggestions for further reading. The case studies consist of a fictitious conversation between various individuals representing different positions and points of view. The authors endeavor to portray each of the positions equally, accurately, and without rancor or prejudice. While the conversations are fictitious, the discussions are so believable that readers may forget that they are not portrayals of actual events or conversations. At first, I found the authors' employment of realistic fiction awkward. But further reading led me to think that this approach allows the opposing viewpoints to be humanized and thereby helps students avoid simplistic and arbitrary decisions.

The commentaries provide background evidence regarding the claims made in the case study as well as identify moral issues and principles useful in guiding the decision-making process. For the most part, the authors avoid interjecting their own views, but they do show their bias against anthropocentric views on occasion. Teachers will find the review questions to be very useful in supporting deeper reflection and dialogue among the students.

Although suitable for any high school–level reader interested in learning more about environmental ethics, this book is especially useful for college courses. Busy professors will appreciate the book's organization as well as the useful teaching tips in the appendix. Anyone interested in reviewing the complex and multifaceted field of environmental ethics will find this text exceedingly helpful.

Stephen M. Vantassel
King's Evangelical Divinity School

Review of
Doing Justice in Our Cities: Lessons in Public Policy from America's Heartland

WARREN R. COPELAND
Louisville, Ky.: Westminster/John Knox Press, 2009. 176 pp. $19.95.

Doing Justice in Our Cities provides a special opportunity to examine the ethical decision-making process of a city commissioner and mayor. Warren

Copeland was appointed as the city commissioner of Springfield, Ohio, in 1988. He was later elected to continue his service as a commissioner and then as Springfield's mayor. What makes Copeland's book even more unique is that he is also a professor of religion and director of urban studies at Wittenberg University. Public service enabled Copeland to apply his expertise in social ethics to Springfield's problems.

Copeland's book is a very good basic primer for citizens, public servants, and religious leaders concerned with enacting their faith as they work to influence the course of public life. Copeland divides the book into three parts beginning with the story of how he became a politician. In the first section of the book he also includes a detailed description of Springfield's demographics. Springfield is a typical Midwestern city in the United States and, as a typical city, struggles to effectively combat problems experienced in most American cities: crime, drug abuse, poverty, job loss, urban sprawl, competing visions for the city's future, and so on. Copeland draws upon the work of expert and consultant on urban policy David Rusk and sociologist William Julius Wilson in his analysis of the promise and problems of Springfield. Copeland and other members of the faculty at Wittenberg University worked with Rusk to study Springfield. Their study of the city underscored the importance of Springfield's "elasticity" and "concentration of poverty."

Copeland focuses on ethical and theological reflection in the second part of the book. He presents an illuminating summary of four ethical perspectives (competitive, populist, pluralist, and planned) that surfaced in public debates while he served on the city commission. Moreover, he describes how each perspective offers a different and sometimes competing vision for the city's well-being. Two additional chapters in this section explore the relevance of biblical stories about the prodigal son and the good Samaritan for justice work in American cities and emphasize freedom and diversity as principles upon which just cities can be based. For Copeland, diversity and freedom are essential to expressing one's full humanity in concrete human communities. Real diversity is evidenced in cities that make available many avenues for individuals to develop their own unique abilities and to use those abilities to contribute meaningfully to the common good. Diversity "requires social justice" and facilitates interchange among different groups of people.

Concrete strategies for creating and sustaining diverse cities are outlined in the third part of the book. Access to good, family-sustaining employment, adequate amenities, and affordable housing are the "Three A's for Creating Diverse Cities." Adequate space, good schools, and safety are keys to preserving a diverse urban environment. Copeland's final chapter, "Catching the Spirit of Public Life," expresses his belief that throughout his service as a commissioner and as mayor he witnessed faith in action when difficult and sometimes compromising decisions were made about the most just course of action for the city to take.

One limitation of the book is the unevenness of the theological reflection; Copeland could go into much greater theological depth. However, what *Doing Justice in Our Cities* lacks in theological reflection is made up for with practical and creative advice for concerned citizens, politically engaged religious leaders, and public servants. The book is a very good case study for individual reflection or for ethics classes in colleges and seminaries.

Elizabeth Hinson-Hasty
Bellarmine University

Review of
Family Ethics: Practices for Christians
JULIE HANLON RUBIO
Washington, D.C.: Georgetown University Press, 2010. 272 pp. $29.95.

In this book, Julie Hanlon Rubio offers a family ethic that reflects both personal and social concerns. In this she joins other recent Catholic writers on the family, such as Lisa Sowle Cahill or Florence Caffrey Bourg; this book is distinctive in its attention to "practices" as the locus for the integration of the personal and social. Throughout, Rubio argues for the moral importance of the "ordinary," the cumulative impact of innumerable daily choices. She offers her own approach as an alternative to "reformist" approaches that advocate policy and structural changes and "radical" approaches that call on Christians to live in sharp contrast to the mainstream society. In her view, the former pays too little attention to the importance of individual and grassroots efforts to bring about social change, and few Christians can meet the heroic standards imposed by the latter. Instead, drawing from both models, Rubio encourages Christians to habituate themselves to moderate but significant changes in five daily practices grounded in family life: sex, eating, tithing (interpreted broadly as curtailment of consumer spending in order to devote resources to the needy), service, and prayer.

In part 1, Rubio mines resources from the Catholic tradition for her family ethic. Chapter 1 draws on the contemporary Catholic marriage liturgy, scripture, and sacramental theology to emphasize both personal and social dimensions of marriage. Chapter 2 analyzes the historical development of Catholic social teaching, attending to the place of the family in key documents. Rubio focuses on the important role of "intermediary groups" in Catholic social thought and considers the family to be one such group. A particularly original chapter 3 investigates the literature of Flannery O'Connor as a resource for family ethics. O'Connor emphasizes the in-breaking of grace in the face of sin and imperfection; Rubio considers this a helpful corrective to an overly idealized and perfectionist approach to the family.

Part 2 consists of five chapters, each focused on a "practice of resistance" (as listed earlier). Rubio proposes moderate yet difficult changes, for example, reducing consumption of beef and dairy products. Throughout, Rubio offers fresh approaches to certain well-trodden subjects in Christian ethics. Rubio's elucidation of married sex as a "practice of resistance" makes an original contribution to sexual ethics. Likewise, in her chapter on prayer, Rubio emphasizes the prevalence of interfaith families and the differing level of religious commitment within most Catholic families. We must take account of such realities and work through them as the grist for a realistic, "ordinary," yet transformative family ethic.

My primary point of discomfort with the book is an overly sharp opposition between family life and political change, a division that seems at odds with Rubio's overall purpose of offering an integrated personal and social family ethic. Though she rightly notes that middle-class families should resist some cultural norms about the use of time and resources, she gives little attention to the ways in which public policies and economic structures affect families and their ability to engage in the practices she proposes. Thus, Rubio emphasizes the integration of the personal and the social within the family itself, but she does not highlight the dialectical nature of political change and the formation of Christian families in their personal and social missions.

This book would be accessible and useful to both undergraduates and graduate students. It could be used as a framework for a course in family ethics; the chapters lend themselves to being read alongside key texts in historical theology, sacramental theology, and Catholic social thought with respect to the family.

Sandra Sullivan-Dunbar
Loyola University Chicago

Review of
God, Science, Sex, Gender: An Interdisciplinary Approach to Christian Ethics

EDITED BY PATRICIA BEATTIE JUNG AND AANA MARIE
VIGEN WITH JOHN ANDERSON
Urbana: University of Illinois Press, 2010. $30.00.

God, Science, Sex, Gender is the result of several interdisciplinary symposia on human sexuality convened at Loyola University, Chicago in 2007. The goal for this collection of papers, the editors say, is to "foster explorations into what, if anything, reflection on information from evolutionary biology along with other disciplines might contribute to a faithful Christian account of human sexual diversity" (9). At stake are Church teaching and its relationship to science over "what is" and "what ought to be" concerning human sexuality.

The volume is arranged into three parts: (1) establishing base points for dialogue; (2) reflecting on human sexual diversity; and (3) examining sexual diversity and Christian moral theology. The introduction reminds the reader that human nature—both biological and moral—is contested space where philosophical disputes, the nature of terms and their meanings, and the weight of authorities as they struggle for normative influence must be given their place. The five essays of part 1 analyze the nature of the relationship between religion and science from the perspective of the Church. Part 2 provides (in six essays) a survey of the diversity of human sexuality from the point of view of evolutionary biology, theology, and social analysis through literature. In the last section, five essays look forward to the implications that the previous chapters offer for rethinking norms for human sexuality.

Several chapters stand out for a rethinking of a theology of sex and gender. Joan Roughgarden, a Christian evolutionary biologist, proposes an alternative scientific narrative of sex roles, one that replaces Darwin's theory of sexual selection with a theory of social selection. In her essay, "Evolutionary Biology and Sexual Diversity," she maintains that relationship systems, not mating systems, account for evolutionary change and reproductive fitness. Reproductive success is renarrated through social networks rather than sexual competition. Although her chapter is replete with the technical language of her discipline, it remains accessible to the novice biologist and moral theologian alike.

John McCarthy looks at the norm of the exclusive male–female gender binary in recent Catholic creation hermeneutics. In "Binary Gender in Catholic Thought," he suggests that the theology of procreation found in Catholic teaching returns to a theology of creation grounded in gift rather than order. With an ontological emphasis on order, Catholic teaching relegates the "betweenness" found in the primary binary of the first chapter of Genesis—that of "created" and "uncreated"—to a "no man's land" (153). Yet it is precisely in this space that Catholic teaching locates the incarnation, grace, and salvation. Eschatology, he argues, repositions the hermeneutics of gender toward hospitality.

In summary, *God, Science, Sex, Gender* addresses with clarity a collective dissatisfaction in contemporary scholarship with the status of Catholic teaching on human sexuality. In response, the essays of the volume successfully expand the tradition's resources to include science and social analysis, thus reinforcing the inductive methodology articulated in the book's introductory objectives. Overall, the historical, theological, and socioaesthetic explorations of these essays are as fresh as the scientific theory they seek to compliment. Conversely, these theological arguments underrepresent Catholics sympathetic with the encyclical tradition concerning sexuality, celibacy, marriage, and the natural law tradition of creational and moral order. The absence of these voices is inconsistent with the goal of interdisciplinary dialogue over messy issues of sex. Nonetheless, the editors do give serious attention to the teachings of John XXIII, Paul VI, John Paul II, and Benedict XVI, and the binary ontology found in natural law and Catholic biblical hermeneutics.

Andrew Watts
Belmont University

Review of

Heterosexism in Contemporary World Religion: Problem and Prospect

EDITED BY MARVIN M. ELLISON AND JUDITH PLASKOW
Cleveland, Ohio: Pilgrim Press, 2007. 232 pp. $25.00.

Out of the Shadows, into the Light: Christianity and Homosexuality

EDITED BY MIGUEL A. DE LA TORRE
St. Louis, Mo.: Chalice Press, 2009. 192 pp. $19.99.

Reasoning Together: A Conversation on Homosexuality

TED GRIMSRUD AND MARK THIESSEN NATION, WITH A
FOREWORD BY TONY AND PEGGY CAMPOLO
Scottdale, Pa.: Herald Press, 2008. 240 pp. $17.99.

Most straight Christians see room for moral disagreement on the matter of homosexuality and therefore find it plausible to cultivate restraint in judgment and respect for adversaries in the fullness of their divergent views. Immune to the harm that received teachings have done to the LGBTQ (lesbian, gay, bisexual, transgendered, queer) community, straights have the psychological, and perhaps logical, space to approach the subject as a matter of long-term conflict resolution. But those who experience harm do not see room for legitimate moral disagreement; they see only violence—sometimes, though less often than in the past, actual physical and verbal attack but also insidious, silent, and persistent violence in Paul Ricoeur's broad sense of "the diminishment or the destruction of the power-to-do of others" (*Oneself as Another* [University of Chicago, 1995], 220). In dozens of ways that straights usually do not even recognize, LGBTQ Christians experience the violation of the respect they are owed. From this point of view, it may well seem disingenuous at best to talk about respectful dialogue because the violation of dignity precedes and inheres in the framework of the conversation and, indeed, infects not only the very subject the discussants endeavor to take up but also the status accorded the participants in the "dialogue."

These three books originated in different settings that have influenced their shape, tone, and aspirations. For purposes of assessment, it matters whether one considers them as a contribution to the project of civil and respectful dialogue on a moral issue that in fact requires further discernment or attends to them as reclaiming declarations from the dispossessed, rising out of the reality of this peculiar, often unrecognized, deceptively polite violence. I will examine the books against both backgrounds, beginning with dialogue because two of the books very specifically identify encouraging respectful conversation as their aim.

Reasoning Together has been developed from a set of public "conversations" between Ted Grimsrud and Mark Thiessen Nation at Eastern Mennonite University. In the spring of 2006 the two faculty members were asked "to participate in a series of public conversations that would voice some of the different opinions related to these issues" (16). The book, which expands these conversations, is offered in the hope that "by persevering in our conversation we have at least provided a model for Christians trying to find their way through this oh-so-difficult terrain" (17).

Reasoning Together offers a vigorous, sometimes biting, and entirely unresolved argument between friends within a religious community, and it can be gathered into the genre of carefully balanced considerations of both sides of the argument, which we have seen in such treatments as *Homosexuality and the Bible: Two Views* (by Dan O. Via and Robert A. J. Gagnon; Fortress, 2003), *Homosexuality in the Church: Both Sides of the Debate* (Jeffrey S. Siker, ed; Westminster John Knox,1994), *Stumbling toward a Genuine Conversation on Homosexuality* (Michael A. King, ed.; Cascadia, 2007; which includes essays by both Grimsrud and Nation), the ethnographic *God, Sex, and Politics: Homosexuality and Everyday Theologies* (Dawne Moon; University of Chicago, 2004), and the volumes on human sexuality and on gender in the "Taking Sides" series offered by McGraw Hill. *Reasoning Together* differs from these other volumes in that it offers a sustained, interactive dialogue with ample opportunity for each participant to question and to respond to the other. Their dialogue, though framed within the Mennonite tradition, is by no means insular. The exchange is rich and revealing as the two bring a great deal of clarity to matters of biblical interpretation, the right understanding and proper place of both hospitality and compassion in the Christian life, the nature of sin and of righteousness, the temptations of "cheap grace," and the sort of structures of mutual constraint that are appropriate among Christians in a fallen world. Despite concessions that each makes to the other and notwithstanding the final chapter identifying "common ground," the authors arrive where they began: at the familiar impasse. It is not clear, then, what notable theological or hermeneutical contribution the book actually makes to resolving the "problem." Recognizing this, the authors offer the book primarily as a practical model for clarifying moral disputes and maintaining friendship despite disagreement.

Out of the Shadows collects seven presentations (by gay, lesbian, and straight speakers) originally delivered at a 2007 conference designed to foster respectful conversation among lay Christians and to create "a network of support for clergy and lay leaders as they continue to deal with gender, equality, and justice issues within their own communities" (vii). The last chapter, "The Church in Action Asking Hard Questions," by James R. Oraker and Janis Hahn, gives an account of the "U-Process of Social Change" (diagrammed on page 134) and the way in which it was used to structure the conference.

There is, to my ear, a certain dissonance between the stated intention of *Out of the Shadows* (and the conference that preceded it) and the stance of several of the authors. A commitment to dialogue is foregrounded and the organizational principles of the conference were reportedly designed "to minimize any political agenda," "spotlight people gathering for dialogue," and emphasize "personal stories rather than theories and/or concepts" (122–23). The ground rules for the conference were, apparently, "no fixing, no saving, no advising, and no setting each other straight" (125). But in the first essay Marvin Ellison writes, "As a gay man and a Christian ethicist, my interest is not tolerance, inclusion, or even acceptance . . . but rather *transformation*, a dismantling of hierarchical social power and of the patriarchal conceptual framework that legitimates gender and sexual oppression" (7). Those guilty of oppression have "skewed notions," employ a "norm-deviant paradigm," and must repent. He wants to "[shift] the problem from homosexuality to heterosexism" (11). It is hard, then, not to wonder whether in the interest of creating a "safe space" for LGBTQ Christians to share their stories, we must necessarily create a very unsafe space for traditionalist Christians to share theirs—certainly traditionalists in my own church body (ELCA) often feel that that is exactly what has happened. In another essay, Irene Monroe lifts up "our common goal" as "creating a multicultural society and a participatory democracy so that no one is left behind, and every voice is lifted up" (56), but she enumerates quite a few voices who are not welcome in her participatory democracy (Christian Right organizations, those guilty of "homophobia, transphobia, sexism, classism, and other oppressions together" [56]). The diversity that is wanted is diversity within the domain of the morally correct. It is hard for me to see how these positions differ, structurally speaking, from the mirroring position that finds truth exclusively in the heterosexual norm and regards LGBTQ sexual activity as a serious sin that needs to be repented. Neither position seems conducive to conversation—respectful or otherwise. Moreover, strictly from the point of view of dialogue, it would seem to be a deficiency of this book that no stories are included from Christians who support traditional teachings.

Heterosexism in Contemporary World Religion signals by its title that for these authors the moral question has been settled, and what is needed is rapid change, not further discernment. Daniel Maguire opens the introduction with the widely quoted assertion that "homosexuality is not a problem: heterosexism is a problem, and not just for sexual minorities." He goes on to remark that "homophobia has, in irony, been called 'the last respectable prejudice,' but, of course, no prejudice merits respect" (1). He identifies religions as "major offenders in fomenting prejudice against sexual minorities" (1) and offers the book as a "remedy" (11). This book is not, then, a contribution to respectful dialogue. Rather, it brings us those voices of protest rising in concert from multiple religious traditions and undertaking constructive work within those traditions from their distinctive social location on the demographic margin. Although not all eight authors belong to sexual minorities, what is most interesting about the book is the kind of work, focus, and insight engendered by their identification with the LGBTQ community.

Although I lack space to consider all of the contributions individually, let me mention a few. Judith Plaskow, in the exploration of Judaism, lifts up "rabbinic discussions of gender variance" (17) and "hermaphroditic disruptions" (22) as an opening that invites and can potentially contribute to contemporary rethinking of "the connection between body and gender" (33) and the regnant cultural assumptions concerning gender dimorphism. Ann-Marie Hsiung examines the Confucian and Taoist traditions historically in order to highlight the differences between premodern Chinese gender culture, with its fluidity and "broad tolerance for variety of sexual relations" (103), and the attitudes that came to dominance with Westernization and the early twentieth-century New Culture movement that rejected Confucianism. This opens, she suggests, the possibility that "reconnecting" to the religious resources of Confucianism and Taoism might actually "offer support to contemporary *tongzhi* and facilitate a change of mind-set and public policy" (134). Ghazala Anwar's treatment of the situation of LGBTQ persons in Islamic contexts begins with same-sex couples in Jakarta and is "undertaken with the hope of reforming and extending Muslim family ethics and law" (71). This essay comes closer than any other in the volume to exploring the need for respectful dialogue (an instance of which she reports). Anwar rests a lot of weight on "the well-established precept . . . that has guided enlightened discussions and debates . . . that 'diversity of opinion within [the scholars of] the Muslim community is a mercy from God' because it gives options and brings ease into the lives of the diverse members of the *unmah*" (70). It is therefore both instructive and poignant that, at about the same time this book was published, she was dismissed from her position at the International Islamic University in Islamabad—by all reports, essentially for her views concerning sexual minorities.

Returning to *Out of the Shadows* after reading *Heterosexism*, one sees that this book, too, may be best approached not in terms of its stated purpose but in terms of what can be learned from voices of protest, especially what can be learned from them about where they themselves find life-sustaining hope. From Luis Leon's story of Cesar Chavez, we learn of a man who developed a strong personal identity in opposition to gender norms and a compelling and transformative Catholic social movement "that did not tolerate intolerance" (97). Although Mona West's primary purpose is to enable LGBTQ Christians to overcome their fear of the Bible, so often used as a weapon against them, so that they can "*trust the formative power of scripture*" (84, italic original), all readers may learn from her what it means to allow scripture to bring us to communion rather than deploying it to protect or enhance personal or collective power.

Reasoning Together also takes on a different cast when viewed against a background of pain and dispossession. It is a dialogue between straights about that which is conceived as "other" (notwithstanding the awareness of both contributors that it is acutely important not to turn the "other" into an object). It does not envision the "reasoning together" that might take place if straight and LGBTQ Christians (or Christians of the full range of genders) were to respect one another enough to talk constructively together, as full equals, about the future of our theology or the requirements of our sexual ethics.

D. M. Yeager
Georgetown University

Review of
Hunger and Happiness: Feeding the Hungry, Nourishing Our Souls

L. SHANNON JUNG
Minneapolis: Augsburg Fortress, 2009. 160 pp. $15.99.

With *Hunger and Happiness*, Shannon Jung offers the third volume of his trilogy on food. In this brief book, he approaches hunger and food systems through the lens of spirituality. He addresses the affluent and middle classes, arguing that our culture of excessive consumption comes at the expense of others whose labor, health, and environment are appropriated for our enjoyment. Benefiting from food systems that ensure cheap and abundant meals, the affluent are complicit (often unwittingly) in the hunger of others. Jung argues that this complicity engenders spiritual discontent—a malaise that can be transformed only when one attends to the hunger of others. He offers inspiration and practical steps for that journey.

Jung draws from three fields of study—theology and ethics, food systems, and sociological research on happiness. The book is accessibly written at an introductory level that is appropriate for church groups. Each chapter is a self-contained unit for discussion. The first four chapters address specific aspects of "cheap food" systems, identifying their detrimental impact on rich and poor alike. Each chapter then turns to sociological and theological resources to consider the spiritual hunger that accompanies complicity. Jung offers possible remedies and asks further questions at the close of each chapter. Chapters 5 and 6 delve more deeply into the psychology and theology of well-being and provide concrete suggestions for transformation and action. The book's structure is a bit disjointed, requiring the reader to keep jumping back and forth between food, happiness, and theology, but these last two chapters help tie things together.

Substantively, Jung addresses the food production systems that yield abundant, inexpensive, and sometimes unhealthy food. Brief vignettes identify hidden costs associated with industrial farming including dangerous working conditions, oil-dependent fertilizers and transportation, environmental degradation, poor nutrition, obesity and ill-health, global inequities, declining rural communities, and expensive government subsidies that enrich agribusiness while encouraging production of grains instead of fruits and vegetables. In Jung's sweeping survey, some issues are developed quite well, but others suffer from oversimplification.

Jung argues that we who benefit from these food production systems are complicit in the harm they cause. Our personal and corporate decisions hurt others and diminish ourselves. The theme of the interconnectedness of life runs consistently through this book as Jung connects the personal, social, economic, and political. He grounds this theme in his theological reflections, which are among the strongest parts of the book. For Jung, relationality both informs his analysis and reveals the solutions. Developing a call to action, Jung appropriates notions of God's desire for the flourishing of creation, Kathryn Tanner's gift-giving economy of God, and the classical themes of the *imago dei* and the imitation of God's sharing.

Closing with practical suggestions for the reader, Jung reminds us of God's abundant creation in which the earth provides adequate resources for all. Hunger is not inevitable; it thrives only as long as we permit it. For Jung, taking concrete steps to end hunger is central to addressing not only the physical hunger of the poor but also the spiritual hunger of the affluent. Lest the reader fear, as I initially did, that Jung might use antihunger work as a tool for the happiness of the wealthy, rest assured. He emphasizes giving and acting not so the donor can assuage guilt or feel virtuous but rather because the dignity of all compels it. That the donor (or the ethical eater) receives spiritual nourishment is a by-product.

This book is especially timely given the resurgence of hunger in our day and the growing interest in the ethics of eating. Jung adds an important dimension as he ties these realities to our spiritual nourishment.

Nancy Arnison
University of Chicago

Review of
Living Well and Dying Faithfully

EDITED BY JOHN SWINTON AND RICHARD PAYNE
Grand Rapids, Mich.: Eerdmans, 2009. 320 pp. $25.00.

This collection of essays grew out of a 2006 symposium at Duke University during which scholars met in the attempt to "refund" the Christian imagination in a way that will enable ways of facing death that are more authentic. A common theme that unites the essays is the desire to expand the limited ways that dying has become medicalized—dominated by prognosis, the etiology of disease, cure, and every other way that patients may become alienated from the experience of their own illness. Yet without minimizing the important function that modern medicine plays, the authors reclaim Christianity's native ability to understand end-of-life matters for their theological significance.

Most of the authors identify and address the ways that medicine has come to inscribe a profound distance between doctors and patients. For example, one need only consider the ways that doctors commonly make clear that they treat illness rather than patients. Yet the practices of medical care are marked by characteristics of modern living more generally: protecting a society from needing to think about death has its cognate in protecting the dying from the demands they might otherwise naturally feel being exerted upon their lives when death becomes real. Death is kept idealized as sudden, unexpected, and freed from burdening others. Therefore, by handing over end-of-life care entirely to the medical professionals, Christians neglect the opportunity to discover God amidst suffering, pain, and death. It is a theological failing, as John Swinton makes clear in his essay. After all, finding God in these things is the work of eyes of faith determined to see all of life through the lens of a crucified Messiah.

Consistent with the volume's intent, most of the essays are practical, rather than theoretical. When the question of theodicy arises, it functions to press for responses in practice rather than in understanding. For example, Tonya Armstrong, in her essay on dying children, accomplishes this by drawing distinctions between love and compassion—the latter committing love both to concrete solidarity with those who are suffering and to perpetual protest against the suffering itself. Relatedly, Therese Lysaught reflects on the practice of the sacraments as modes of preparing for death, although she argues against understanding them instrumentally, emphasizing instead the ecclesial nature of practices that bind individuals to the church in life. John Swinton notes the poverty of our language, particularly in an ethos dominated by scientific and medical terminology. He commends the lament psalms for how they model an appropriate and genuine use of language for those whose dying threatens to put them at a loss for words.

Most of the authors avoid technical philosophical language and normative moral formulations. This benefits its intended audience: caregivers and those working in medicine, pastoral ministry, and hospice who wish to be aided in allowing Christian practices to be given a primary role rather than being tacked on as an afterthought. Daniel Sulmasy's essay on human dignity seems out of place in this collection. By first developing moral rules about dignity as an intrinsic quality based on tracing the idea from Greek thought through Kant, Salmasy must then argue that "intrinsic dignity is the foundational notion of dignity for Christianity" (238). This way of arguing reverses the general trend of these essays, which more often foreground both questions of practice and something unique that Christianity brings to bear on the question of care. These pages abound with wisdom and good sense that will serve many readers and enable Christians to recover some sorely neglected resources.

Craig Hovey
Ashland University

Review of

Biotechnology and the Human Good

C. BEN MITCHELL, EDMUND D. PELLEGRINO, JEAN
BETHKE ELSHTAIN, JOHN F. KILNER, AND SCOTT B. RAE
Washington, D.C.: Georgetown University Press, 2007. 271 pp. $26.95.

God, Science, and Designer Genes: An Exploration of Emerging Genetic Technologies

SPENCER S. STOBER AND DONNA YARRI
Santa Barbara, Calif.: ABC-Clio, 2009. 243 pp. $49.95.

New developments in science and public policy occurred almost daily in the weeks I read these books and wrote this review. Given the vast amount of change and the huge import of the issues involved, can any pair of books adequately capture even a small snapshot of the panorama of biotechnology? The short answer, of course, is no, but this negative assessment is not due to the books chosen but rather to the complexity of this field. Nevertheless, these two books do offer, each in their own way, a helpful overview of what is clearly becoming one of the major ethical challenges of this half century.

I successfully used *Biotechnology and the Human Good* in my graduate course on contemporary critical issues in ethics. This book is seamlessly written by a multidisciplinary team of authors who address the foundational theological, philosophical, and ethical issues connected with biotechnological development as well as the deeper cultural and societal perceptions of these issues. Regardless of their training or interest, scientists, philosophers, and theologians—as well as the general public—will certainly profit from and value the careful attention with which this book interweaves science with theological and philosophical reflection in a way that is both excellent and accessible.

As a younger scholar, I recall watching on television the *Six Million Dollar Man*, which starred Lee Majors playing the astronaut Steve Austin, an accident victim rehabilitated and enhanced with bionic implants that enabled him to become a military superhero. In today's economy, the cost of these implants would certainly be much higher—and perhaps would raise some ethical questions concerning the military's role in their use. However, there has been surprisingly less development in the show's framing of the relevant moral issues—that is, its ironic twist on the "Is/Ought" principle: "Gentlemen, we can rebuild him.

We have the technology. We have the capability to build the world's first bionic man. Steve Austin will be that man—better than he was before. Better, stronger, faster." Certainly many would agree that "if" the technology exists then certainly it "ought" to be used. Nonetheless, the authors of this work recognize that the issues involved are far more complex and so as a "multidisciplinary group of physicians, scientists, philosophers, ethicists, theologians, and a lawyer" they set out to grapple with them so as to reach a deeper "way of thinking about technology—especially biotechnology" (ix).

Chapter 1 helpfully describes the wide array of biotechnologies available or in development (such as genetic manipulation, cybernetics, robotics, and nanotechnology) before turning, in chapter 2, to the principal narrative philosophies that provide arguments—both pro and con—for technological expansion. Here the authors adopt a careful middle ground that accepts biotechnology as a qualified good to be pursued with both vigor and caution. Chapter 3 then moves to the spectrum of different worldviews that ground and inform our various attitudes toward biotechnology—from philosophical naturalism, which would cede "no room for immaterial human components that cannot ultimately be reduced to physical or material substances" (36), at one extreme to radical environmental biocentrism, on the other, which would oppose most biotechnological intervention since "animals, and some plants perhaps, are entitled to the same moral considerations and respect owed to human beings" (49). The authors stand somewhere in the middle, proposing a Judeo-Christian theism, which in their view offers the best way "to frame the goals of biotechnology because it offers a view of human dignity combined with a purposive history that warrants therapeutic applications of biotechnology without either sanctioning the wholesale modifications of the human species or overprotecting the environment to the detriment of the human species" (x).

Chapters 4 and 5 take up the concepts of human dignity and moral autonomy as they relate to biotechnology and the quest for control, while chapter 6 focuses on the notion of a morally responsible stewardship related to the goals of medicine. Chapter 7 concludes the discussion by presenting principles in the form of questions that the authors hope will provide a philosophical and theological framework to "help assess biotechnologies philosophically, theologically, and practically" (137). Beginning with questions rather than judgments is methodologically helpful in complex areas such as biotechnology. However, my students and I observed (when we discussed this book in class) that in their conclusion the authors fall a bit too much into a dichotomous oversimplification, which they largely avoided in the bulk of their presentation. For example, we were asked to reply with a clear "yes" or "no" to a principle question such as "Does the technology require or promote the commodification or destruction of human life?" or an either/or choice of deciding whether technologies ought to "facilitate healing or restoration from disease or disability" or be used for "reengineering (so-called enhancement)?" (139). Even a generation ago our *Six Million Dollar Man* would give us a "both/and" reply to the latter query and probably a nuanced "it depends" response to the former question. Nonetheless, the concluding sections following these principle questions summarize the core philosophical and theological considerations grounding the authors' own belief system, which most readers of this journal should find compelling.

Based only on its title, it might seem at first glance that our second book, *God, Science, and Designer Genes: An Exploration of Emerging Genetic Technologies*, takes and builds on the foundation of *Biotechnology and the Human Good* by delving in greater depth into the core philosophical and theological issues it raised. However, the authors, who teach biology and theology, respectively, at Alvernia University, seem to have intended this book as an undergraduate textbook to be used in a cross-disciplinary course justifying a core course requirement in either science or religious studies. Part 1 offers a rather rudimentary biological, theological, and ethical background before turning to a consideration of the opportunities, challenges, and risks connected with genetic technologies in part 2. Part 3 consists of a single nineteen-page chapter that discusses biotechnological challenges in a quick sketch of contemporary theories of justice—but again at a rather basic introductory level. Unlike *Biotechnology and the Human Good*, it is very clear just who wrote what in *God, Science, and Designer Genes*. This is not necessarily a fatal critique, but a better synthesis of voices of the biologist and theologian would have helped the book considerably.

In their own ways, these two books helpfully analyze a complex field, even though their intended audiences are quite different. I am not sure if the *Biotechnology and the Human Good* would work well with an uninitiated undergraduate audience, but I would recommend it in a graduate course; *God, Science, and Designer Genes* would not engage a more sophisticated audience but serves well as an introductory text.

James T. Bretzke, SJ
Boston College School of Theology
and Ministry

Review of
Stem Cells, Human Embryos and Ethics: Interdisciplinary Perspectives
EDITED BY LARS ØSTNOR
New York: Springer, 2008. 271 pp. $49.95.

Sacred Cells? Why Christians Should Support Stem Cell Research
TED PETERS, KAREN LEBACQZ, AND GAYMON BENNETT
Lanham, Md.: Rowman & Littlefield, 2008. 272 pp. $37.95.

The Nature of Our Humanity: The Ethics of Genetics and Biotechnology
PAUL JERSILD
Minneapolis· Fortress, 2009. 188 pp. $25.00.

The ethical and political debate over human embryonic stem cells has recently been revived: first by President Obama's executive order (in 2009) overturning previous restrictions; second by Chief Judge R. C. Lamberth's ruling (on August 24, 2010) challenging its legality, followed by the Obama administration's appeal to this ruling; and third by the Pontifical Council for Culture's initiative with Stem Life Foundation (in May 2010) promoting research on adult stem cells. *Sacred Cells?* and *Stem Cells, Human Embryos and Ethics* (both published in 2008) extensively address stem cell research with a specific focus on human embryonic stem cells. Paul Jersild's 2009 volume, *The Nature of Our Humanity*, comments on this research within the context of broader theological reflections on science and religion.

Stem Cells, Human Embryos and Ethics, edited by Lars Østnor (professor of systematic theology in Oslo), targets an interdisciplinary readership. It emerged out of an international multidisciplinary two-year-long effort involving scientists, philosophers, and theologians from Norway, other European countries, and the United States. The book identifies the status of the human embryo as the exclusive ethical issue that needs to be addressed. The authors are divided on whether embryos should be used for research. While some support deriving stem cells from embryos (because they accord moral status to the embryo only after implantation), others oppose doing so (because they believe that the moral status of the embryo results from fertilization).

The section on scientific data will be appreciated by readers with interests or expertise in natural sciences; it is a well-documented introduction to further ethical reflections. The essays in this section describe well the alternative ways to produce embryonic stem cells without using human embryos (e.g., altered nuclear transfer and dedifferentiation of adult somatic cells that might make them pluripotent, i.e., induced pluripotent stem cells). In essays on the social and political aspects of stem cell research, the authors analyze current legislation throughout the world, particularly Europe. In addition, Theo A. Boer gives a constructive understanding of pluralism aimed at promoting moral empathy, which he discusses in relation to the appropriate personal and social dispositions needed to help us make better political decisions. The philosophical pieces struggle to define the beginning of human life by focusing on potentiality, by relying on logic, by contrasting descriptive and normative approaches, and by dealing with contextual data. Personally, I would have preferred a philosophical contribution that analyzed the arguments that have dominated the extended debates on the status of the embryo in recent decades and that offered new insight into these debates. Finally, the theological essays by Norwegian and German scholars give an overview of the positions taken within Christianity (including Orthodox, Protestant, Roman Catholic perspectives) and briefly discuss the contributions of select theologians chosen to represent the spectrum of current positions (including R. M. Doerflinger, Lisa Sowle Cahill, Gilbert Meilander, and Ted Peters). A more consistent engagement with these and other authors would have strengthened this theological section.

As with many volumes like this, I was left wondering whether this book could have had more coherence among its various sections and essays. It could have benefited from editing redundant descriptions of scientific techniques and procedures, expanding the sections on social and political perspectives and theological insights, and making the philosophical section more incisive.

In *Sacred Cells?* Ted Peters, Karen Lebacqz, and Gaymon Bennett (each belonging to different Protestants traditions) provide theological and ethical arguments in support of embryonic stem cell research that also presuppose a commitment to respect human life and dignity. They discuss current ethical approaches to stem cell research by distinguishing three frameworks on the basis of their respective emphases: (1) protecting the embryo; (2) protecting human beings from the dangers of scientific and biotechnological developments; and (3) promoting the future wholeness of human beings and society by stressing the beneficial potential of regenerative medicine. They also analyze exemplars of each framework: first, the Vatican documents, which aim to protect human embryos from the point of fertilization; second, Leon Kass' scholarship and his leadership of President George W. Bush's Council on Bioethics (2001–5) as indicative of a secular approach to stem cell research that focuses on human protection; and third, the authors' approach, which seeks to promote future human wholeness.

The authors' ambitious position seeks to integrate religious insights not only from the Christian tradition but also from Jewish and Muslim bioethical scholarship. Among other things, the authors seek to deconstruct fears of creating chimeras, to advocate for patenting and justice in accessing the therapeutic benefits of this research, to propose a renewed understanding of "ensoulment," and to separate stem cell research from abortion. To respect the dignity of the embryo while pursuing research on human embryonic stem cells, the authors identify implantation in the mother's uterus, which occurs around the fourteenth day after fertilization, as the crucial event that defines the embryo's moral status. They also argue that this is the point at which any previous biological and genetic indeterminacy ends; in this event, there occurs "the rudiments of the nervous system necessary for sentience, the adherence to the uterine wall necessary for any future development, and the shutting off of the possibility of twinning" (81).

The book opens with an interesting account of the beginnings of stem cell research in the late 1990s and of the role played by Peters and Lebacqz in the Ethics Advisory Board of Geron Corporation, which is committed to cutting-edge research on stem cells. The authors' account of this important period in the history of bioethics and in scientific research demonstrates the value of interdisciplinary collaboration. As Christians, they combine a commitment to respect human dignity from the beginning of human life with an unwavering support for any scientific research that would benefit persons in need, thus promoting medical beneficence. In developing their argument, they draw on current scientific data on implantation. In other words, they use current scientific data to support their ethical stance. Their approach is coherent and inspiring, but it leaves me wondering about the role they give to scientific explanations and data in shaping an ethical approach, which I fear risks falling into the "naturalist fallacy" the authors seek to avoid. Moreover, although the authors' commitment to justice is clearly affirmed throughout the volume, their focus is on distributing medical benefits and on guaranteeing access to future treatments could have been enhanced by a more comprehensive understanding of justice. For example, they do not examine the fact that the various settings for research throughout the world have differing economic resources or that there can be research centers in the developing countries that do not employ researchers from the host countries.

Written in an accessible style, the book has the potential for a wide readership: scholars, students, and interested readers. Although Lebacqz and

Peters draw on the insights and methodology of their previous published work, their joint contributions to this book represent a successful collaborative achievement.

In *The Nature of Our Humanity*, Paul Jersild offers an equally accessible volume to a wide readership. On the one hand, he draws on the past in his treatment of the following: discussing evolutionary biology from a Christian perspective; avoiding scientific reductionist materialism; proposing a holistic understanding of human nature; and rejecting any scientific explanation of our religious beliefs. On the other hand, he turns to the future by addressing the ethical issues raised by stem cell research and human genetics (with a discussion of the expected therapeutic benefits and of the blurred line between therapy and enhancement). The volume concludes with reflections dealing with mortality and the pursuit of immortality.

Throughout the book, the Bible is the first source of theological inspiration; this is clear not only when the author refers to it directly but also when he uses it implicitly to inform particular ethical assumptions (e.g., that of "relationality"). Second, Jersild relies on a holistic and dialogical theological anthropology rooted in Christian revelation, which leads him to rethink human nature and our being created in the image of God in light of what we know about biological evolution. Third, when reflecting on scientific materialism, the author engages influential authors who dominate the current debate (e.g., E. O. Wilson, S. J. Gould) by critically examining their arguments. His approach leads him to support human embryonic research because of its therapeutic benefits and because he too identifies implantation as a pivotal event determining embryo development and the assignment of human dignity (see 144–47).

The timely character of the topics this book addresses and its interesting methodological approach invite readers to further develop its theological approach. We are invited not only to reflect on the communal and global dimensions of human nature (thus expanding Jersild's understanding of relationality) but also to relate these dimensions to other developments in biotechnology mentioned in the volume (e.g., nanotechnology and neurosciences).

Andrea Vicini, SJ
Boston College

Contributors

John P. Burgess is professor of systematic theology at Pittsburgh Theological Seminary. His publications include *The East German Church and the End of Communism*, *Why Scripture Matters: Reading the Bible in a Time of Church Conflict*, and *After Baptism: Shaping the Christian Life*. He also edited *In Whose Image: Faith, Science, and the New Genetics*, and coedited *What Is Justification about? Reformed Contributions to an Ecumenical Theme*. His current research focuses on the efforts of the Russian Orthodox Church to shape national identity in post-communist Russia.

Charles E. Curran is the Elizabeth Scurlock University Professor of Human Values at Southern Methodist University. He has served as president of three national professional societies—the American Theological Society, the Catholic Theological Society of America, and the Society of Christian Ethics. Curran has received the highest awards from the Catholic Theological Society of America and the College Theology Society. He is a member of the American Academy of Arts and Sciences. His 2008 book *Catholic Moral Theology in the United States: A History*, from Georgetown University Press, won the 2008 American Publishers Award for Professional and Scholarly Excellence in Theology and Religion. His latest book, published in 2011, is *The Social Mission of the US Catholic Church: A Theological Investigation*, from Georgetown University Press.

Tommy Givens, ThD candidate at Duke University, is an instructor of New Testament studies at Fuller Theological Seminary. His research focuses on the meaning of the election of Israel for Christian ecclesiology and discipleship, particularly in dialogue with John Howard Yoder and Karl Barth. He researches also modern understandings of peoplehood and national appropriations of the election of Israel, related issues in political theory, and the exegesis of the Gospel of Matthew and Paul's Epistles. He is a member of the board of the National Society for Scriptural Reasoning and has an article on Jürgen

Habermas and theology in dialogue with Nicholas Adams forthcoming in *Journal of Scriptural Reasoning*.

Amy Levad is assistant professor of moral theology at the University of St. Thomas in St. Paul, Minnesota. Her book *Restorative Justice: Theories and Practices of Moral Imagination* is forthcoming from LFB Scholarly Publishing. In addition to ongoing work on the ethics of criminal justice, she is also researching food ethics.

Douglas F. Ottati, past president of the Society of Christian Ethics (2010), is the Craig Family Distinguished Professor of Reformed Theology and Justice Ministry at Davidson College. He is a general editor of the Library of Theological Ethics series published by Westminster John Knox Press, and his most recent book is *Theology for Liberal Presbyterians and Other Endangered Species* (Geneva Press, 2006).

Kathryn Getek Soltis is the director of the Center for Peace and Justice Education at Villanova University. Her research focuses on issues in virtue ethics, punishment, and Catholic social teaching. She received her PhD from Boston College in 2010. She has served in ministerial and education roles in prison systems in the Boston and Philadelphia areas.

Lloyd Steffen is professor of religion studies, university chaplain, and director of the Center for Dialogue, Ethics, and Spirituality at Lehigh University in Bethlehem, Pennsylvania. He is the author or editor of seven books, including the award-winning *Executing Justice: The Moral Meaning of the Death Penalty* (Pilgrim 1999) and, most recently, of *Holy War, Just War: Exploring the Moral Meaning of Religious Violence* (Rowman & Littlefield, 2007). He has served as a board officer for the Religious Coalition for Reproductive Choice and as that organization's nongovernmental organization representative to the United Nations.

Cristina L. H. Traina is a professor and director of graduate studies in the Department of Religious Studies at Northwestern University, Evanston, Illinois. She is the author of *Erotic Attunement: Parenthood and the Ethics of Sensuality between Unequals* (University of Chicago Press, 2011). She favors an interdisciplinary approach to ethics, drawing on research in philosophy, anthropology, psychology, history, and other fields.

Michael R. Turner is a doctoral candidate in religious ethics at the University of Chicago Divinity School. His research interests include theological engagements with economics and ethics; business ethics; neuroethics; free will and determinism; and religion, literature, and film.

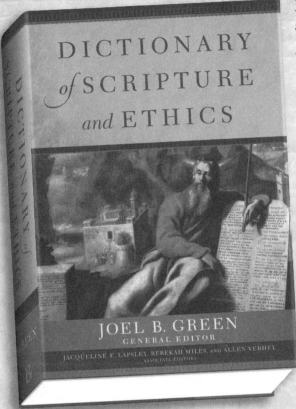

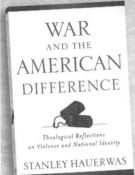
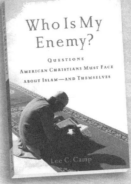
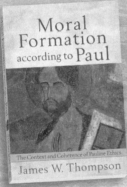

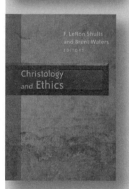

NICHOLAS WOLTERSTORFF
JUSTICE IN LOVE

"In this exquisite new book of political theology, Wolterstorff tours the perennially contested questions of eros and agape, rule and equity, discipline and mercy, responsibility and forgiveness, justice and righteousness. Learned, judicious, strikingly innovative, and crystal clear, this book has all the marks of yet another Wolterstorff classic in the making."

— John Witte Jr.

"Wolterstorff has gotten justice right."

— Miroslav Volf
in *Books and Culture*

"In this brilliant work Nicholas Wolterstorff does what many thought impossible: he brings fresh insights to a debate that long ago grew stale and predictable. *Justice in Love* is exemplary in its clarity and balance. This beguiling new work burnishes Wolterstorff's reputation as one of our most important and original religious philosophers."

— Jean Bethke Elshtain

ISBN 978-0-8028-6615-8 • 294 pages • hardcover • $35.00

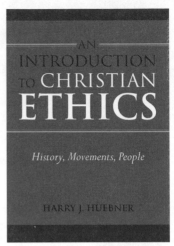
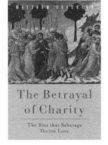

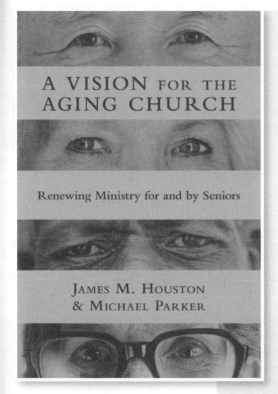

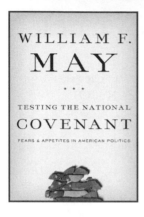
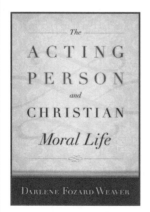

UNDERSTANDING

Transhumanism and Transcendence
Christian Hope in an Age of Technological Enhancement
Ronald Cole-Turner, Editor

"This is the most important Christian debate on transhumanism that I have ever read. Those who prefer fawning acceptance or frightened rejection of human enhancement can find simplistic monographs aplenty. But if you want to think theologically about the transformation of humanity through technology — what's already here, and what lies ahead of us — this collection is mandatory reading."

—*Philip Clayton, Claremont School of Theology*

978-1-58901-780-1, paperback, $32.95

Communicating the Word
Revelation, Translation, and Interpretation in Christianity and Islam
David Marshall, Editor
Afterword by Archbishop Rowan Williams

"There are very few people, specialist or otherwise, who will not learn much from this rich and varied volume. It is rare for interreligious exchange to take place at such a sustained level of quality, and much of the authors' contributions manage to feel both erudite and direct."

—*Caner K. Dagli, College of the Holy Cross*

"Holy writings, received as revealed, are central to both Islam and Christianity. This welcome collection will open the debate."

—*Janet Soskice, Cambridge University*

978-1-58901-784-9, paperback, $24.95

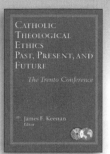

978-1-57075-941-3
304 pp pbk $40.00

Catholic Theological Ethics
Past, Present, and Future
The Trento Conference
James F. Keenan, editor

Theological ethicists confront key questions and issues from around the globe to provide a "state of the art" twenty-first century moral theology. This volume includes the most current thinking on ethics and interreligious dialogue, the interaction between history and theology, missing and marginalized voices, moral reasoning, political ethics, health issues, identity and familial relations, and the future of theological ethics.

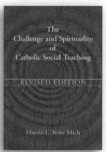

978-1-57075-945-1
272 pp pbk $22.00

The Challenge and Spirituality
of Catholic Social Teaching
Revised Edition
MARTIN L. KRIER MICH

Offers readers the insight and inspiration to live out the gospel of Jesus Christ, the "glad tidings to the poor," here and now. This revised and updated edition focuses on key themes of Catholic social teaching. Mich weaves together the biblical tradition and the wisdom of Catholic social teaching with the stories of saints and spiritual leaders, contemporary and historical.

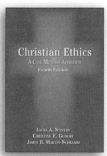

978-1-57075-966-6
320 pp pbk $26.00

Coming in Spring 2012
Christian Ethics
A Case Method Approach
4th Edition
LAURA A. STIVERS, CHRISTINE E. GUDORF,
JAMES B. MARTIN-SCHRAMM

This classic text now includes ten new cases on immigration, homelessness and foreclosures, water, ethical issues in the workplace, closing hospital emergency rooms, executive pay, living together v. marriage, same-sex marriage, and physician-assisted death. "Highly recommended." —*New Theology Review*
February 2012

RECENT BOOKS *from* EERDMANS

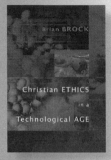

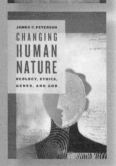
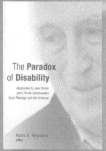

Apply Today

2012-13
Workshops & Colloquies

Application Deadline
January 16, 2012

WABASH
CENTER
For Teaching and Learning
In Theology and Religion

www.wabashcenter.wabash.edu

Funded by Lilly Endowment Inc.
Located at Wabash College

Celebrating 15 Years
Promoting Teaching Excellence
1996-2011